TAMIN

PANZERS

Monty's Tank Battalions, 3rd RTR at War

PATRICK DELAFORCE

SUTTON PUBLISHING

This book was first published in 2000 by
Sutton Publishing Limited · Phoenix Mill
Thrupp · Stroud · Gloucestershire · GL5 2BU

This new paperback edition first published in 2003

British Library Cataloguing in Publication Data
A catalogue record for this book is available from the British
Library

ISBN 0 7509 3197 3

Typeset in 9.5/11pt Benguiat.
Typesetting and origination by
Sutton Publishing Limited.
Printed and bound in Great Britain by
J.H. Haynes & Co. Ltd, Sparkford.

CONTENTS

ACKNOWLEDGEMENTS

Two of my published books, *Monty's Marauders* and *The Black Bull*, have covered some of the history of the famous 3rd Battalion, Royal Tank Regiment. Famous because they fought all the way through the war from Calais, to Greece, to the terrible ebb and flow of the North African desert campaigns and, finally, to the last year of desperate hostilities in France, Belgium, Holland and the Third Reich.

I have a vested interest in writing about 3rd RTR: 13th Royal Horse Artillery, in which I was a troop leader in Normandy and Forward Observation Officer (FOO) in Holland and Germany, supported 3rd RTR in every battle in north-west Europe (except the Ardennes). I like to think that our barrages and 'stonks' helped them on their way from the Normandy beaches to the Baltic. There are many individuals I must thank for their great help: Major Bill Close MC, who, uniquely, fought with 3rd RTR in every campaign except the Ardennes, and was rudely unhorsed on at least seven occasions. His remarkable journal *A View from the Turret* has been enormously helpful to me.

Major-General 'Pip' Roberts DSO, MC, who commanded 3rd RTR briefly in the desert and, as GOC 11th Armoured Division, led them with great dash to VE Day, gave me permission to quote from his autobiography.

Lieutenant-Colonel Cyril Joly MC allowed me to use extracts from his *Take these Men* and George Morris permitted me to quote from his *The Battle of Alamein and Beyond*.

Dick Shattock's journal and his superb collection of personal photographs taken in the desert have enhanced this book. Les Slater produced a number of Comet photographs and David Fletcher, Curator of the Tank Museum, Bovington, has unearthed some rare 3rd RTR photographs of First World War, Calais and Greece.

Jim Caswell and Fred Dale have sent me their very interesting 3rd RTR journals; Lieutenant-Colonel Bill Reeves DSO has allowed me to quote from his account of the battle of Gravelines; Jack Kempton's *Third Tanks in Ardennes*, Robin Lemon's *Goodwood* and Johnny Langdon's *Aller* battle have amplified crucial actions.

Peter Ross's book *All Valiant Dust*, and contributions from Johnny Dunlop (verses), Bill Jordan, Bert Jobson, Reggie Keller,

J.A. Kempton, 'Buck' Kite, R.C. Payne, 'Geordie' Reay, Jock Watt, Barry Whitehouse, Cliff Wicks, A.C. Wilson, R.N. Wilson, George Witheridge, F.J.C. Wollaston and Nancy Langmaid (Friends of the Tank Museum) have also been of great help.

My only regret is that the indomitable South African Bob Crisp who won the DSO in Greece and an MC in the desert battles died a few years ago. I have used extracts from his two vivid books, *The Gods were Neutral* and *Brazen Chariots*. Although I have tried many avenues, I have failed to trace his family. He was perhaps the biggest swashbuckler of all the gallant 3rd Tanks. I like to think that he would have enjoyed reading *Taming the Panzers* for he most certainly did his best to do just that.

INTRODUCTION

Shortly after General Bernard Montgomery arrived in the North African desert destined to transform Britain's Eighth Army and march from victory to victory – he caused a sensation. A dedicated professional infantryman (the Royal Warwickshire Regiment) he put a gleaming silver First World War tank – the cap badge of the Royal Tank Regiment – on his beret and wore it with pride throughout the rest of the war. Shortly after the end of hostilities in 1945 he wrote:

> We learnt our lesson the hard way – as is so often the case in the history of British arms. It took the early successes of the German panzer divisions in 1940 to convince us that the tank, if used properly, was a decisive weapon in modern land warfare. By then it might have been too late. But we were saved from disaster because of the efficient tank schools which the Regiment had established in peacetime and by the splendid body of reservists which they had trained. These made it possible to effect a rapid expansion of our tank forces, Regular and Territorial, and eventually to put into the field a hard core of highly efficient armoured units – which bore the brunt of the fight for two long weary years. Finally at Alamein in October 1942, we gained the advantage over the enemy, utilising our superior numbers and equipment – after which we never looked back. And it was the same in other theatres of war. The Regiment won praise wherever it fought.
>
> I know this better than most. It was my great honour and privilege to have had under my command at varying times during the late war most of the units of the Royal Armoured Corps – Regular, Territorial and units specially for the war. Among all these, I can speak with authority of the technical efficiency, and tenacity and skill in battle of the units of the Royal Tank Regiment.
>
> When the Second World War was over, the Regiment asked me, an infantry soldier to become one of its Colonels Commandant and it was a notable moment for me when my appointment as such was approved by the Sovereign – Colonel-in-Chief of the Regiment. Let us never forget the immense debt

which the whole nation owes to the officers and men of the Royal Tank Regiment. I have always considered the Royal Tank Regiment to be outstanding in the Royal Armoured Corps – second to none when it comes to efficiency in battle. By determination in peace and valour in war, the Regiment worthily established, and has unflinchingly maintained, the right to its inspiring motto – 'Fear Naught'.

Field Marshal Viscount Montgomery of Alamein KG, GCB, DSO.

This is the story of perhaps the most famous British fighting formation of the Second World War. A bold claim perhaps? The 3rd Battalion, Royal Tank Regiment had a distinguished reputation in the First World War, earning a fine Victoria Cross, but some 30 years later the two main adversaries acknowledge their prowess. Winston Churchill stated that the week-long defence of Calais in May 1940 (in which 3rd RTR were the only tank formation) gave the British Expeditionary Force (BEF) extra time for the crucial evacuation from the Dunkirk beaches. In the spring of the next year the re-formed, refitted battalion fought the panzers again in the ill-fated campaign in Greece. (The only RTR unit to do so.) Adolf Hitler was furious since the six-week campaign delayed Operation 'Barbarossa'. His panzers might have reached Moscow that much sooner before the Soviet armies could regroup and the dreadful Russian winter arrived.

3rd RTR fought and fought again in all the main African desert battles, eventually under the command of General Montgomery. Finally 3rd RTR fought in all the desperate battles in Normandy; took part in the 'Great Swan' to capture Amiens and Antwerp, then acted as right-flank protection in Operation 'Market Garden'; helped halt the panzers in the Ardennes; and, equipped with brand new Comet tanks (the only RTR unit in the British Army to be so), took part in the many river crossing battles on their way to the Baltic.

A truly magnificent record.

1

BIG WILLIE (MOTHER), LITTLE WILLIE AND THE SAVAGE RABBITS

Despite the views of the senior professional soldiers still fighting the Boer War, the politicians in the early days of the First World War took a great deal of interest in the development of an armoured vehicle capable of breaking into and through enemy lines of trenches. Lloyd George was impressed by the new invention and Sir Douglas Haig read with great interest a memorandum entitled 'Attack by Armour', written by Winston Churchill, who after the Dardanelles saw front-line action in France. A Tank Supply Committee was formed under Lieutenant-Colonel Stern and the first hundred tanks were manufactured by the firms of Fosters of Lincoln and the Metropolitan Carriage Company of Wednesbury. The first Mark I tanks would operate in pairs, one with two 6-pdr guns, attacking enemy artillery, while the other carrying four Vickers machine-guns (MGs) would tackle the enemy infantry. Known as 'male' and 'female' respectively, they were soon christened 'Big' and 'Little Willie'. The latter, a chaperone tank defended 'Big Willie', but it was Big Willie that was nicknamed 'Mother'.

The specifications of the Wilson 'Big Willie' model (Lieutenant W.G. Wilson and Lieutenant A. Stern were pioneer tank designers in 1915) created a fighting vehicle 8 feet in width and height and 31 feet in length. The maximum speed was 4 mph and it could cross an 8 foot trench and climb a 4½ foot high parapet. A crew of eight men was needed to drive and man the two naval 6-pdr guns, one on each side. The engine was a 105-hp Daimler and when loaded with crew and ammunition the vehicle weighed 28 tons, 8 cwt. The protective armour was 12 mm thick in front of the driver, 8 mm at the sides, and 6 mm on top. Poor reception inside the tank precluded use of the primitive wireless and short-range communication was by means of metal discs (semaphore) and small flags (Morse code); for long range carrier pigeons were used. Naval compasses were also provided. The new formation was christened, 'Fred Karno's army, the ragtime ASC'.

In early 1916 Colonel Ernest Swinton, perhaps the main advocate for the development of tanks, commanded the new Tank Department based at Siberia camp, Bisley, where the Motor Machine Gun Service had their training school. For reasons of secrecy the name was changed in May to the Heavy Section, Machine Guns Corps. Secrecy was paramount and officers and men were told to say the 'cars' were a new type of water tank intended for the Russians! So Russian letters were painted on the side of each tank before leaving the factories.

The war establishment was for six companies, each with 25 brand new tanks (or land ships, or land cruisers) since with Lloyd George's help the initial order was increased to 150. Each Company, named initially 'A' to 'F', had four sections with a total of 28 officers and 255 other ranks. 'C' Company which became later the 3rd Battalion, was commanded by Major A. Holford-Walker MC of the Argyll and Sutherland Highlanders and his Adjutant was Captain B.E. Williams MC.

There was a dearth of officers and men, so several batteries of the Motor Machine Guns were disbanded to form a nucleus. Officers volunteered from infantry units in France who had experienced trench warfare and from newly formed cadet schools in Oxford, Cambridge and Bristol. The new companies were based at Bull House Camp, Bisley, a large secure area of heath and woodland 15 miles square where training with Hotchkiss and Vickers machine-guns and 6-pdr guns could take place. The area was guarded night and day by 450 men of the Royal Defence Corps and turned into a realistic Flanders Fields battlefield. Besides the British front and French supply lines, a substantial No Man's Land and German first, support, and second and third defence lines were created.

Colonel Swinton in a memorandum 'Notes on the Employment of Tanks' urged not only secrecy, but the vital need for concentration of numbers combined with an infantry assault. The element of surprise would enable these great monsters to force and breach the enemy lines. Training on Lord Iveagh's Elveden estate near Thetford in Norfolk took place as tanks emerged from the factories. Driving, mechanical maintenance and six tank section manoeuvres took place and training notes in concise form were issued.

The new formations were inspected by King George V, by Mr Lloyd George and by numerous sceptical generals at Bernersfield Camp training area, Thetford.

Field Marshal Sir Douglas Haig, the new Commander-in-Chief, succeeding Sir John French, had sent Major Hugh Elles, a Royal Engineer officer to make enquiries in 1915 about the new 'Caterpillar' project. Elles with front-line warfare experience was promoted to lieutenant-colonel to lead the new secret force into battle.

Haig wanted tank support for the massive Somme offensive he was planning to launch on 1 July 1916, but Colonel Swinton was able to point out that very few *trained* units would be available by then. Once the offensive began and the appalling casualty lists appeared showing 58,000 killed or wounded, Haig and his staff were demanding tank support, even if only to raise the morale of his troops. Colonel Swinton visited Haig's HQ on 19 August and was shown on a map the sectors in which the new tanks would receive their baptism of fire. The French tank design plan (introducing 14-ton Char Schneider and 23-ton Char St Chamond vehicles) was six months behind that of the British and they wanted a large synchronized tank launch in a spring 1917 offensive. Lloyd George, now War Minister, supported delaying the introduction of tanks into the New Year.

So 'His Majesty's landships – HMLS' were shipped from Avonmouth in mid-August to Le Havre; Second Lieutenant A.M. Henderson with his vehicle C43 was in one of the first tanks to land on French soil. 'C' Company in two instalments, followed by 'D' Company had their side sponsons fitted at Conteville. By the 25th in Yvrench near Abbeville at an improvised training centre they were fitted with armour for the first time. By the end of August fifty tanks and ten spares had arrived, with no clear plan as to how they were to be used! There was no training cooperation with infantry and insufficient mechanic training. Major Holford-Walker's 'C' Company became a circus turn for visiting VIPs for a time when they concentrated at the Loop, a rail centre near Bray-sur-Somme close to the front line.

Besides Sir Douglas Haig, Marshal Joffre, General Rawlinson (his opinion being that the tank would 'never be any use'), and HRH the Prince of Wales, all took a keen interest. The tank stunts by 'C' and 'D' took place from 0900 to 1000 hrs and again at 1400–1500 hrs. Crews needed to repair, tune and clean their tanks, adjust their new guns, test the spare engine parts and practise gas drill with their clumsy box respirators. Each member of the crew (officer and seven men) carried haversack, water bottle, iron rations, field dressing kit, goggles, a leather helmet and two gas helmets, and were individually armed with a revolver. Also on board were 33,000 rounds of ammunition, a spare Vickers machine-gun and four replacement barrels, a lamp-signalling set, a hundred yards of cable so that messages could be sent back, drums of engine oil and grease. Last but not least food for two or three days and a basket of carrier-pigeons!

The first commander of the joint 'C' and 'D' Companies was Lieutenant-Colonel John Brough, who after correctly demanding more time for preparation and questioning their form of deployment in penny packets, was almost immediately fired. Lieutenant-Colonel R.W. Bradley succeeded him. The GHQ plan was for each infantry division to have a section of 6 tanks on a 1,200-yard frontage: 16 were allocated to 'XIV' Corps, 18 to 'XV' Corps, 8 to 'III' Corps and 6 to the Reserve Army.

After three whole days of incessant artillery bombardment, at dawn on 15 September Captain H.W. Mortimore of 'D' Company in D-1 was alone entrusted with the task of clearing enemy posts near Delville Wood. A German newspaper journalist witnessed this attack as the English infantry rolled up in waves behind the 'devil's coaches'. The main attack Zero Hour was at 0620 hrs and only thirty-six tanks reached their start lines, due to engine trouble, track problems or ditching in trenches and collapsed dugouts.

'C' COMPANY AT COURCELETTE – 15 SEPTEMBER 1916

The CO was Major Allen Holford-Walker, his adjutant was Captain R.E. Williams and the Technical Officer was Second Lieutenant T.L. Wenger.

No. 1 Section was commanded by Captain A.M. Inglis and the six tanks (half 'male', half 'female') were commanded by Lieutenant A.G.C. Wheeler, Lieutenant F.W. Bluemell, Second Lieutenant S.D.H. Clark, Second Lieutenant G.O. Campbell, Captain A.M. Inglis (was OC C-5) and Second Lieutenant J. Allan.

No. 2 Section was commanded by Captain H.H. Hiscocks (was OC C-8), Second Lieutenant A.L. Arnaud, Second Lieutenant

T.E.F. Murphy, Lieutenant L.J. Bates, Lieutenant H.B. Elliot, Second Lieutenant C.F. Ambrose.

No. 3 Section was commanded by Lieutenant Sir John Dashwood (was OC C-13), Second Lieutenant F.J. Arnold, Second Lieutenant E.L. Purdy, Lieutenant J.E. Tull, Second Lieutenant J.P. Clarke, Second Lieutenant L.V. Smith.

No. 4 Section was commanded by Captain Archie Holford-Walker (was OC C-19), Lieutenant G. MacPherson, Lieutenant H.H. Vincent, Lieutenant B.L. Henriques, Second Lieutenant A.M. Henderson, Second Lieutenant H.R.C. Cole.

Tank names included 'Champagne', 'Cognac', 'Chartreuse', 'Chablis', 'Crème de Menthe', 'Cordon Rouge', 'Corunna', 'Casa', 'Clan Leslie'.

No. 1 Section supported 2nd Canadian Division, No. 2 Section supported the Guards Division, No. 3 Section the 56th and Guards Divisions and No. 4 Section, 6th Division.

'C' Company had an undistinguished start on 15 September supporting the Guards, 6th and 56th Division of 'XIV' Corps and the Canadian Corps on the Reserve Army front. Of the three supporting 56th Division attacking near Combles and Bouleau Wood, one, Second Lieutenant Purdy in C-16 proved helpful opposite Combles trenches and according to the infantry 'thoroughly frightened the foe'. Another broke a track and the third, Second Lieutenant Arnold in C-14 cruised round the wood, became ditched and was abandoned as its crew was bombarded with hand grenades. No 'Mother' tank nor infantry was there to support them. Three set off to support 6th Division in its attack on Morval, two failed to reach the start point with engine trouble and a broken 'tail' (stabilizer wheel at the back of the tank) respectively. The third, Lieutenant Henriques in C-22 opened fire on its *own* infantry, but then briskly enfiladed the German front line without support and with both sponsons holed.

Ten tanks were allocated to the Guards Division. Three had mechanical trouble, two were ditched on the way up, one broke its 'tail' at the start, and then there were four. Two sprayed the *wrong* trench for several minutes and then returned. The last two started late, then strayed off course, one became ditched and the other turned back as its petrol ran low.

On the 2nd Canadian Division front six tanks in two groups helped the attack on a fortified sugar factory barring the road to Courcelette. One had track trouble, three became ditched, but two did rather well. The commander of C-6 'Cordon Rouge' was Second Lieutenant John Allen, who kept to the line of Sugar Trench, silenced several machine-guns and was awarded the MC. C-5 'Crème de Menthe' commanded by Captain Arthur Inglis nearing the sugar factory, persuaded fifty Germans to surrender. One shouted 'there is a crocodile crawling into our lines'. Using his 6-pdrs, C-5 smashed through walls, barricades and destroyed MG emplacements round the factory. Inglis was awarded the DSO and his driver Sergeant G.B. Shepherd the DCM. On the whole the Canadian infantry were encouraged and the resulting German prisoners were badly shaken. It must be admitted that 'D' Company had a brilliant start. D-1 did its stuff and D-6, D-16, and D-17 were crucial factors in the capture of Flers. D-6 and D-5 occupied Gueudecourt unsupported and Second Lieutenant Storey won the DSO.

Field Marshal Sir Douglas Haig in his despatches was quite generous with his praise. 'The Somme 1916. At 6.20 a.m. on 15 September the infantry assault commenced and at the same time the bombardment became intense. Our new heavily armoured cars known as "Tanks" now brought into action for the first time successfully co-operated with the infantry and coming as a surprise to the enemy rank and file gave valuable help in breaking down their resistance. The advance met with immediate success on almost the whole of the front attacked. At 8.40 a.m. our tanks were seen entering Flers followed by large numbers of troops. . . .' The national press were more enthusiastic than the higher military circles about the debut of 'C' and 'D' Mk I Tanks. Haig requested the building of a hundred more Mk Is and then a further thousand. Lieutenant-Colonel Bradley was replaced by Lieutenant-Colonel Hugh Elles on 29 September and moved the Heavy Section ('A' and 'B' Companies had arrived by now) to Beauquesne and then to Bermicourt near St Pol. Lieutenant-Colonel B.S. Baker-Carr now commanded 'C' Battalion. The four companies were formally brigaded as 1st Tank Brigade after the Somme offensive ended on 19 November and Baker-Carr became their first brigadier. In his memoirs *From a Chauffeur to a Brigadier* he wrote, 'My Adjutant came from a box factory in Wallasey, my Equipment Officer was a Welshman and the best bee-keeper in Wales, my Recce Officer was a London lawyer, my Engineer Officer came from the Hillman Car Co of Birmingham, my Medical Officer came from the South Pole after two years with Shackleton.' The Brigade Major was Cox of the Gloucesters, Tapper was the Staff Captain and Williams-Ellis, the Recce Officer.

The War Office notified GHQ that the four companies in France were to expand into twelve and form four battalions, each of seventy-two tanks. However, in early 1917 this was reduced to an establishment of thirty-six tanks.

Colonel Elles expanded his command to an area of 24 acres with workshops, stores, hangars, and a driving and mechanized school with its own training ground. The staff increased to 1,200 officers and men with a compound of 500 Chinese labourers! The next standard model was the Mk IV without a wheeled tail, and with smaller sponsons. To reduce the risk of fire an armoured 60-gallon fuel tank was mounted outside on the back of the tank. Ditching was still the main problem and many small modifications of tracks and un-ditching gear were made. To keep the factories going 150 Mk Is were to be built, then 50 each of Mk IIs and Mk IIIs (with no tail wheels, thicker armour and new cast-iron rollers). The remainder of the 1,000 order were new Mk IVs with Lewis guns instead of Hotchkiss.

On the first day of the New Year, 1917, 'C' Company became 'C' Battalion Heavy Branch MG Corps. Lieutenant-Colonel S.H. Charrington DSO was the CO, No. 7 Company was under Major Holford-Walker (later by Major Haslam); No. 8 under Major Kyngdom; No. 9 under Major Forestier-Walker. Each company had four sections and the battalion was stationed at Erin. Private H.E. Emans wrote,

Erin was a small scruffy village. We were billeted in old barns and stables, wire netting bunks, just two blankets and the coldest winter in France for 50 years – it was perishing. We settled down to training as no new tanks were available, we made contraptions of wood and canvas, about 9 feet by 6, with slits in the canvas to represent slits on the tanks. With a man in each corner we used to *walk* about the fields in these, to get used to finding our way across country when in action. What the French farmers thought we were up to, I do *not* know. . . . With the arrival of the new tanks, training started in earnest.

We had to learn about the Lewis machine gun. We had previously used the Vickers with a water jacket for cooling purposes. It was vulnerable to concentrated fire from German MGs. The Lewis was air-cooled and could stand quite a bit of battering before being put out of action. We used to practise stripping and assembling it, blind folded, in the kitchen of the local shoemaker.

In February 1917, the 2nd Tank Brigade was formed with 'A' and 'B' Battalions and their new GSO2 was Major J.F.C. Fuller, destined to become one of the Army's brilliant tank warfare experts.

General Allenby's Third Army held the sector at Arras where the Hindenburg Line defences ended. An attack by massed tanks supported by infantry could turn the flank of the enemy's line by a surprise attack. The new Mk IV, 240 of them, were promised for delivery in late April. They were late and when the great spring offensive went in only a modest collection of sixty Mk Is and IIs, vulnerable to German armour-piercing (AP) bullets, were available. Again these were spread thinly along the entire line; 40 tanks of Baker-Carr's 1st Tank Brigade were divided, 16 each to 'VI' and 'VII' Corps attacking south of the River Scarpe and 8 to 'XVII' Corps attacking north of the river. A further 8 tanks would cooperate with the Canadian Corps attack on Vimy Ridge and the remaining 12 would operate with Sixth Army at Lagnicourt near Bulecourt. The attack on the Arras front started on Easter Monday, 9 April 1917.

'C' Battalion again had mixed fortunes. Moving into position they took a short cut across a valley of the River Crinchon near Achicourt, south of Arras. The causeway was formed of brushwood and railway sleepers, laid across the worst of the swampy ground. The top crust was over a deep bog, and one after another the first six tanks were engulfed. So they were down to twenty-six operationals to help in the main attack south of the River Scarpe. Eighteen of 'C' and 'D' Battalions (including 8th Company of 'C') were used in successful attacks on Telegraph Hill and a stronghold called 'The Harp'. Most of 8th Company were later bogged down or put out of action by hits. Four tanks of 9th Company made a pincer attack on Tilley-les-Mofflaines; Second Lieutenant Weber's 'Lusitania' helped clear the Railway Triangle, south of the Scarpe and silenced several machine-guns. Then lying stranded on the edge of an enemy trench, it was finally destroyed by *British* artillery! In support of

15th Division Weber was awarded the MC for his help in the capture of Feuchy Redoubt and Chapel, as was Second Lieutenant S.I. Norman. Corporal J. Fleming and Sergeant W. Watson won the Military Medal (MM) in the same action. North of the River Scarpe all eight tanks of 7th Company were bogged or knocked out by gunfire. The eight with the Canadian Corps further north were ditched in appalling conditions *before* H-hour! Most of the second day was spent digging out the dozens of ditched tanks. On the third day, 11 April, three 'C' Battalion tanks out of six that started took Monchy-le-Preux almost by mistake! Zero hour had been postponed by two hours but the message had not reached infantry or tanks. The 'C' Battalion tanks set off without the usual predictable artillery barrage – and so crossed the snowy wastes of No Man's Land and subdued the defenders – before the infantry caught up! On 14 April, Major-General H.P. Williams GOC 37th Division wrote, 'The advance of the six tanks of 'C' Bn Heavy Branch MG Corps to Feuchy Chapel and thence to Monchy in time to co-operate with the attack of the 111th and 112th Brigades early on the morning of 11 April was a great achievement and in itself more than justified their existence. The officers and men concerned deserve the highest credit.'

Lieutenant G.C.T. Salter, whose tank was blown to pieces by artillery fire causing six casualties, earned the MC, as did Lieutenant C.H. May. But Second Lieutenant C.F.N. Ambrose won the DSO. His tank was bombed, blown in by shellfire, and pierced by AP bullets. All his gunners were casualties so he kept up a brisk fire on the infantry surrounding and attacking his tanks with bombs. Corporal Vyvian won the DCM and Sergeants Saker and Haugh, MMs. The attack on Bullecourt was a disaster and tragedy and the Australian troops viewed the new tanks with great distrust. Surprisingly, however, Lieutenant General Haldane wrote to Baker-Carr, 'My first experience of tanks. I certainly never again want to be without them when so well commanded and led.'

The offensive was renewed on 23 April and Second Lieutenant Victor Smith's tank helped 51st Highland Division at Mount Pleasant Wood and supported the attack on Roeux, driving the enemy out with his 6-pdrs. He won the MC, as did Second Lieutenant C.M. Le Clair at Gavrelle. Sergeant J. Noel knocked out a series of machine-guns and helped the Gordon Highlanders capture the Chemical Works. For this he won the DCM and *Medaille Militaire* from the French Army. Sergeant Milliken won the MM at the Gavrelle action and Corporal R.J. Williams a bar to his MM.

The remnants of 'C' and 'D' returned to Bermicourt to refit and 'C' Battalion were then posted to Lieutenant-Colonel Hardress-Lloyd's 3rd Tank Brigade along with 'F' Battalion fresh from home. Each battalion was given two spare tanks and also six Mk Is converted into petrol and ammunition supply tanks.

In July King George V inspected the tank brigades, now called 'The Tank Corps', with a new arm badge – a Mk I tank (without rear wheel) sewn high up on the right arm sleeve. And the colours of the corps of brown, red and green were selected and suggested by Fuller to mean, 'From mud through blood to the green fields beyond.' He also proposed the motto for the new corps of 'Fear Nought'.

Records show the composition of the 3rd Battalion in July 1917 when all tanks were 'christened' with a name beginning with the letter 'C':

NO. 7 COMPANY
Section 1, Captain Bates; 'Canada', 'Ceylon', 'Cape Colony', 'Cyprus'
Section 3, Captain Youll; 'Carstairs', 'Cumbria', 'Caithness', 'Culloden'
Section 4, Captain Gates; 'Ca'canny', 'Cuidich'n Righ', 'Celtic', 'Clyde'
Section 2 (Supply), Captain Tull; 'Cork', 'Crewe'

NO. 8 COMPANY
Section 5, Captain Sir J. Dashwood; 'Curmudgeon', 'Cynic', 'Crusty', 'Curiosity'
Section 6 (Supply), Captain May; 'Corncrake', 'Celebrity', 'Censorship'
Section 7, Captain Hiscocks; 'Crocodile', 'Crab', 'Crustacean', 'Caterpillar'
Section 8, Captain Elliott; 'Centaur', 'Caliban', 'Cannibal', 'Cyclops'

NO. 9 COMPANY
Section 10, Captain Keppel Palmer; 'Challenger', 'Conqueror', 'Caesar', 'Cleopatra'
Section 11, Captain Weber; 'Chaperon', 'Consort', 'Coquette', 'Chanticleer'

Section 12, Captain Purdy; 'Crusader', 'Cayenne', 'Chili',
    'Comet'
Section 9 (Supply/Wireless), Captain North; 'Chameleon',
    'Carnation', 'Communiqué'

For the Fifth Army's offensive under General Gough – the Third
Battle of Ypres – the 3rd Tank Brigade (now including 'C'
Battalion) were allotted to 'XIX' Corps.

Half the forty-eight tanks which started on 30 July were
ditched or hit, but many proved helpful to the infantry. Two
helped overcome the Frezenberg strongpoint and two more the
defenders of Spree Farm. The reserve echelon of twenty-four
were delayed crossing the River Steenbeck by marshland and
arrived late for the actual assault. MCs were won by Captain L.J.
Bates for an action in the vicinity of Beck House and by Captain
S.L. Keppel-Palmer whose flag tank was disabled; he tried
another which became ditched and completed a successful
action in a third. Lieutenant T.E.B. Chalmers was ditched near
Wilde Wood and his seventh effort to salvage his tank under
heavy fire was successful; Second Lieutenant E.J. Rollings led his
section across the Steenbeck River into action. DCMs were won
by Corporal D.C. Jenkins who took charge of a section of two
tanks when his officer was killed, and by Corporal W. Myleham
who drove tanks for 13 hours; two were ditched and unditched
under fire. Gunner L. Frankcombe won the MM when he drove
through the Pommern redoubt, dispersed four enemy MG crews,
captured a machine-gun and returned safely to the Tankodrome
(base). Private A. Dryden won the MM when, with Corporal S.
Print, he salvaged a derelict tank near Wilde Wood. Other
decorations were issued for actions at the Steenbeek River,
Frezenberge redoubt, Hill 35 (where Second Lieutenant E.M.
Wolf won the MC, in action for 26 hours, breaking up counter-
attacks with his Lewis guns), the Pommern redoubt, Glencose
Wood (Corporal V.J. Guiver won the DCM as chief wireless
operator on duty for 18 hours; the aerial masts of his wireless
station were shot away ten times, each time being repaired by
him) and Inverness Copse. Altogether 'C' Battalion gained
twenty-five decorations in the Third Battle of Ypres.

On 11 September 1917 'B', 'C' and 'F' Battalions were
withdrawn from the front. When a tank was destroyed or written off
new names were conceived such as 'Clan Leslie', 'Crossmichael',
'Celebrity', 'Comme Ca', 'Creme de Menthe', 'Carnaby', 'Casa',

'Crewe', 'Cork', 'Cardiff', 'Cirencester' and 'Charlie Chaplin'. There must have been a lot of discussion in each tank crew and possibly a democratic choice was made.

The most famous battle in the history of the war in which tanks were to play a significant role was now being planned. The objectives were (a) to break through the main Hindenburg Line from Bleak House to the Canal du Nord and capture the village of Ribecourt, (b) to penetrate beyond and breach the Hindenburg support line and (c) to exploit northwards towards Cambrai. No less than 476 British tanks – all three tank brigades – were to take part in this major offensive.

At the central workshops at Erin, great fascines of brushwood bound together with heavy chains had been constructed to help get across the enemy's three lines of deep and wide trenches. Some 350 fascines were constructed, each with 60 bundles of wood, weighing 2 tons. It took central workshops three weeks to construct them, working night and day. A fascine would be carried on the nose of the tank and released from inside by a special trigger.

J.F.C. Fuller, now Lieutenant-Colonel, had planned the new method of attack. It was a game of chess. The 'lead' or advance tank of a section of three would advance and flatten the wire, turn sharp left *before* the enemy trench, shooting up its occupants. The two 'follow up' or 'main body' tanks each with a fascine would pass through the gap in the wire, select a dropping-off point in the enemy trench, drop its fascine in it, cross and deploy sharp left, while the third back-up tank would do the same and deploy sharp right after dropping in, and crossing over its fascine. The advance guard tank would then return and cross over one of the fascines, and drop its own fascine in the next line of trenches.

'C' Battalion (and 'F') tanks were allocated to 12th Division of 'III' Corps; 24 tanks plus 4 in reserve to 35th Brigade, and 12 plus 2 to 37th Brigade. Each tank brigade had 18 supply/gun-carrying tanks and 3 wireless tanks. The 3rd Tank Brigade trained with 12th Division near Bermicourt, where the first large-scale infantry/armour manoeuvres took place.

From Bray-sur-Somme they entrained for the front in mid-November. Brigadier-General Hugh Elles issued a Special Order No. 6, dated 19 November 1917 and went into action inside 'Hilda' tank of 'H' Battalion in the centre of the six-mile line of attack.

Initially all went well and the Hindenburg front-line system was quickly overrun on 20 November, but several pockets of resistance remained. One was at Bleak House on the Peronne–Cambrai road, where on the extreme right of the front, tanks of 'C' and 'F' Battalions led 12th Division along the Bonavis Ridge. The stronghold was taken after a sharp fight. Lateau Wood was taken by 1100 hrs and 12th Division managed to hold the Bonavis Ridge overlooking the Canal de L'Escaut. When 'C' and 'F' Squadrons rallied at midday on the H Support line, 55 of the original 76 tanks were still operating, 12 had been hit by artillery fire and 9 ditched. By noon on the 20th a great success had been won, with the enemy's two main lines of defences overrun. On the first day of the Battle of Cambrai tank casualties were 179: 65 by direct hits, 71 by mechanical breakdown, and 43 by ditching. That night 3rd Tank Brigade rallied at La Vacquerie.

As a result of the actions on the 20th MCs were won by Captain R.A. Youll at Bleak House, Captain H.A. Johnston on the Gonnelieu Ridge and Bleak House, by Second Lieutenant M.T. Archibald at Lateau Wood (and on the 21st bringing in a ditched tank in enemy lines), Second Lieutenant G. Walker at Pam Pam Farm, and Second Lieutenant W. Moore at Lateau Wood. Lance Corporal A. Budd won the DCM on Gonnelieu Ridge (when his tank received a direct hit wounding all the crew, he bombed the enemy away from his tank which was stuck on top of an enemy trench).

Enemy counter-attacks came in and on 23 November Major-General Harper's 'Duds', the 51st Highland Division, were given extra tank support to try to recapture Fontaine. On the right flank 88 tanks were involved in 'IV' Corps' assault on the Bourlon position, 10,000 yards from Cantaing-Tadpole Copse. Some 36 tanks of 'B', 'H' and 'C' Battalions lined up in the sunken Premy Chapel–Graincourt road with the battalions of Highlanders to attack Fontaine. At 1030 hrs 3 'C' Battalion tanks made for La Folie Wood, and 13 of 'B' and 6 of 'C' Battalion set off towards Fontaine followed by 6th Battalion Gordon Highlanders.

The 6-pdr 'male' tank of 'C' Battalion attacking La Folie Wood was hit immediately by shellfire and put out of action. The other two reached the wood and dispersed many groups of German infantry, but without 6-pdr support could not deal with accurate MG fire from La Folie Château in the centre of the wood. The combined nineteen 'B' and 'C' tanks reached Fontaine village but as the infantry had been ordered by General Harper (who did not believe tanks had a future) to stay well back, they were halted by fire from houses and a château. They went on alone under a hail of MG fire and grenades thrown from houses. Only three tanks of 'B' Squadron got back to base at the end of the day, with crews of four others. Meanwhile, 12 tanks of 'H' Battalion and 3 of 'C' Battalion swung left past Fontaine and led 6th Seaforth Highlanders without a check into Bourlon Wood.

Second Lieutenant M.T. Archibald's tank did great damage to the enemy in the streets of Fontaine. He rescued the entire crew of another 'C' Battalion tank which was on fire and with sixteen wounded persons on board took his tank out of the village. This too was set on fire by AP bullets but Archibald got both crews out and back to the rallying point. Second Lieutenants Walker and Moore fought their tanks with great bravery, the latter being severely wounded. Gunner C.W. Green won the DCM in La Fontaine expending all the 6-pdr rounds, as his tank with sixteen on board, of which eleven wounded, eventually escaped to safety.

In the Battle of Cambrai twenty-one officers and men of 'C' Battalion received awards for gallantry. In addition Major T.S. Dick in charge of 'C' Battalion workshops was awarded the DSO.

By 1 December tanks fought their final action in the Battle of Cambrai. Of 4,000 Tank Corps officers and men who took part, 1,153 were killed, wounded or missing. Of the 474 tanks who started the battle less than a third returned to base and most needed extensive repairs. The end of the ten-day battle was a stalemate.

Although Sir Douglas Haig was generous with his praise for the work of the Tank Corps, discussion and controversy continued at the War Office. Mk V tanks (designed to be faster, and carrying Hotchkiss machine-guns), Mks VI and VII and finally the Mk VIII were agreed and development begun in December 1917, but inevitably they arrived too late for the battlefields of 1918.

'C' Battalion was still commanded by Lieutenant-Colonel S.H. Charrington with a DSO, and later a *Croix de Guerre* and CMG. The battalion were soon equipped with the brand new Medium A or Whippet tank designed to exploit a breach in the enemy lines. Its speed was 8 mph, it weighed 14 tons and had a petrol endurance of 80 miles. Its two 45-bhp engines each drove one track and the tank was steered by varying their speeds. General Elles christened them the 'Savage Rabbits' which may have been a compliment.

By March 1918 the original nine battalions which had fought at Cambrai were reinforced by five more and exchanged their lettered titles for numeral ones; thus 'C' became 3rd Battalion Tank Corps (3rd RTC). The five tank brigades were next in action against the massive German offensive of March 1918. 3rd Battalion was in reserve for the Third Army at Wailly in the Bapaume area, with Lieutenant-Colonel Walker Bell as the new CO of 3rd (Light) Tank Battalion.

An action at Colincamps on 26 March earned Corporal A.F. Ebsworth the MM as he drove his tank with great skill and courage. As a 'first' driver he had fought in the Battles of the Somme, Arras, Third Ypres and Cambrai. In each action his tank had received a direct hit from enemy artillery. Twelve Whippet tanks went north from Bray towards Serre and from Colincamps swept forward into the two leading German infantry battalions, took them by surprise and chased them to Sere. The German breakthrough by the river line of the River Ancre was thus repulsed.

The next month on 24 April saw 3rd Battalion in great form. Captain Tommy Price with seven Whippets was in reserve on 24 April near the Bois de L'Abbé. A reconnaissance aircraft dropped a message that two enemy battalions were halted in a hollow near Cachy. Price had already won the DSO and MC and his action at Villers-Bretonneux now earned him a bar to the MC. This is his report of the action:

I assembled my section and tank commanders and quickly gave them the information ('X' Coy 3rd Bn to go and assist in the defence of Amiens) 7 Whippet tanks with Lieutenants Hore and Elsbury; with 58th Infantry Division; enemy massing 2 Bns for attack 1,000 yards east of Cachy and ordered them to form line facing south at 50 paces interval between tanks . . . cross the Cachy switch and chase at full speed southwards dispersing any enemy on the way. On reaching the skyline I indicated, they were to turn back and charge through the enemy again on the way back. Met Captain Sheppard of the Northamptons. The country was beautifully open and undulating and ideal for tanks. My deduction as to the position of the enemy proved correct. The charging tanks came upon them over a rise at point blank range apparently having a meal as several bodies had laid aside arms. The tanks went straight through them causing great execution by fire, and by running over many who were unable to get away. They turned and came back through the remnants again utterly dispersing them. We lost one tank, KO'd by a battery placed in Hangard Wood. We counted 400 dead of the enemy later. We left Point A at 10.30 am and were back again at 2.30 pm and the second phase of the attack on our lines never materialised.

Price had five casualties out of the twenty-seven tankmen in the action, while three other Whippets were damaged by a German battery and a huge A7V German tank. The intrepid Price took his surviving tanks out again the same evening and was in a brisk action. Lieutenants Elsbury and Hore were awarded MCs, Corporal A.E. Lucas a bar to his MM and Sergeant C. Parrott and Corporal E. Till, both received MMs.

By mid-May 1918 the British tank strength was 600, of which 82 were Whippets and the remainder mostly Mk IV and Vs. For the Battle of Amiens on 8 August the 3rd Tank Brigade of Whippets which included 3rd Battalion was placed under command of the Cavalry Corps.

South of the Somme a gap of eleven miles opened up on the German front but the 3rd Cavalry Division to which 3rd Battalion were attached made slow progress. The logic of using cavalry against MG nests and field guns was, of course, after four years of attritional warfare, a complete absurdity. However, the battalion was in action on the 8th at Le Quesnel and Beaucourt and at Rouvroy the next day. Major H.A. Grayson won the MC and Chevalier Order of Leopold and Second Lieutenant W.P. Whyte who had done so well at Cachy, now won the DSO. He was wounded three times; his tank broke down and he directed his section on foot under intense fire. At Beaucourt Sergeant H. Hibbert won the DCM though wounded in neck, face, thighs, arms and groin and continued to fight his tank, inflicting heavy casualties. Corporal A. Budd already had the DCM, but now gained an MM, driving away by fire the enemy serving two 6-inch naval guns.

For the Third Army's attack planned for 21 August, 3rd Battalion formed part of 1st Tank Brigade, and in actions at Achiet-le-Petit, MCs were gained by Captains C.F. Weber (a bar) and I. Bower; Sergeant F. Howells was awarded the DCM when he silenced a large nest of twelve enemy machine-guns. His tank was hit and he blew it up to prevent it falling into enemy hands. MMs were won that day by Corporal Edwards and Gunners

Young, Gillie and Witty. In the next few days fierce fighting continued for the battalion at Biefvillers, Favreuil and Bapaume. On 25 August Sergeant W. Goward, already the holder of two MMs, won a third at Bapaume in charge of a Whippet badly ditched close to the enemy. He took out his guns and formed a strongpoint 350 yards *ahead* of the supporting infantry. Captain Le Clair won a bar to his MC at Biefvillers as did Captain Monk; Second Lieutenant Thomas at Favreuil received six bullets in his arm as he held a steel helmet over a porthole cover, shot away by a machine-gun. Later he fell unconscious under his tank and was rescued by the infantry.

The Tank Corps were awarded three Victoria Crosses in the First World War. Lieutenant Cecil Harold Sewell earned one of them on the afternoon of 29 August 1918 in front of Fremicourt following the enemy's retreat from Bapaume. He got out of his Whippet and crossed open ground under heavy fire to rescue the crew of another tank of his section (commanded by Lieutenant Rees-Williams) which had sideslipped into a large shell hole, overturned and caught fire. He dug away the side of the shell hole, reached the tank door and released the trapped crew. Then he rescued one of his own crewmen who was lying wounded behind his tank, was hit, then hit again fatally in the act of dressing his wounded driver. The whole action in full view of enemy MG and rifle pits took place at Beauquatre. One of his fellow officers wrote: 'As a soldier he was absolutely fearless. On 8 August I saw him doing things which even a brave man might well shrink from and all the time he was laughing and treating it all as a joke. On the 29th there is no doubt whatever that he lost his life in saving the lives of three others. We found him (riddled by machine-gunners who were all around us) with his arms round his dead driver Gunner W. Knox.'

Further action took place in October. On the 3rd, Second Lieutenant G.M. Finnsberg won the MC at the Masnières–Beaurevoir line. Near Estrées he was wounded in five places when his gunner and driver were *hors de combat*. He then attacked two German strongpoints; when his Whippet was ditched, he evacuated it, was wounded again and taken prisoner. After three hours he escaped and survived, although wounded altogether in seventeen places. On the same day at Serain Lieutenant L.E. Minchin won the MC. After his Whippet had been knocked out and his crew killed, he joined the infantry and helped them consolidate under heavy fire. Private

T.C. Cronie drove his tank for seven hours; when it broke down he mended it under shellfire, brought it to the objective despite railways and sunken roads, and enabled his gunners to get successfully into action, and was awarded the MM.

By 8 August 819 tanks had been completely written off. The Tank Corps had suffered over 3,000 casualties, a third of those involved. The Hindenburg Line was stormed during September with 230 surviving tanks taking part. 'V' Brigade with 3rd RTC were by then in reserve. On 17 October King George V became Colonel-in-Chief of the Tank Corps. When the ceasefire came on 11 November the British Armies had managed an advance of just 40 miles beyond the Hindenburg Line. The resources of the Tank Corps were by then exhausted. During the First World War 'C' or 3rd Battalion won a Victoria Cross, a Commander St Michael and St George (CMG), 5 Distinguished Service Orders (DSOs), 31 Military Crosses (MCs) (and 3 bars), 15 Distinguished Service Medals (DSMs), 64 Military Medals (MMs) (and 7 bars) and 4 Military Service Medals (MSMs). It was a magnificent record.

2

BETWEEN THE WARS – WEARING THE BRUNSWICK GREEN

Five tank battalions were sent to Germany as part of the occupation forces and the officers returned to the Tank Corps Depot in Bovington. In November 1919 3rd Battalion was reconstituted as a training centre under Lieutenant-Colonel H.K. Woods. Two years later it was sent to Dublin for garrison duties under Lieutenant-Colonel W.J. Shannon and numbers were made up from infantry, cavalry and AS Corps. One company was sent south to 6th Division, another to 5th Division in the centre, another to 1st Division in Ulster. A total of 10 tanks and 72 armoured cars were employed in escort work and patrolling. They foiled an attempt to burn the Customs House in Dublin and dispersed a number of hostile raiding parties. In 1922 3rd Battalion returned to Wareham, Dorset and recruited officers and men from the Machine Gun Corps.

On 18 October 1923 the Tank Corps was granted the distinction of the 'Royal' prefix by the King in recognition of 'the splendid work performed by Our Tank Corps during the Great War'. Service lanyards with distinctive colours were allotted to the senior battalions – Red to 1st, Saffron Yellow to 2nd, Brunswick Green to 3rd and Blue to 4th. The Regimental March Past tune for the battalion was 'The Quarter Deck'. The black beret was now officially adopted as the RTC's head-dress, in place of the standard field service cap, approved by the King in March 1924. There were now only the four regular tank battalions. The battalion left Wareham for Lydd in the Eastern Command which was to be their depot until the outbreak of the Second World War fifteen years later.

During the General Strike in May 1926 a group was formed in London commanded by Lieutenant-Colonel Shannon, comprising a tank company and two Peerless armoured car companies from

3rd RTC. It was based in Chelsea Barracks to maintain order and escort food convoys from the docks. The next year an Experimental Mechanized Force was formed, and was the first attempt at a genuine 'armoured division'. Lieutenant-Colonel F.A. Pile was the CO of 3rd Battalion RTC which consisted of RHQ, two companies each of ten armoured cars and a company of 'tankettes', (eight Morris and eight Carden-Lloyd vehicles). The 5th Battalion RTC, 2nd Battalion Somerset Light Infantry, 9th Field Brigade Royal Artillery (RA), 9th Light Battery RA, 17th Field Company Royal Engineers (RE) and four RAF squadrons formed the composite group. This unique motorized group included Vickers Mk II tanks, 'tankettes', armoured cars, wireless tanks, motorized machine-gun units, towed and half-track field guns and howitzers, plus RAF air cover. Guderian and Rommel would have been proud of this 'panzer' unit. Lieutenant-Colonel Pile was the driving force within the group.

Private F.W. Fertherstone, No. 5 Section, 'B' Company, 3rd RTC was stationed at Lydd, Kent on 14 February 1926. He wrote: 'We are worked to death here. This is an average day. Reveille 6.30. Breakfast 7.15. Drill order parade 8.15 to 9.0. Sometimes a few minutes drill between 9.45 and 10.15. Next parade 11.0, sometimes PT which means kicking a football about; Dinner 2.30. Finished at 2.30 each day. This company hasn't any tanks. Before they left Germany 3 weeks since they were ordered to blow up all the tanks before returning to England.'

Lance Corporal J.F.C. Wollaston was a 2nd Gunner and hull Vickers gunner in 3rd RTC and noted, 'All arms collective training occurred each year after the harvest. In 1928 "A" Coy 3rd Bn RTC moved from Lydd to Colchester to train with Eastern Command. The OC was Major A.J. Clifton and we had 16 Vickers Medium MK II tanks. No. T-74 of No. 1 Section was under Corporal E. ("Nutty") Bolton; driver Lance Corporal Jimmy Grainger. On the way back from exercises, just south of Colchester on a country road with a steep bank on the left, eight foot high, the driver managed to overturn the tank. It needed three tanks to retrieve it. The photographs in the local papers showed the rescue.'

Winston Churchill, then Chancellor of the Exchequer, was in charge of the special demonstration of 280 armoured and other vehicles which took place on Salisbury Plain that year. Field Marshal Sir George Milne, Chief of the Imperial General Staff (CIGS) was a convert to the mechanization of the Army, with the tank in the principal role. Armoured mobility was the key innovation, while the petrol engine, the tank and the aeroplane were also changing the concept of warfare, particularly in France. The year 1928 saw the first stage in the conversion of the cavalry from horses to armoured fighting vehicles (AFVs), although the cavalry generals took another decade to accept the reality that gallant Dragoons, Lancers and Hussars could not compete with machine-guns, let alone tanks and AFVs. Winston Churchill, a cavalry officer of the 21st Lancers by choice, became the godparent of the tank. He demanded that the cavalry units be abolished or mechanized. But the diehards of the General Staff persuaded the Secretary of State for War to disperse the armoured force after a two-year 'experiment'.

However, in 1929 new experiments revolved round two infantry brigades, the 6th in Aldershot Command, and the 7th in Southern Command. Two light tank battalions from 3rd and 4th Battalions RTC (under Lieutenant-Colonel H.D. Carlton and Lieutenant-Colonel M. Kemp-Welch) each with three companies of sixteen light tanks, were part of each brigade. Manoeuvres continued in the 1930 and 1931 training seasons with 3rd and 5th Battalions RTC taking part. In one exercise both RTC battalions covered a 60-mile march as a fighting advance between 0300 hrs and early afternoon with minimal casualties. The year 1931 saw the formation of a complete brigade of tanks under Brigadier Charles Broad which included 2nd, 3rd and 5th Battalions RTC. Each unit had a mixture of 95 light, 85 medium and close support tanks. The armament comprised 85 3-pdr guns and 350 Vickers machine-guns. Lieutenant-Colonel Percy Hobart was CO 2nd Battalion; Lieutenant-Colonel M. Kemp-Welch CO 3rd and Lieutenant-Colonel J.C. Tilly CO 5th Battalion. Brigade HQ was at the Royal Military College, Sandhurst.

The Disarmament Conference in Geneva brought immediate constraints on spending, tank design and development and Army estimates were reduced. Although sixty-six light tanks were manufactured in 1931–2 only nine were built in 1932–3. The unfortunate 3rd Battalion, now commanded by Lieutenant-Colonel R.H. Broome had to make do with Carden-Lloyd machine-gun carriers. To 2nd RTC went the new Mk II light tanks.

In 1933 the reduced tank brigade was not reassembled, not even for training. The 3rd Battalion became part of the 1st Division which trained around Aldershot. In November, Colonel P.C.S. Hobart, Inspector of the Tank Corps was designated to command a new 1st Tank Brigade. It was formed on 1 April

1934 with 2nd, 3rd and 5th RTC with the new 1st (Light) Battalion. The 3rd was still based at Lydd as a 'medium' battalion with 49 tanks (18 medium, 21 light, 6 close support and 4 for HQ). Early that year Bill Close joined 3rd RTR at Lydd. Five years later as a troop sergeant he trained on the Vickers Mks I and II at Lulworth, a sandy heathland south of Brighton: 'They were handy little tanks produced in early 1920s, weight 12–14 tons, a crew of five, a speed of 18 mph, a 23-pdr gun and up to 6 machine guns.' Trooper Bill Jordan recalled: 'Our regimental bus at Lydd used to take the lads on the nights of Friday, Saturday and Sunday to Hastings to enjoy the fun to be had at the Railway Hotel. Shepherd Neame's bitter was threepence a pint.'

Colonel Hobart (known as 'Hobo') was a skilled tank commander, irascible, intolerant but a dominant leader and brilliant organizer who later created no less than three armoured divisions. So exercise followed exercise often in conjunction with the RAF. The development of tank movement at night was to prove important but unfortunately was to be little used in the early desert campaign in North Africa which lay ahead. Lieutenant-Colonel H.H. Dean took over command of 3rd Battalion in March 1935 and Hobart carried out six extensive brigade exercises that year. The 3rd Battalion joined 4th Division, and Captain K.C. Johnston-Jones became responsible for the training of all the Tank Brigade transport personnel (99 vehicles with 34 ammunition, 23 petrol and 21 fitters' lorries). The next year Hobart planned nine brigade exercises including a 'Tank versus Tank' action and night-firing exercises. The brigade was at Tilshead with few tanks, few men, few officers and with lorries representing AFVs. The latest light tank, the Mk VI, was under-equipped, the suspension was faulty and it had to be fitted with Triplex glass windows.

Disarmament was now of major importance to all politicians except those in Germany, and Winston Churchill. The years 1935-7 were the nadir of the fortunes of the RTC, although eight cavalry regiments were destined to become mechanized.

In April 1936 Bill Jordan arrived at Wool Station (nearest to Bovington) and found Bovington Camp just a mass of wooden huts. Together with Corporal Jack Orr and Lance Corporal Fyffe and others they joined 3rd RTC at Lydd:

We were then entering a different life altogether. We were distributed between "A", "B" and "C" Companies. I went to "B" and fell into trouble. Pancakes on Shrove Tuesday (1937) were on the dinner menu. The supply of clean plates ran out so Bill and others ate their pancakes with their hands. So he was put on a charge before Major Mahoney the OC. Jordan found 'the officers a race apart wearing khaki trousers similar to old fashioned plus-fours with puttees and with a stand-offish attitude. During the war many NCOs were commissioned and then there was a different feeling throughout the regiment. A high-ranking officer told us Britain would be at war with Germany in four years time. We could not understand why no new tanks were being produced, as the mediums and Mark VIBs were no use whatsoever. Every summer training took place at Tilshead on manoeuvres. This was the pattern every year. We used to say that in the event of another war, as long as the enemy came to Salisbury Plain we were bound to win!

When Colonel Martel, Assistant Director of Mechanization, visited Soviet Army manoeuvres he was much impressed by the 1,200 tanks he saw. The most up-to-date had a maximum speed of 30 mph, few mechanical problems and were powered by 300-bhp *aircraft* engines. On his return many tank designs and prototypes were considered: the A-6, A-7, A-8, A-9 (a stopgap medium, 100 were ordered), the Carden A-10, A-11 (eventually 139 were built and it became the Infantry Tank Mk I), A-12 (Infantry Tank Mk II, the Matilda), A-13 (the Mk III became the Cruiser Tank Mk V, or Covenanter), A-14, A-15 (Cruiser Mk VI, the Crusader). But any attempt to mount a bigger gun than the 2-pdr would cause severe production delays!

In January 1938, the CO of 3rd RTC was Lieutenant-Colonel R.M.W. Gross. His battalion had a strength of 26 officers, 7 WOs, 33 sergeants and 322 other ranks. Three months later the Director of Artillery approved a specification for a 6-pdr gun which then took 20 months to reach the a prototype stage!

The Wireless Wing 3rd RTC in 1938 was in the new barracks at Warminster. Sergeant Sandy Powell was i/c and the other instructors of the No. 7 and No. 9 wireless sets were Corporal Hugh 'Smudger' Smithson (later to be captured at Calais), Corporal Jock Cunningham, Corporal Frank Peel (later commissioned in the Middle East in 1943), Corporal Bob Redmile, Corporal Tommy Potts and Lance Corporal 'Monty' Mount. Driver/operators received an extra trade pay of 1s 3d per day – riches indeed!

Private A.E. Jobson was posted to 3rd RTR in 1938. He was a good hockey player but could not get into the RTR team which included Lieutenant D. Coulson (who played for Ireland), Sergeant Twigg in goal, 'Tich' Kemp, J. Cornwall and Paddy Bingham. They were in the Army final 1938/9. Bert was a waiter in civilian life and worked in the officers' mess – Colonel Gross, Major Mahoney, Captain R.H.O. Simpson, G.B. Moss, I.B. Fernie, Captain 'Polly' Blank, Captain Reeves. The Quartermaster was Reggie De Vere. 'At the outbreak of war we moved out of the new barracks at Warminster, then under canvas, next to Hitchin, then on to Fordingbridge and our every move was mentioned by "Lord Haw Haw"', recalled Bill Jordan.

The Secretary of State for War Leslie Hore-Belisha announced in Parliament on 4 April 1939 that the cavalry and RTC battalions would be combined into a single corps, the Royal Armoured Corps. The RTC battalions became the Royal Tank Regiments (RTR). During that year 3rd Battalion occupied the newly built Hore-Belisha Barracks on the edge of the Salisbury Plain military training area. At the outbreak of war on 3 September they were stationed at Swinton Barracks, Warminster. At 1800 hrs mobilization orders were received and on 30 October Lieutenant-Colonel R.M.W. Gross moved the battalion, part of 1st Heavy Armoured Brigade, to Fordingbridge in the New Forest. The George Ship and Royal Arms public houses did some good business!

3

CALAIS – 'A TERRIBLE WAY TO START A WAR'

The 3rd RTR was now commanded by Lieutenant-Colonel R.C. Keller, part of 3rd Armoured Brigade (the original Tank Brigade of 1934–8) in the 1st Armoured Division. Reggie Keller (a regular tank officer from the First World War) had taken command on 11 December 1939. Captain E.G.D. Moss was the Adjutant. 'A' Squadron OC was Major J. McCaffrey MC, 2 i/c Captain J.E. Deighton. 'B' Sqn OC was Major I.B. Fernie, 2 i/c Captain R.H. How, 'C' Sqn OC was Major W. Harrison MC, 2 i/c Captain Evered.

Battalion HQ with 175 strength were ensconced in the Riverside Hotel, Fordingbridge, 'A' Sqn with 154 strength were in the Greyhound Hotel, 'B' Sqn strength of 146 were in 'Woodlands', Sandleheath and 'C' Sqn strength of 155 were in 'Bowood', Boweswood Road. There were four tank parks in Alexandra Road, Park Road, Victoria Road and Church Square.

Their tank strength in late 1939 comprised of Battalion HQ, 2 cruiser Mk I A-9s (with another cruiser and 2 light Mk VIBs to come); 'A' Sqn had 5 light tanks (with 2 to come), 3 cruisers with guns, 1 without! 'B' Sqn had 5 light tanks (plus 2 to come), 2 cruisers with guns and 2 without. 'C' Sqn had 5 light tanks (with 2 to come), 3 cruisers with guns, 2 without. The Medium Tank Group had 5 medium Mk III tanks. 'B' Echelon had a total of 164 vehicles.

Early in 1940 manoeuvres were planned to take place with 1st Armoured Division in France and orders were received to move to Pacy-sur-Eure in Normandy to complete their training. In the spring about a third of the battalion had been taken away to form a new unit and were replaced by officers and men from a training regiment, while some also came from the North-West Frontier in India. The tank strength was now 21 light Mk VI tanks of 5½ tons weight, a crew of three with a .505 and .303 Vickers machine-gun. They were powered by a Meadows 89-bhp engine which gave a maximum road speed of 35 mph and fuel endurance of 130 road miles. They were lightly armoured and vulnerable to the German anti-tank (A/Tk) guns. Two squadrons were also equipped with a total of twenty-seven cruiser tanks. These were largely A-9s with a crew of six, a 2-pdr gun and three Vickers machine-guns (one coaxial, two in auxiliary turrets), with a maximum road speed of 25 mph, powered by an AEC six-cylinder 150-bhp engine. There were a few A-10s armed with a 3.7-in mortar for close support. The remainder were Mk I A-13s of 14¾ tons, a crew of four, and a 2-pdr gun with a coaxial Vickers .303 machine-gun. The A-13's Nuffield Liberty I, 340-bhp engine produced a maximum speed of 30 mph. The thin 14-mm armour was vulnerable but the 2-pdr gun was effective against tanks.

Commander of 'XVI' Panzer Corps, General Guderian's plan for the invasion of France was to capture the vital Channel ports of Dunkirk, Calais and Boulogne by the coordinated advance of his three Panzer Divisions: the 1st (under Lieutenant-Colonel Balck), the 2nd, and 10th (earmarked for the capture of Dunkirk). By the night of 20 May the panzers had reached the sea beyond Abbeville and were moving northward along the coast by Etaples towards the three Channel ports. Prime Minister Winston Churchill knew the area well: 'the inundation system between Calais and Dunkirk and the significance of the Gravelines waterline'. The sluices had been opened and every day the floods were spreading. Churchill wrote: 'The defence of Boulogne, but *still more of Calais*, to the latest hour, stood forth upon the confused scene and garrisons were immediately sent there from England. Boulogne isolated and attacked on 22 May was defended by two battalions of Guards, one of our few A/Tk batteries with some French troops.' After nearly two days of fighting the Guards were rescued by eight Royal Navy destroyers with a loss of only 200 men. The Lord Gort, GOC of the British Expeditionary Force (BEF), was responsible for the defence of the three Channel ports. Churchill continued:

I now resolved that Calais should be fought to the death and that no evacuation by sea could be allowed to the garrison (30th Infantry Brigade) which consisted of one Bn of the Rifle Brigade, one of the 60th Rifles, the Queen Victoria Rifles, the 229th A/Tk battery RA and (3rd) Bn of the Royal Tank Regiment with 21 light and 27 cruiser tanks and an equal number of

Frenchmen. It was painful thus to sacrifice these splendid, trained troops, of which we had so few, for the doubtful advantage of gaining two or perhaps three days. The Secretary of State for War and the CIGS agreed to this hard measure.

The 30th Infantry Brigade units mentioned by Churchill were a scratch formation originally planned to land at Trondheim in mid-April as the reserve unit in the small British Expeditionary Force (BEF) in the ill-fated Norwegian expedition. So now this brigade was sent with all despatch to Calais to hold it against all odds. 3rd RTR would operate as a mobile threat to the flank of the German panzer advance. Trooper Bill Jordan of 'B' Sqn: 'The tanks were taken to Southampton and before loading onto the ship (*City of Christchurch* on 19 May), all petrol had to be drained from them into 2 gallon cans; all .303 machine-guns were removed from their mountings and covered in mineral jelly and placed in their boxes. All this time all troops were confined to the town area. Early in the evening NCOs were going round all the pubs, the cinema and other places warning all our men to pack their kit and to proceed to the station as we were leaving at midnight for France.' Major Mahoney, the 2 i/c was in charge of loading and unloading the tanks and echelon vehicles. Major Simpson was OC 'A' Sqn, Major W. Reeves OC 'B' Sqn and Major F.V. Lyons OC 'C' Sqn. Captain Evered was OC HQ Sqn.

By midnight on the 21st all but ten men and one officer were collected and the troop train took the battalion to Dover, arriving at dawn. 'We sailed on the *Maid of Orleans* a Southern Railways cross-channel steamer,' recalled Sergeant W.H. Close. 'On board we were told "our tanks will be delivered there (Calais) and you will prepare them for action immediately. Light enemy forces have broken through somewhere to the north. We will find them and deal with them."' Close, his troop sergeant 'Socker' Heath, an Army boxing champion, and 'Tubby' Ballard from Northants were all both part of the battalion's Recce Troop under Lieutenant Morgan. Their Daimler Dingos were under 5 foot tall, with a crew of two, and could travel at 55 mph forwards *or* backwards. Armament was a single mounted Bren LMG. The Commander observed from the gun cockpit and the No. 2 did the driving. Close's driver was Trooper Billy Barlow who once ran a fish and chip shop in Lydd.

The *Maid of Orleans* left Dover at 1100 hrs on 22 May in a thick mist which cleared on arrival at Calais revealing the spire of

Notre Dame church and the clock tower of the Hotel de Ville. The ship tied up at the Gare Maritime at 0115 hrs. 'The glass from the windows of the Customs House and restaurant was strewn all over the quayside and railway platform', wrote Major Bill Reeves. 'Black smoke was belching forth from most of the quayside buildings and warehouses and the whole area was pock-marked with bomb craters. We made our way in single file round the edge of the lagoon to the sand dunes on the far side where there was some cover. The heat was terrific. I was weighed down with both pack and haversack on my back, a second haversack at my side, a gas mask at the alert on my chest and a gas cape rolled on top of my pack on my shoulder. In addition of course was weapon, ammunition, compass, binoculars and map cases. The idea of a crew fighting *in* a tank in all this regalia was of course ludicrous. . . .'

Other 3rd RTR characters to arrive in Calais were Sergeant Major George Witheridge who became a Squadron Commander later on in the African Campaign. Lance Corporal 'Buck' Kite, a talented footballer, was a reserve driver/gunner and optimistically brought two footballs with him. Sergeant Stan Cox took over a mature A-9 tank armed with a 3.7-in mortar which could only fire smoke rounds, as the high-explosive (HE) shells were still in England.

On the same day, Winston Churchill flew to Paris to encourage the French to continue fighting just as 2nd Panzer Division reached Boulogne and surrounded 2nd Guards Brigade on their landward side. At the same time 1st Panzer Division had reached the outskirts of Calais and invested it, while 10th Panzer Division remained in reserve. At Dover, 3rd RTR's CO, Lieutenant-Colonel Keller was told 'there is no enemy north of St Pol', although 6th and 8th Panzer Divisions were already west of there. Keller wrote several reports after the siege and fall of Calais. 'There was no one to meet the Bn beyond the Station Troops Officer who did not know much.' Eventually Colonel Holland, then OC troops in Calais and his HQ were located in the western part of the town on the Boulogne road. The battalion was 'put up in the sand dunes to the NE of the Bassin des Chasses'. Colonel Holland asked Keller to billet the battalion for the night in the Baraques area, but it was not suitable for tanks. None of the battalion had been issued with BEF military identity cards and zealous gendarmes refused to allow the CO into the Hotel de Ville. Keller went back to the docks and there met Lieutenant General Brownrigg (Lord

Gort's Adjutant-General) and General Loyd. The orders were specific: 3rd RTR when unloaded were to proceed into harbour in the Forêt de Boulogne, 19 miles due south and east of the town and then get in touch with Brigadier Fox-Pitt, Commanding Officer 2nd Guards Brigade. Moreover, two liaison officers were to be sent to Wimereux, just north of Boulogne to Lieutenant-General Brownrigg's HQ. 'I was also impressed with the necessity for speed', Keller wrote. He was sure that he needed a full 24 hours to unload. He was also told that a small German battlegroup of seven light and four medium tanks were in the Boulogne–Calais area. The *City of Christchurch* with all tanks and vehicles arrived at 1600 hrs. Lieutenant R.W. McCallum noted, 'All our tanks were left in their own boat. All of our personnel on another. If either had sunk the Bn would have been useless.' Rumours were already circulating that the German panzers were definitely approaching Calais and had *already* invested Boulogne.

All the tanks had been loaded at the bottom of the ship's hold, with vehicles above and on the open deck, crateloads of petrol drums piled high. The unfortunate 2 i/c Major Mahoney was in charge of the unloading operation. French dockers responsible for manning the cranes disappeared every time an air-raid warning sounded. The ship's crew, and the stevedores also downed tools when the sirens wailed. Major Mahoney had to put some of the crew under guard. At 2100 hrs they all went *on strike* and unloading did not begin until the next morning. But officers and men worked throughout the night without sleep to clean the guns and prepare them for action. Some of the machine-guns had no shoulder pieces and radio sets lacked parts. As Second Lieutenant Quentin Carpendale recalled: 'I remember the crews sitting on the sands thumbing rounds of ammunition into belts and thinking this was the most extraordinary way to go to war.' Trooper P.A. Howe, a cruiser tank driver, noted that there were not enough HE shells for the close support guns. 'The Germans were surprised to be fired on with smoke shells!' Sergeant 'Bill' Close: 'The ship's crew were reluctant to work. Electricity supply to quayside cranes more often off than on. Eventually sappers and 3rd RTR did most of the unloading. The heavy A-13 tanks and cruiser tanks at the bottom, light tanks on deck above, scout cars on top. Ammo, spare parts, radio accessories tucked away in corners. Most of .5 ammo rounds for light tanks were packed *loose*. A mechanical device (none of course on the boat) forced individual rounds firmly into the MG feed belts.' A very laborious job, however, by hand. Cleaning the guns of mineral jelly, oiling, testing and adjusting them, was just as hard.

On the evening of the 22nd a Major Bailey, liaison officer at Lord Gort's HQ at Hazebrouck 40 miles away, arrived in Calais by car. He brought verbal orders for 3rd RTR to go *immediately* to St Omer, 25 miles south-east of Calais and 'seize crossings over the Aa canal at St Omer and Watten', to extricate Gort's HQ from encirclement by 8th Panzer Division! This new order flatly contradicted Lieutenant-General Brownrigg's. Keller took Major Bailey to see Colonel Holland and jointly they decided that this new order was genuine. Unbelievably, a few hours later Keller received a cipher message from Lieutenant-General Brownrigg, now safely back in Dover, confirming the order to go south to Boulogne! Keller decided that he needed more information of enemy movement so the Recce troop was split up into two groups. Lieutenant Morgan took five Dingos and headed north towards Gravelines and Dunkirk; Sergeant Bill Close took the rest south-east towards Guines. He noted: '. . . driving through streets of red brick houses, through crowds of refugees in lorries, pushcarts, prams, bicycles piled high with household goods. Enemy planes were flying overhead. Along the canal for a few miles, there we saw troops with vehicles half hidden under trees by the side of the road having breakfast. The enemy had sited A/Tk guns. Billy reversed across the road over the ditch into a field with half grown crops. Two Dingos behind were hit or had taken the ditch too sharply, both overturned. No one got out.' The radio did not work. The CO was cross when Close reported back with only one Dingo surviving out of five. There was no news of Lieutenant Morgan's other four Dingos. RSM Stannard told Close the CO was getting a string of contradictory orders. As squadrons were formed, and as the tanks were unloaded off the boat, squadron commanders did not get their own tanks; in some cases not even their own crews, because the light tanks had a crew of three, and the cruisers a crew of four. 'It was a bit of a mix-up as vehicles came off the ship, we were allocated to them piecemeal.' Gunner Alan Wollaston was in Major Warren's squadron. 'I was put in a cruiser tank as gunner, Lieutenant "Ginger" Moir as commander, and "Tich" Newman as driver.' In their first engagement the tank gun struck a tree. 'My left wrist smashed.' With the rest of the wounded Wollaston was allowed onto the last ship to leave Calais.

The battalion rallying point was the farm pond at Coquelles, 1½ miles south down the main road. The CO gave out his orders: 3rd RTR were to advance immediately to St Omer to protect GHQ. At 1300 hrs the battalion moved off.

Captain Hugh O'Sullivan 2 i/c of 'B' Sqn, was just back from service in India and had joined 3rd RTR a few days before and did not know his crew properly. His force consisted of a troop of three light plus three cruiser tanks and a Sqn HQ in two A-9s. Their No. 9 wireless sets were not in working order. On their way to recce river crossings on the Guines road,

I saw a large mechanized force advancing up main Calais road. The German tanks halted on the road in position behind trees. We were deployed on the fields advancing towards them. The enemy had superior firepower on our 3 or 4 cruisers. We concentrated our MGs on enemy lorries. (In the 35 minutes of action) our light tanks, naturally ineffective were forced to withdraw over the crest of the hill, having knocked out the lorries to block the road, and KO'd two German heavy cruisers and two light tanks. My A-9 tank hit by 2 pdr shell, smashed its offside suspension and track. We swung broadside to the enemy, crawled down a bank into a well camouflaged hull down position. The suspension was damaged beyond repair and the tank settled into the marshy ground.

O'Sullivan ordered his crew to keep lorries under fire while he went to find Colonel Keller, 200 yards in the rear on a road behind the crest of a hill. He was told a right-flank attack was intended with a light tank section coming to join and to distract the enemy's attention. 'Two light tanks and a cruiser subsequently appeared, all KO'd in a few minutes. The cruiser however knocked out another enemy cruiser. The Germans were using both A/Tk guns and tank guns.' O'Sullivan had no HE for his mortar and neither of the two front MGs would fit into their mountings. Gunner Brown was wounded, so O'Sullivan got out the third MG and fired from the top of the tank.

The Germans were infiltrating through woods and opened fire with A/Tk guns at 600 yards range. Galbraith and Price were firing an MG co-axial mounted with the mortar. Deuchar was in a light tank. No sign of battalion. Shelling heard; heavy opposition behind wood. 20 minutes after seeing the CO, two shells hit the tank in quick succession killing the two crew and putting the smoke mortar and MG out of action. Only now one MG on the bank engaged enemy for 10–12 minutes, silenced fire of one A/Tk gun in wood. More hits now on the empty tank. Enemy started to withdraw. Isolated, I decided to rejoin Bn in Calais with remaining four men.

On the way back O'Sullivan and his crew joined up with Major Hardcastle's First Searchlight group. With a very mixed force of men they put up a good fight at the crossroads at Les Attaques. They were overwhelmed by a panzer division. O'Sullivan was the first RTR officer to be captured by the Germans. He told his captors that the *whole* of 1st Armoured Division was defending Calais with a new *monster* tank! The gallant O'Sullivan escaped from POW camp in Germany, made his way to Switzerland, then down through Spain to Gibraltar. On the way home the destroyer *Wild Swan* in which he was sailing was sunk in the Bay of Biscay. He spent two days in a lifeboat and reached the UK in September 1941.

Was it coincidence that Guderian's advance was so cautious? There were now five panzer divisions within a radius of 25 miles, with *Oberst* Kruger's assault group of 1st Panzer Division in the lead. A German report stated: 'His group tried to take Calais from SE by crossing the Guines canal and cutting the Calais-St Omer road. He beat off an attack by 3rd RTR between Hames Boucres and Guines and his light tanks advanced to Les Attaques 13 kilometres due south. There held up for 3 hours by Lieutenant Barr's 'C' Tp 1st Searchlight Battery.'

All the roads were congested with French Army lorries, refugees and French troops marching towards Calais. Sunken roads and the railway impeded progress. The CO, Keller, noted, 'After St Tricat my advance guard reported a column halted on the road to the south on the road from Pihen-lès-Guines to Guines. It was raining at the time and visibility was very bad. I went forward with my HQ but was unable to tell whether the column was French or German. Eventually Major Mahoney my 2 i/c saw men removing A/TK guns from the lorries so I ordered fire to be opened and the battle commenced.'

Second Lieutenant Carpendale led a troop of 'B' Sqn across country. 'We came upon the column which was stationary and resting and they were as surprised to see us, as we them. There was only twenty yards between us when I realised they were

Germans. An officer fired a revolver at my head as I was looking out of the turret.' His OC Major W. Reeves wrote, 'Very shortly after this report the troop leader, Lieutenant Williams, reported a large column of German tanks from west to east in the next valley at a range of about 2,000 yards. The CO then decided to take up a position on a hill to the south of Guines and attack the column in the left flank. We had no supporting artillery, no anti-tank guns, no infantry and our own guns were far out ranged by those of the enemy. We in front took up our position, less one squadron which had difficulty in crossing the railway line.'

Sergeant Jimmy Cornwell of 'B' Sqn in a leading Mk VI light saw possible enemy movement on high ground a mile to his right. He halted his tank and climbed into a hedgerow to use his binoculars. As he did so the Adjutant came charging past in an A-13 tank. 'He had not gone very far – a worthwhile target. That A-13 was our first casualty – a nice "brew up".' Later on, 'I saw no other British tanks and realised they were all charging back towards Windmill Hill.' He then met Jock Duncan in an 'A' Sqn light and suggested they jointly carried out a pincer movement. Discretion won. 'We headed after the rest. It was a terrible way to start the war.'

'It was very impressive to see the reaction of the German column on being attacked. They very quickly dismounted from their vehicles and got their anti-tank guns into action and soon shells were whizzing past our ears.' Major Bill Reeves in an A-9 cruiser had a small mortar with a coaxial MG. 'I could only watch other tanks fighting and not hit back myself. Soon one tank after another was put out of action. It was obvious that we were out-gunned and out-numbered and the only thing was a withdrawal back to Calais.' Three 'smoke' tanks put down a screen and the remains of 3rd RTR withdrew to a ridge between Coquelles and Calais.

The CO's report continued: 'Owing to the ground I was unable to see the right flank. I tried to get my flank guard out to the right but they found this impossible as the Germans had A/TK guns in position and several heavy tanks were on that flank. The shooting of my unit was very good but made no impression on the German heavy tanks. A field gun was soon in action against us and by this time several tanks had been put out of action.' The panzer heavy tanks with a crew of five and a 7.5-cm gun dominated the battlefield, as did the enemy field artillery. Keller's command tank was hit and its gun put out of action. In all 3rd RTR lost twelve tanks in the action, while the Germans lost three medium and two light tanks, three A/Tk guns and many lorries and transport vehicles.

3rd RTR then took up a battle position on a ridge towards the south-west, 3 miles south of the centre of Calais. Major Bill Reeves of 'B' Sqn could see the German columns slowly wending their way towards Calais, only 8 miles away. Keller received orders from the brigadier at about 1900 hrs to withdraw into the town. Reeves's A-9 shed a track and he arrived back at about 2100 hrs. 'Dark, eerie, deserted except for a few drunken Frenchmen lolling about in the wine shops.'

Now Keller sent a patrol of light tanks after dark under Second Lieutenant Mundy to proceed along the Ardres road to St Omer. They found the town in flames but *no enemy* and returned to Calais early on the morning of the 23rd (0200 hrs). Major Bailey would not believe the news and urged the CO to send the whole of the battalion to St Omer. Reluctantly a second patrol of three light tanks of 'A' Sqn under Second Lieutenant Eastman set off at 0630 hrs. In St Omer they lost touch with Major Bailey in a town crammed with refugees and stragglers. Three miles south of Ardres the patrol found an RASC convoy of twenty-five supply lorries under fire from infantry of 8th Panzer Division. Eastman forced the enemy to withdraw and put two of their armoured cars out of action. He then tried to escort the convoy back to Calais, but 8th Panzer Division heavy tanks and A/Tk guns knocked out two of the RTR light tanks. Major Bailey was wounded near Ardres but returned to Calais to tell Keller at 1330 hrs that Lord Gort had given a direct order that 3rd RTR *must get through to St Omer!* Battalion HQ was at La Beusinque farm near Coquelles on the south-west perimeter of Calais. Most of 3rd RTR tanks now laboriously unloaded were parked in the leafy Parc St Pierre opposite the Hotel de Ville. It was fortunate at the time that Keller was brave enough to ignore Lieutenant-General Brownrigg's orders as Assault Group Kruger of 1st Panzer Division had just occupied the Forêt de Boulogne!

By now the British garrison of Calais was composed of 4,150 troops with Brigadier Claude Nicholson as their CO. There were 750 men of the 1st Battalion Rifle Brigade under Lieutenant-Colonel Chandos Hoskyns; 750 men of the 2nd Battalion 60th Rifles under Lieutenant-Colonel Euan Miller; 566 men of 1st Battalion Queen Victoria's Rifles (a Territorial formation) under Lieutenant-Colonel Ellison-Macartney; 630 men of 3rd RTR under

Lieutenant-Colonel Reginald Keller and a further 1,460 officers and men of AA/Searchlights. Lieutenant-Colonel R.M. Goldney was OC Air Defence of Calais. The 6th Heavy AA Regiment had seven 3.7-in guns installed around Oyez Farm. A direct phone line to Dover and thence to the RAF produced two patrolling Spitfires to ward off enemy bombers. There was no transport to bring twelve Vickers 2-pdr naval guns into action as their mountings were left behind near Lille. The Queen Victoria Rifles, before leaving England on 18 May, handed over their twenty-two scout cars to 3rd RTR; they were later seen on the quayside of Calais without any drivers. They had handed over their valuable 3-in mortars to another unit and they only had smoke bombs, and no HE, for their 2-in mortars.

The large sprawling town of Calais had at its centre a defence system of a Louis XIV Vauban-built Citadel, plus eight bastion forts in an area 450 yards north–south, 300 yards west–east and a perimeter of 3,000 yards square. Two naval 'Bassins', des Chasses (west–east) and Carnot (north–south) were additional defence barriers. The whole perimeter of the town defences extended to 8 miles. The Old Port was an island surrounded by water and the industrial suburb of St Pierre was bounded by canals and drainage ditches.

So soon after 1400 hrs on 23 May most of the battalion went into action as their CO relates: 'Very much against my better judgement I decided to make up composite squadrons with an equal number of cruisers. I only had one tank for my HQ as 4 tanks had been shipped with the Bays. I heard, via my rear link in Calais that some more cruisers were on the way, but that there were still 3 cruisers and 2 light tanks in the docks, not available for another hour.' Keller decided to advance via Guines and south of Ardres direct on St Omer. A German column was known to be advancing towards Calais from Marquise, 20 miles south-west, and Keller wanted 3rd RTR to pass ahead of the advancing panzers, and avoid direct confrontation.

Corporal G.R. Basford's tank had topped a rise on the first reconnaissance and was promptly knocked out. He made his way to the main park in Calais used by 3rd RTR as a rendezvous. Two tanks were missing and the echelons were drawn up under a brick wall to protect them from German shells. Corporal H.T. Jarvis noted that many of the refugees swarming into Calais carried in their arms lambs and chickens, pigs and dogs, as well as children. The Germans bombed the central park with its lake, bandstand and greenhouse. Jarvis took shelter in the boiler house of the greenhouse. 'When I came up there was nothing left of it. We saw some French 75s *left* beside the road with stacks of ammunition as well as some French tanks. The Germans kept shelling the park but there were few hits on the vehicles.' Some of the French shopkeepers sold Corporal Jarvis and his RTR companions beer and bread each night.

Sergeant Percy Stuteley's lorry was first off the ship. In it he took some of the tank crews in the direction of Boulogne to bivouac until the tanks arrived. Back in Calais, he bedded down in a railway truck in a siding. When the train was bombed he moved to a truck with a dozen RTR men inside. He posted one on the top of the truck with a machine-gun to keep guard. Serg Major T.A. Kemp while helping to unload the transport, petrol and oil thought 3rd RTR were going into a camp near Calais for *training*! Next day at dawn tank patrols were sent out. Kemp had a party of Royal Engineers in his lorry as he drove in Sergeant Stuteley's unit towards Calais. Sergeant John Maskell saw a French gendarme hold up a senior Dutch officer and shoot him dead, evidently a German spy masquerading and in disguise. Later, when the evacuation was ordered and all the Echelon lorries were being destroyed, Maskell fired a bullet at the tyre of his lorry. 'It bounced back and nearly killed me,' he said. Sergeant Kemp said of the Echelon personnel evacuated on SS *Kohistan* 'discipline was perfect'.

Mysterious wireless messages were received by the CO as 3rd RTR were regrouping on the high ground south-west of Coquelles. Keller was still under shellfire and replied, 'Get off the air, I am trying to fight a bloody battle.' Brigadier Claude Nicholson, newly arrived to take command of all forces in Calais, was trying to establish contact for a conference! They met at 2000 hrs and Sergeant Bill Close described the new commander of the Calais garrison. 'A tall, slim quietly spoken officer who gave one confidence. Before the war was CO 16/5th Lancers before taking over command of 30th Infantry Brigade.' Captain Moss, 3rd RTR's Adjutant told Close to place his Dingo at the disposal of Brigadier Nicholson, at Brigade HQ in the Boulevard Leon Gambetta, a large house with cellars which was at the time a medical clinic.

Nicholson had already sent out a strong patrol of 3rd RTR tanks of two cruisers and two light tanks under Captain R.H. (Dick) How, down the road south-east of Calais towards Ardres. They ran into German motorcyclists 4 miles along the road and dispersed them, but 2 miles further on an A/Tk gun and field gun firing point-blank from the Les Attaques area forced How's patrol to withdraw. Dick How told Major Reeves on his return, 'I had to run the gauntlet both ways, having received 18-pdr fire from the Germans and A/TK and MG fire from our own troops – an unhealthy trip!' Nicholson's orders were for 3rd RTR to move into Calais after dark, fill up with petrol, await orders in the Parc St Pierre opposite the Hotel de Ville. At 2300 hrs Nicholson asked Keller to send out a patrol towards Marck, a few miles due east.

On the evening of the 23rd, Guderian, after the various spirited actions by 3rd RTR (and the Searchlights), was convinced that the British would land more troops at Calais, so he reluctantly committed 10th Panzer Division to the capture of the town instead of sending it to attack Dunkirk. Prime Minister Churchill's message to General Ismay and the CIGS (dated 23 May) was urging that a clear line of supply be opened up at the earliest moment to Gort's army by Dunkirk, Calais or Boulogne. 'If the regiment of armoured vehicles including cruiser tanks has actually landed at Calais this should improve the situation and should encourage us to send the rest of the 2nd Brigade of that Armoured Division in there. This coastal area must be cleaned up if the major operation of withdrawal is to have any chance. The intruders behind the line must be struck at and brought to bay.'

In a highly mobile war the panzer divisions were exploiting the Pas de Calais almost at will. By the night of 23 May 1st Panzer Division had blocked the Marck road with A/Tk guns. Nevertheless, Adolf Hitler personally halted the advance of all panzer divisions at 1130 hrs on the 24th. The British War Cabinet was getting out-of-date information just as the panzer commanders round Calais were tightening their noose, despite their Fuehrer's command. Field Marshal Von Runstedt's plan was to halt panzers along the line Lens–Bethune–Aire–St Omer–Gravelines. The encircled BEF could then be destroyed by Stukas, Junkers and Messerschmitts of the Luftwaffe.

At 2300 hrs on the 23rd, by the light of a full moon, Major W.R. Reeves's 'B' Sqn with an A-13 cruiser and three light tanks (the survivors of the afternoon battle near Guines) set off to force the road east to Gravelines via Marck. Gravelines was held by the British 69th Brigade. Sergeant Cornwall commanded the point tank of the light troop followed by Lieutenant Peter Williams, the troop commander. 'I (Major Reeves) followed close behind ready to give covering fire with my 2 pdr. Before starting I had carefully tuned in my wireless set to Bn to pass back any information as to whether the road was taken or otherwise.' After 2 miles they met a roadblock of old lorries towed across the road. 'We got through. There was no turning back. The Germans were present in large numbers on both sides of the road. We had three alternatives. Firstly, getting right through to Gravelines, secondly getting captured, or thirdly getting killed.' The Germans in the darkness thought the RTR tanks were German. 'Some of the German troops waved to us and we returned the compliment.' Peter Williams stopped his tank on one occasion thinking the soldiers were French and said, 'Parlez-vous Anglais?' Two miles further on German despatch riders switched their torches onto Reeves's A-13 tank 'and made off rapidly as if to report. No one fired at us.' On arrival in Marck eight tank mines were seen on the canal bridge connected by a strip of metal. Major Reeves exploded two with 2-pdr fire, but Sergeant Cornwall bravely volunteered to attach the tow rope of his tank to the mines and clear the bridge. The next hazard were coils of anti-tank wire which brought the first two tanks to a complete standstill. With wire cutters and 20 minutes' hard work the patrol continued and the 'B' Sqn tanks reached Gravelines at about 0200 hrs on the 24th, where a Provost Corps captain gave Major Reeves a situation report.

Airey Neave's *The Flames of Calais* gives an excellent account of the superb defence put up by the 2nd King's Royal Rifle Corps (2nd KRRC), 1st Rifle Brigade (1st RB), two crack regular units, and the territorials of 1st Queen Victoria Rifles (1st QVR). French troops under *Capitaine de Frégate* Carlos de Lambertye had cobbled together a mixed force of 800; one and a half infantry companies, and an MG company with two 75-mm field guns (based on the Citadel). His HQ was in Fort Risban on the west side of the Avant Port. The coastal defence guns in the fort and bastions on the sea front were manned by French sailors. Later in the siege *Commandant* Le Tellier arrived from Dunkirk to take command of the French troops. Unfortunately there were a considerable number who took no part in the fighting and hid in cellars in the town suburbs. 1st RB and 2nd KRRC were allocated the defence of the town ramparts and 1st QVR manned the town outposts.

Brigadier Nicholson received an order to escort rations for 350,000 men to Dunkirk *overriding all other considerations*. As the convoy formed up, 10th Panzer reached the slopes to the south of Calais town and began shelling.

After the first bombardment, civilians, refugees and some inexperienced RTR soldiers took refuge in air-raid shelters. Sergeant Reg Ellis had to threaten a young RTR private at gunpoint to get him out and back to his duty.

While Major Reeves was pushing his patrol into Gravelines early on the 24th, Major-General R.H. Dewing, Director of Military Operations at the War Office sent a cable to Brigadier Nicholson. 'Evacuation decided in principle. When you have finished unloading your two MT ships, commence embarkation of all except fighting personnel who remain to cover final evacuation.' By 0700 hrs it was known that this would be planned for the evening of 25 May, but not necessarily to Winston Churchill who on 24th sent a message to General Ismay: 'I cannot understand the situation around Calais. The Germans are blocking all exits and our regiment of tanks is boxed up in the town because it cannot face the field guns planted on the outskirts. Yet I expect the forces achieving this are very modest. Why, then, are they not attacked? Why does not Lord Gort attack them from the rear at the same time that we make a sortie from Calais?'

On the 24th 'A' Sqn fought a spirited engagement at Porte de St Omer and Sergeant Stuart's troop of medium tanks KO'd two German tanks. Several other actions were fought in the streets but snipers picked off crews repairing RTR tanks with track trouble.

The large ration convoy for the BEF set off at 0400 hrs on 24 May along the Dunkirk road. Major Hamilton-Russell OC 'B' Company 1st RB, with five tanks of 'C' Sqn 3rd RTR under Major F.V. Lyons were followed by three carriers, three platoons in trucks, and two platoons in the rear. In between the escort were the many 10-tonners with the 350,000 rations. After 2 miles between Le Beau Marais and Marck the column found a strong German roadblock with A/Tk guns among the houses and allotments on both sides. The tanks were forced to stop. The RB platoons worked their way around the German flanks. A spirited action lasted until daylight. Brigadier Nicholson, present with the convoy, was clear that it would be surrounded and reluctantly withdrew.

The two panzer divisions surrounding Calais had a combined strength of 550 tanks. Of 3rd RTR's original 48 tank strength, only 9 cruisers and 12 light tanks remained in fighting condition.

Churchill had now been informed that an order had been sent at 0200 hrs to Calais that evacuation had been decided in principle, 'but surely this is madness' he wrote to General Ismay. 'The only effect of evacuating Calais would be to transfer the forces now blocking it to Dunkirk. Calais *must be held for many reasons*, but specially to hold the enemy on its front.'

Meanwhile, the intrepid Major Bill Reeves, Lieutenant Peter Williams, Sergeant Cornwall and the four tanks of 'B' Sqn were soon involved in the defence of Gravelines. In addition to French troops there was a battalion of Green Howards. Reeves made a plan with the French commander to cover the main drawbridge and two smaller bridges over the canal to the west of the town. Because of the vast number of refugees the drawbridge remained down, but the four tanks were in fire positions on the east bank of the canal. Air bombardment began at 0800 hrs and shells and mortar bombs started along the line of the canal. The drawbridge was now closed and in close-quarter fighting Major Reeves's tank accounted for five German Mk II tanks and two troop carriers of 1st Panzer Division. 'I think the Germans must have thought there were several more tanks in Gravelines than there actually were. We kept on running back into the town and appearing in new fire positions.' Sergeant Jimmy Cornwall: 'We barely had time to Recce good fire positions when we experienced our first dose of real shellfire – quite frightening. Light artillery and mortars seemed to be following us about. We soon saw our first dead men. Two German tanks moved up but not firing. Getting quite brave we engaged first one and then another with the .5 (Corporal Willey had joined me as gunner). . . . We were given a free hand manning the outer defences and by changing position regularly gave the impression there was a sizeable armoured unit inside the town.' The attack on Gravelines died down about 2030 hrs and Reeves's fighting patrol reached Bergues (12 miles south-east of Dunkirk) at midnight. The next day they moved east via Poperinge to Ypres.

Reduced now to three tanks, Reeves's force linked up with Major Forrester's A/Tk battery and took part in the defence of Ypres. Major Forrester kept fifty pigs in the cellar of the local HQ and stocks of champagne. On 28 May a recce was made to Dikkebusch where Reeves's tank broke down. Another had a broken bogie wheel. Sergeant Cornwall was forced to destroy his Mk VI as its batteries were flat. From Ypres the RTR group headed back to Dunkirk. 'We ran into heavy shelling as the enemy had ranged on cross-roads and junctions. Lieutenant Peter Williams said he was going to make it on foot.' Cornwall and other survivors found an abandoned rowing boat off the Dunkirk beaches, reached a waterlogged minesweeper which despite two air raids landed them safely at Margate. Eventually the other survivors reached England via Dunkirk. Their destroyer was bombed and put out of action and a small Dutch ship took some of them to safety. Major Reeves was awarded an immediate DSO, Lieutenant Peter Williams, the MC and Sergeant Jimmy Cornwall the DCM.

Back in Calais by 1800 hrs on the 24th Nicholson had completed plans to withdraw 60th Rifles and 1st QVR to the inner perimeter; 3rd RTR tanks spent the day patrolling the streets and engaging tanks outside the perimeter. In the heavy shelling and bombing of the town 3rd RTR lost one officer and two ORs killed in action. Major Lyons's 'C' Sqn helped in the defence of the west side of the town.

Lieutenant-Colonel Keller was told by Nicholson at 0700 hrs on the 24th that Calais was to be evacuated within 24 hours. 'I asked him what was to happen to my tanks and he said that they would have to be abandoned and burnt. I thought I should require three hours to do the job.' He and the 2 i/c Major Mahoney agreed that the cruiser tanks must under no circumstances be allowed to fall into enemy hands. Sergeant Stan Cox was personally ordered by Keller that tanks should be abandoned or destroyed. 'We soaked some old overalls in petrol, set them on fire and dropped them into my A-9.' Cox then, tankless, swam out to a French boat anchored 50 feet from the quay, and thence to safety.

Nicholson told Keller to send back to the UK 'B' Echelon and all 3rd RTR men not required for tank crews. All echelon transport was to be burned or rendered useless but regrettably two cruiser tanks were set on fire by their crews. They blazed on a sandy space near the Gare Maritime and created a deplorable impression, as Colonel Holland later reported to the War Office. The steamer *Kohistan* took a packed collection of wounded and the echelons of five regiments. Enemy tanks were now seen east, south and north of the town; Calais was indeed surrounded. Dark clouds rose over blazing fuel dumps. The noise of fighting rose and fell as the garrison were penned in. Brigadier Nicholson's HQ was moved from the Gare Maritime to the Citadel. Sergeant Close was freed from his driving duties and destroyed his Dingo with a grenade under the bonnet. He was taken back to Dover in a trawler under shellfire. The Stukas were queuing up in the Channel to dive-bomb Royal Navy destroyers and every vessel leaving Calais. Bill Jordan wrote: 'All useless mouths were to proceed to the docks to board an old coal freighter, SS *Kohistan*. I was one of the fortunate few of the Regiment to get home. Several came back later in dribs and drabs. So many fine men were taken PoW. It was terrible to see our transport vehicles being driven over the harbour edge, others set on fire.'

The transports that sailed on Friday 24 May took back not only the non-combatants and the wounded, but also the stevedores and much-needed ammunition, vehicles and weapons. In the afternoon 10th Panzer Division made a determined effort to break through the defences, with bitter fighting in the west and south, getting a foothold in the outskirts of Calais. The panzers paid a high price and attacking units lost almost half of their equipment. Guderian asked Major-General Schaal if he wanted the Luftwaffe to complete the obliteration of the town. Stukas were dive-bombing the defenders, and another threat came from snipers who had infiltrated with refugees, firing from houses in the town. Bad weather and RAF sorties aided the defenders, but Guderian's panzer troops already had four bridgeheads over the Aa canal. Admiral Ramsay's six Allied destroyers bombarded the panzers' positions, but had three ships sunk or damaged.

By dawn on the 25th Keller had three cruisers and four light tanks still battleworthy. Battalion HQ was in the north-west corner of the Bassin des Chasses. General Fagalde, GOC 'XV' French Corps in command at Dunkirk forbade the local French commander *and* Brigadier Nicholson to continue with the evacuation 'for the sake of Allied solidarity'. A War Office message now advised that the defenders would be assisted by 48th Division, which was totally untrue! Still in this strange terrible 'Alice in Wonderland' war, Lieutenant-General Brownrigg, now on a destroyer in mid-Channel ordered the unfortunate Keller to carry out his original orders and proceed to Boulogne which was by then in German hands! Keller went aboard the Royal Navy yacht *Gulzar* moored in the harbour, which was used as a wireless station. He told Brownrigg the orders were impossible. With two patrols missing, and tank crews in shell holes near the Gare Maritime he could only just contribute to the defence of Calais. A cruiser tank was stationed at the east end of Boulevard Gambetta as part of 60th Rifles defences, and another cruiser from Pont Jordan moved forward to defend the railway bridge area. Three more light tanks supported the Green Jackets as German tanks appeared north of the Boulogne road and were held off.

The Brigadier had by now received two German demands for surrender. But by 0800 hrs on the 25th the Swastika flag was flying from the Hotel de Ville. Three hours later RTR tanks were supporting 'I' Company of the Rifle Brigade at Pont Mollien under fire from Stukas; Second Lieutenant McCallum commanded the four light tanks. A cruiser tank which helped them force a road block was hit in the turret by two shells from an A/Tk gun opposite the Hotel de Ville and set on fire, killing three of the crew. The badly burned driver brought the tank back to the sand dunes. McCallum climbed up and put the fire out. 'On the bottom were two severed heads. My squadron CO told me to get the bodies out and bury them. I told him this was impossible. He climbed up to look for himself.' There was no suitable explosive to blow up the canal bridges. A few RTR tanks in reserve on the road behind the Gare Maritime were an obvious target for Stukas and German artillery.

The Foreign Secretary, Anthony Eden, sent the beleaguered garrison a message by Royal Navy minesweeper. (He was a Green Jacket and was desperately upset at their probable fate.) 'Eyes of the Empire are upon the defenders of Calais. HM Government are confident you and your gallant regiment will perform an exploit worthy of the British name.' They did just that.

Shortly before Lieutenant-Colonel Hoskyns, CO of the Rifle Brigade was mortally wounded, at 1600 hrs on the 25th, he asked Keller for a patrol to help a counter-attack along the Quai de la Loire. Keller sent a cruiser and two light tanks under Second Lieutenant Mundy. He sent Second Lieutenant Gregg with a light tank to the eastern flank to bring fire on the embankment south of the Bassin des Chasses. Captain How's troop of three cruisers knocked out six German tanks.

Eventually Keller told his 2 i/c Major Mahoney to get the few surviving tanks and all the remaining tankless crews onto the beaches and try to make their way to possible safety at Gravelines. He wrote: 'The men had done their utmost in conditions for which they had not been trained, were very tired but still full of fight.' The battalion was now mostly armed with revolvers. It was a scene of utmost confusion with French civilians and troops swarming all over the beach. By 1800 hrs the Germans had reached the beach but Major Mahoney with several tanks got the front half of the survivors through. The rear party were just too tired to go on. The battalion padre stayed with the wounded. The CO and Major Simpson walked along the beach; several miles along the shore they came across the last of the 3rd RTR tanks, abandoned, out of petrol, driven into the sea and useless to the enemy. By 2230 hrs their party had reached the river estuary near Port Philippe. The current was very strong and only the two officers could wade across. They eventually reached Gravelines and thence to Dunkirk by lorry on 26 May, then by trawler to Dover.

The savage fight in the centre of Calais continued on the 26th. The 69th German Rifle Regiment (10th Panzers) stormed over the quays and platforms of the Gare Maritime. By 1530 hrs they captured the Bastion de L'Estran and forced the Rifle Brigade to surrender at Bastion I after savage fighting and heavy losses on both sides. At 1600 hrs the 86th Rifle Regiment surrounded the old Citadel of Vauban. Led by a *Feldwebel* they crossed the courtyard and captured Brigadier Claude Nicholson (who later died in captivity). Finally Lieutenant-Colonel Euan Miller ordered the survivors 'sauve qui peut'. HMS *Conidaw* and *Vesper* took off 165 men. The Belgian yacht *Semois* went in four times and took off wounded, while the yacht *Gulzar* rescued 47. HMS *Mona's Isle* embarked 1,420 mostly echelon troops. The 2nd KRRC, Rifle Brigade and 1st QVR lost about 60 per cent casualties. When Gunner Alan Wollaston's train from Dover arrived in London, he saw King George VI acting as volunteer 'ticket collector', helping the wounded onto various hospital trains.

Of the 575 all ranks of 3rd RTR slightly more than half had returned. These were mainly 'B' Echelon: fitters, drivers and armourers. About 100 men were reported killed or missing. Of Sergeant Bill Close's friends, 'Tubby' Ballard was missing, 'Socker' Heath was captured, and 'Ginger' May and 'Tich' Kemp were dead. 'We'd gone to war on a Tuesday night a regular battalion with 50 tanks. By Saturday we had lost all our vehicles, tracked and wheeled and nearly half our strength.' Close went on: 'Lessons: the A-10s might as well have stayed in England, with no HE, but *only* smoke bombs! The A-13s only had AP, no HE. The Germans set up A/Tk guns in ruined houses and fired into the sides of A-13 cruisers. Solid shot from two pounder was useless on this type of target.'

There are three postscripts to the siege and loss of Calais. Winston Churchill wrote, 'Calais was the Crux. Many other causes might have prevented the deliverance of Dunkirk, but it is certain that the three days gained by the defence of Calais enabled the Gravelines water line to be held, and that without this, even in spite of Hitler's vacillations and Rundstedt's orders all would have been cut off and lost.' After the withdrawal of the BEF, Brigadier V.V. Pope, head of AFV branch at GHQ wrote a report to Brigadier A.G. Kerchington, Deputy Director SD (AFV) at the War Office:

(1) There must be a Commander Royal Armoured Corps in the field with adequate staff to command and control all RAC troops as directed by the General Staff, otherwise we shall continue to fritter away our tanks. We must model ourselves upon the German lines. 3rd RTR has been thrown away at Calais. (2) We must have thicker armour on our fighting tanks and every tank must carry a cannon. The 2 pdr is good enough *now*, but only just. We must mount something better and put it behind 40 to 80 mm of armour. (3) Our tanks must be mechanically simple and reliable. 75% of our casualties have been due to mechanical failure and slow repairs. (4) We want the highest road speed compatible with the above. The A12 Mk III is too slow. The A13 is OK in this respect. (5) Moves by rail cannot be relied upon. The Boche can always cut the lines by air attack. All our tanks must be capable of moving long distance at reasonably high speeds by *road*. (6) The Morris armoured cars are not tactically or technically good enough. The armour must not be very thick – though the thicker the better, but the car must mount a gun – a 2 pdr will do.

Brigadier Pope continued, 'The RAC has done extraordinarily well but has suffered enormously. 1st Army Tank Brigade walked through everything it met but mechanical failures have wrecked it. The Boche has succeeded solely because of his mass of tanks supported by air attacks. Dive bombing followed by tank attack is too much on our extended fronts.'

Spare a thought for Lieutenant-Colonel Reggie Keller, as his battalion was thrown straight into the fray piecemeal, with conflicting orders and conflicting priorities: in the first action at Coquelles attacking a superior armoured force and getting a bloody nose; being ordered to protect GHQ; then ordered to send a huge ration convoy north to Dunkirk; and protect

Gravelines; then above all help Brigadier Nicholson's infantry brigade defend Calais against Stukas and three panzer divisions; 3rd RTR did their very best in impossible conditions. John Dunlop an Officer Cadet Training Unit (OCTU) cadet from 3rd RTR wrote a series of 'doggerel' verses:

> They gave me an A10 and I drove her
> From Fordingbridge onto the train
> We matelot'd to Calais from Dover
> and soon matelot'd back home again.
>
> Chorus: Oh I wear a green tab on my shoulder
> and a little white tank on my arm
> 'Twas the Third Tanks that taught me to soldier
> and with them I will come to no harm.

4

THE GREEK CAMPAIGN – 'THE STUKAS' PLAYGROUND'

The 3rd Battalion was rapidly re-equipped, and reinforcements arrived to replace the many experienced men lost at Calais. Trooper Bill Jordan and other survivors were initially put under canvas at Dean Hall estate near Corby, Northants. They gave Winston Churchill a lacklustre cheer when he and VIPs visited the area. Sergeant Bill Close recalled that the sergeants' mess was re-opened in a field at Newbury Park near Cambridge. 'Tiny' White became the new RSM; Stannard had only just survived the Channel escape after his ship was hit. Lieutenant-Colonel Reggie Keller was back in command with several experienced Squadron Commanders including 'Bill' Reeves with his well-deserved DSO, Majors 'Simbo' Simpson and 'Bimbo' Warren. The battalion mustered at first at Bottisham near Newmarket and then at Deans Park, Kettering after various moves. Initially the War Office planned to send the battalion back to France as soon as it was fully equipped. Churchill wrote to General Ismay on 2 June, two days *before* Operation Dynamo (the evacuation of troops from Dunkirk) ended. 'The BEF in France must immediately be reconstituted, otherwise the French will not continue in the war. Even if Paris is lost, they (the Chiefs of Staff) must be abjured to continue a gigantic guerrilla. . . . A large army can be developed in a Brittany bridgehead.'

Twenty-two tanks of 2nd and 5th RTR (3rd Brigade) had managed to reach Cherbourg. Some of their experienced crews joined 3rd RTR at Bottisham Park. Later, new A-13 cruisers and ten smart new Dingo scout cars (commanded by Second Lieutenant Bob Crisp) were collected at Newmarket. First the battalion joined 22nd Armoured Brigade and eventually 2nd Armoured Division under General Tilly. By July when new Crusader tanks arrived and the battalion was fully equipped the situation in France had gone beyond hope. At one stage most of the wireless equipment was arbitrarily removed and Lieutenant-Colonel Keller risked official displeasure before the equipment was returned.

Dick Shattock and Ken Farquarson joined in September 1940. Shattock recalled: 'One of the constant air raids was in progress at the time and rail movement a lottery. Captain Cyril Joly was in the next carriage.' They joined 'A' Company OC Major 'Simbo' Simpson. 'One of the survivors of the "Calais" shambles, still much affected by the harrowing experience.' Captain Dennis Bartlett, Lieutenant Eric Niedermeyer, Second Lieutenant Houghton L. Upcott-Gill, known as 'George', and Second Lieutenant Dudley Easterbrook made up the officers of 'A' Company. 'The battalion was equipped with A-10 tanks, surely ranked as the worst in history. As an engineer I quickly realised this. The tracks broke every few miles, literally. The engines, ex-AEC London bus engines, were installed with the radiator cooling fan placed on one side of the tank, the radiator itself placed on the opposite side. The so-called cool air then passed over the overheated engine via the red-hot exhaust through the radiator.' Dick Shattock expressed the views, 'that the designers of the A-10 must be in the pay of the Nazis. In mid-October we were ordered northwards to an area between Corby, Peterborough and Stamford. "A" Squadron in the mansion and grounds of Blatherwycke Hall, the others in Bulwick, Southwick and Apethorpe.'

Captain Cyril Joly in *Take these Men* wrote his assessment of the A-9 and A-10.

The A-9 was the first of the new range of tanks developed in peace time and just beginning to come off the production lines at the outbreak of war. It was armed with a high-velocity armour-piercing gun, firing a two-pound solid-steel shot, with a Vickers machine-gun mounted co-axially with the two-pounder, and with two further Vickers guns in two sub-turrets, one on each side of the driver, who was located forward and below the centre of the main turret. These latter sub-turrets were cramped and of only limited value. Due to a shortage of crews, they were seldom manned, the space thus freed being used to stow extra ammunition and the hundred and one other things needed on a tank. The armour thickness, though not great, was proof against any other tank-mounted guns at that time, though not against some of the higher-velocity ground-mounted anti-tank guns. The main fault of these tanks, and of the

A-10, which gradually replaced them, was that their transmissions and tracks were unreliable. The engine, being similar to those of the London buses, was admirable, but the drive from the engine to the sprockets, which transferred the power to the tracks, was weak. The tracks themselves, and particularly the pins joining the track-plates, were also not robust enough for the hard, stony ground normally met in the desert. The A-10 was basically the same vehicle, but with a Besa machine-gun in place of the Vickers, and only one of these mounted next to the driver, instead of the two sub-turrets in the A-9. It entailed hard work and not a little expert knowledge to keep these tanks running for months on end and over long distances.

The battalion was then re-allotted to 3rd Armoured Brigade and sailed for North Africa from Liverpool in October 1940. 3rd and 5th Battalions RTR with Brigade HQ sailed in the *Stirling Castle*. The regimental tanks were carried in a Clan Line freighter. After a few days at sea, Keller was told that the battalion would disembark at Gibraltar and be taken swiftly by a naval cruiser to Alexandria as reinforcements were urgently needed. Keller noted. 'November 1940 was not one of the happiest times for a Mediterranean cruise.' The project was cancelled. The long voyage in convoy, dodging U-boats and Luftwaffe planes, via the Azores and the Cape, ended as the battalion disembarked at Suez on Christmas Eve 1940. The OC troops (on his third voyage) sent a personal message to Lieutenant-Colonel Keller thanking him for the excellent turnout, behaviour and discipline of his men during the voyage.

'After Calais (recalled Private Bert Hobson) we remustered at Fleet. After being made up to strength again I went back to my role as Wireless Operator. We then sailed from Scotland, King George V Docks for the Middle East in November 1940. 5th Tanks were in the same convoy. The "Windsor Castle" was the convoy Flagship. I was on the "Clan Lamont" with 32 others and the tanks. Lieutenant Tony Greig was in charge. We pulled into the 'White Mans Graveyard' (Sierra Leone) and then Durban. We reached Suez on Christmas Eve but were held up on the 'Bitter Lakes' because a shipload of Italian PoW were coming through.'

Second Lieutenants Dick Shattock, 'Squirrel' Oxberry and Oscar Bamford with fifty ORs were selected as battalion reinforcements and sailed from Liverpool on the troopship SS

Andes, a first-class liner with menus of virtually unlimited choice. A six-week journey by sea to Port Said then ensued.

The 3rd Armoured Brigade was then ensconced in the tented town of Amariya, a transit camp on the outskirts of Alexandria. Early in January 1941 the battalion was warned to stand by for a move south with 4th and 6th Indian Divisions to the East African theatre. After standing by for some time this move was cancelled. The impressive-looking near-obsolete cruiser tanks A-9s, A-10s and A-13s were in the vast base workshops in Alexandria having their camouflage altered from the brown and green of rural England to an exotic shade of red and yellow; Second Lieutenant Robert Crisp a tall, strong young subaltern who had played test cricket for South Africa noted, 'As plainly as a banner headline, it revealed to the crews who manned the tanks that they were booked for the Sudan.' He went on, 'We were equipped with ancient A10s and A13s and even some A9s dragged out of various war museums and exhibitions. They were ponderous square things like mobile pre-fab houses and just about as flimsy. Their worst failing was their complete inability to move more than a mile or two in any sort of heavy going without breaking a track or shedding one on a sharp turn.'

In mid-January the intention to move to the Sudan was cancelled and a 1st Armoured Brigade recce party set off due west into the desert to 'Charing Cross' the railhead for the main desert war, based on the Italian frontier. Major Bill Reeves DSO, and the other squadron COs, and Lieutenant Bob Crisp for the Recce Troop were by the 21st on the outskirts of the south-west corner of Tobruk. Roughly 25,000 Italian troops were in the town about to be taken prisoner by General Wavell's advancing army. Crisp could see the dark umbrella of treacly smoke curling upwards from the burning oil tanks in Tobruk harbour. A mile or so away was 4th Armoured Brigade which included 2nd RTR, 7th Hussars and 2nd KRRC who on 8 February were to win the astonishing Battle of Beda Famm.

Lieutenant-Colonel Keller and the 3rd RTR recce party returned from 'Charing Cross' to Amariya, dusty, tired and browned off. Bob Crisp resented the tents, the NAAFI, the Shafto cinemas and the squadron messes. On 1 February 'A' and 'B' Sqns departed in penny packets back to 'Charing Cross'. 'C' Sqn to their chagrin were left behind at Amariya as Divisional HQ reserve squadron. But Crisp and the other subalterns and most of 'C' Sqn had a good time in Alex in the nightclubs and cabarets (the Excelsior and Phalaron were very popular). '"Bimbo" Warren was very understanding about allowing us out of camp', Crisp recalled. The *Egyptian Gazette* recorded daily Wavell's early victories with the towns and harbours of Tobruk and Benghazi duly captured.

A few weeks before, Prime Minister Winston Churchill had written to his Chiefs-of-Staff. 'Although perhaps by luck and daring we may collect comparatively easily the most delectable prizes on the Libyan shore, the massive importance of keeping the Greek front in being, must weigh hourly with us.' After the capture of Tobruk, assistance to Greece was given priority over *all* other operations in the Middle East.

Lieutenant-Colonel R.C. Keller with 'A' and 'B' Sqns returned and all the 3rd RTR tanks were sent to the big RAOC depot at Quassasin on the other side of the Delta. Tank camouflage was to be changed for the second time from hot yellow to olive green! On the first day of February 3rd RTR reluctantly handed over their two squadrons of A-13 tanks to 5th RTR and equally reluctantly received in return a motley collection mainly of A-10s. These had very badly worn tracks which became later a source of much trouble – even disaster. The battalion was placed on 48 hours' notice to move although a four-day training exercise over the Sweet Water Canal was cut short abruptly. Battledress in which the battalion had arrived from England was replaced by an issue of khaki drill and *thick woollen* underwear. Crisp's 'C' Sqn subalterns nicknamed 'Oxo' and 'Dicky' and Australian 'Harry' Maegraith were all baffled about their destination. 'Dicky' a regular with an Indian North-West Frontier ribbon suggested, 'Nepal, hot in the day time, cold at night.' Harry suggested the curious kit issue was 'designed to fool the enemy' as Axis spies were thriving in Alex and Cairo. Brigadier Charrington rushed off to see Sir Henry 'Jumbo' Wilson for an explanation. The result – battledress and winter jerkins were issued to all ranks.

Major Basil Carey the 2 i/c was a very efficient regular soldier who expected very high standards from his colleagues. He had lost an eye as a result of an accident in his youth and was nicknamed 'Wahid Shufti' behind his back by old desert hands. After his capture at the end of the Greek campaign (for that was where 3rd RTR were destined), he was released by the Germans, considered to be unfit for further military service, which certainly was not so. Major Bill Reeves DSO (won at Calais) commanded 'B' Sqn, Major 'Bimbo' Warren 'C' Sqn and Major R.H.O. Simpson 'A' Sqn. MacMillan was the reliable Regimental Medical Officer,

Captain Plews was OC the Light Aid Detachment (LAD) which was kept busy helping to maintain the aged tanks. The Regimental Quartermaster Sergeant (RQMS) was Paddy Hehir, and Lieutenant Tom Eeley had taken over Bob Crisp's command of the troop of Daimler scout cars. Captain String was the Adjutant and Captain George 'Withers' Witheridge was 2 i/c 'B' Sqn.

From Quassasin near Tel-el-Kebir, some sixty mature cruiser tanks, now sprayed green, were loaded onto long flat trains and sent through the teeming Delta, no doubt observed and counted by the Axis spies. The move to Alexandria docks took place on 1 March. Captain G. Witheridge supervised loading of the tanks and with a team of drivers sailed with the cargo ship. 'The tanks were loaded on a merchantman and tank crews embarked on the cruiser *Bonaventure*. The sailors told us (Jim Caswell 'B' Sqn) we were going to Greece. Although the Mediterranean was then full of enemy U-boats, warships and aircraft, we were assured by the sailors that this cruiser was unsinkable.' The cruiser tanks were loaded fairly unobtrusively onto the *Singalese Prince* and *Clan Macaulay*. 'B' Echelon lorries and trucks were lifted into holds and strapped down on decks. Drivers accompanied their tanks (two engines were fitted on the voyage by the battalion fitters and RAOC) plus a selection of officers and NCOs. Trooper Fred Dale, 3rd Troop 'A' Sqn and his crew worked all night with the fitters to change their A-10 tank engine on the quayside. 'The workshop was alongside the water where there were numerous mosquitoes. My eyes were closed with bites. I had to be led up the gang plank.' The 4th Hussars (with Mk VI light tanks with MGs), 9th KRRC, 2nd Royal Horse Artillery (2nd RHA), the Northumberland Hussars (with 2-pdr A/Tk guns) sailed in the convoy escorted by the 8-in gun cruiser *York* and the 6-in gun cruiser *Gloucester*.

'We discussed with our naval hosts', recalled Crisp 'the inadequacies of our tanks, describing with affectionate abuse the thin armour, the ridiculous 2-pdr gun and the inability of the whole outfit to move more than a few miles in heavy going without shedding a track. If we were going anywhere from Athens, we would have to go by train, tanks and all.'

The Greeks were confident that they could hold out against their Italian attackers, but nevertheless asked for at least six divisions from Churchill. General Maitland Wilson's expeditionary force consisted of five divisions totalling 60,000 men (24,100 British, 17,125 Australians and 16,532 New Zealanders). In the van of the expedition was the British 1st Armoured Brigade, the NZ Division and 6th Australian Division to be followed by a Polish brigade and 7th Australian Division. The task of the 1st Armoured Brigade group known as 'W' Force was to observe and guard the Florina pass between Greece and Yugoslavia on the farthest north-west frontier.

The war correspondents Alan Moorhead, Alexander Clifford and Edward Ward of the BBC drank a champagne toast to the 'new Dunkirk at Salonika'.

Steaming at 31 knots the convoy reached Piraeus – a voyage of 558 miles – in about 24 hours. The sea was rough and there were no lifebelts for the troopers. The 'unsinkable' *Bonaventure* was sunk within a few days of landing 3rd RTR. The German Embassy staff in Athens duly noted the details of the new arrivals and were still observing three weeks later. By 11 March 1941 the troops were reunited with their tanks and the battalion moved initially to a tented camp 3 miles east of Athens in a wooded area by the sea. At the loading dock in Piraeus, Crisp had noted: 'Some of the people waved to us, there were many smiles, but no evidence of any particular jubilation at the arrival of British forces to help their own brave soldiers keep the sacred soil of Greece inviolate.' All the Greek men were away fighting, those too old or too young were at work on the roads.

The battalion spent a week in the glades of Glyphada, a green but smart suburb of Athens, with woods, beaches and esplanade within walking distance. 'Bimbo' Warren reminded young Bob Crisp, 'the Parthenon is an ancient ruin, not the name of a pub'. But ouzo with its distinctive aniseed smell proved popular. The cruiser tanks were now named. Lieutenant Harry Maegraith's troop, 'C' Sqn, were 'Cecilia', 'Cynthia' and 'Cymbeline'. 'Oxo' had 'Catherine', 'Clara' and 'Columbine' and Crisp, 'Cool', 'Calm' and 'Collected'. 'Dicky' with his Indian background had 'Cawnpore', 'Calcutta' and 'Calicut' on the grey armour plating of his troop. Sadly, Crisp wrote in his *The Gods were Neutral*: 'But we had no future together. Toby and Dicky with a good fifty per cent of the tank crews were to be left behind in Greece. Bimbo (the OC), Oxo and Harry were unlucky enough to get away . . . back to the desert. They lie there still, the sands above them, marked by the simple monument of a cross.'

All the 'B' Echelon vehicles under Major R.N. 'Dicker' Wilson left on 15 March for the north of Greece. A forward recce party with the CO and Adjutant in one car, and HQ Sqn staff in another, had left three days earlier. Their route was Eleusis–Thevai–Levadeia–Atalante–Lamia (very tricky through the passes), then Larissa–Elassoma–Servia to Kozani. It had snowed heavily on the day of the move. The roads were in a poor state of repair, very narrow and full of potholes. Many high passes had to be crossed through scores of hairpin bends. The highest passes were snowbound and a way had to be dug through the snow. The road journey took four days but was made without casualties. HQ Sqn with 'A' and 'B' Echelons commanded by Major R.N. Wilson made its HQ in a dry gully at a small village called Padeha some 6 miles south of Regimental HQ. On arrival in Kozani, Lieutenant-Colonel Keller called on the Greek General Kotoulous who appeared very tired and did not seem to think much of the situation!

The tanks went north by rail.

As the warning came of snow the temperature dropped fast, we (Trooper Fred Dale, 3rd Troop 'A' Sqn) changed into battledress, then boarded the train on flat cars. We had no chains so we had to bolt planks to the wooden floors. There were no carriages for the crews so we had to make bivveys on the back of the tank flats. By this time blizzards were howling down from the mountains. When they stopped the views were fantastic. As we got higher the ice began to build up on the tracks and we started to slip about. The railway tracks were only feet away from sheer drops. It took us nearly three days to get to our destination. It was hell under the tarpaulins not knowing whether the tanks or you would slip off the side of the flat car. We arrived at Florina, our destination, and unloaded the tanks. We still had a long way to go to the Yugoslav border. The railhead at Florina was full of dirty cafés and the roads full of holes.

Trooper Jim Caswell, 'B' Sqn remembered:

The train thundered along night and day, through tunnels and round passes. We stopped occasionally mainly to take on water, then we dashed to the engine to get some boiling water to brew some tea, to swill the bully beef and biscuits down. The train driver at first a little puzzled, became quite cooperative as time went on. We eventually arrived at Amyntaon station, unloaded the tanks and drove them to an olive grove and covered them with local greenery. As in the desert we slept alongside the tank protected from the cold with the tank sheet, but it was snow we had to contend with, not sand.

Second Lieutenants 'Squirrel' Oxberry, Ken Farquarson, De Bergh-Sidley and Dick Shattock, plus NCOs and men, were battalion reinforcements left behind at Glyphada. 'We were free for several weeks to enjoy ourselves – the lull before the storm. We hired a sail boat, climbed the local hills and frequented the Athens cafés and night spots,' recalled Dick Shattock. After an attack of dysentery he arrived at Katerini to be ordered by the RMO 'Doctor Mac' to go to an Australian field hospital. Later, after various adventures on a train which ran beside sea marshes alongside Mt Olympus, and myriad noisy frogs, he reached Katerini station. Battalion HQ gave him a 15-cwt truck and driver with sealed orders to take to Brigade – but first he had to find it a hundred miles away over mountain tracks.

Bill Close was now Squadron Quarter Master Sergeant (SQMS) (the QM was Captain Reggie de Vere) with a 15-cwt truck and 3-ton lorry, and supplied his squadron with rations, ammunition and personal requisites such as cigarettes and toothpaste. He also drew the squadron pay in Greek drachma. Commerce at the battalion camp was largely on a barter system: eggs and butter from the Greek civilians in exchange for tins of bully beef, Army biscuits and cigarettes. In the local shops flat loaves of unleavened bread and casks of earthy retsina wine could be bought. Mutton chops appeared on the menu and tank crews for a modest sum bought an entire sheep roasted whole in the oven at the communal bakehouse. Much time was spent on turret drills and gunnery tactics but there was little tactical handling of the vehicles because of the shortage of track pins and plates.

The squadrons had taken up positions, 'C' Sqn on the right of the battalion frontage and 'B' around Sotei, a village directly under Florina and the mountains to the west. So SQMS Close noted: 'Tanks had to crawl over rutted trails, sometimes waterlogged, sometimes frozen iron hard, to isolated locations. Covering approach roads, low ground was a morass. At night the crews bivouacked in snow holes alongside the A-10s. Constant patrols interspersed by football matches against a Greek AA battery. The spares for the tanks arrived – *for A-15s and A-13s*, but none for A-10s. We had plenty of tea and sugar but no A-10 tank plates.' All track pins had been welded. This meant that any break in the track necessitated the pins being cut with a cold chisel. It took five times as long to repair a track as it would had normal track pins been fitted. The tracks were all right on soft going but a hammering on road or rocks meant endless trouble.

Meanwhile, the forward recce party learned at Kozani that 3rd RTR was to proceed to Amyntaon just to the east of Florina, the railhead for the Greek armies fighting in Albania and about 20 miles south of the Yugoslav frontier, to cover the Monastir gap. Brigade HQ was at Edessa and the rest of 1st Armoured Brigade, 4th Hussars and the gunners were round about Salonika. The town mayor of Amyntaon was a helpful Greek colonel; soon Battalion HQ was established in a house by the railway station owned by a family with strong Axis sympathies (duly ejected by the town mayor). The CIGS and Foreign Secretary, Anthony Eden visited Florina, and were told about the worn tank tracks. Anthony Eden was shown a tank demonstration but every possible manoeuvre failed to cause any of the known track faults. Later on spare tracks were seen lying at Larissa station during the withdrawal but they were too late to be of use. Corporal G.R. Basford went with his squadron to Sotei village and settled down, playing football matches against the villagers. At Easter they presented the squadron with 128 eggs, 2 for each man. When Anthony Eden visited, he handed his smart black shoe to Sergeant Pass to extract a nail. Eden displayed a hole in his sock for all to see!

Amyntaon lay at the foot of the Veve pass which commanded the roads from Monastir and Edessa. To the south was the village of Sotei and above it the Sotei Ridge which overlooked the whole area from the foot of the pass. General Karassis the CO of the area Greek cavalry regiment was very helpful. An enormous dump of food, petrol and ammunition was established a mile south of Sotei ridge on the main road. The 3rd RTR were in reserve but nevertheless reccied all roads and tracks in the area. The rest of the brigade, some 40 miles away, were building road blocks, digging trenches, and making tank traps to halt the German attack when it came. The Aliakhmon line through Veria to Edessa, on the Yugoslav frontier, had to be defended. On 27 March 1941 a coup d'état in Belgrade brought Yugoslavia into the Allied camp and the next day the Royal Navy under Admiral Cunningham sank several Italian warships in the Battle of Matapan. But a few days later Benghazi in Libya was captured by Rommel's newly arrived Afrika Korps, and because the Greek

Army was more than holding its own against the Italians, Hitler launched attacks on Yugoslavia and Greece. As spring came, like wolves on the fold, 9th Panzer Division and Adolf Hitler's 1st SS *Liebstandarten* Division thrust south on 6 April.

On a recce of the Monastir gap, through which road and rail traffic linked Greece with central Europe, Bob Crisp realized that this was the main route south for the panzers. On the border with Yugoslavia excited armed frontier guards refused to allow the RTR recce party across; they had no valid passports! At 0300 hrs on the 6th Lieutenant Eeley and Lance Corporal Percy Stuteley in the armoured car section on the border, noted the destroyed road bridge and Greek soldiers on motorbikes being chased by uniformed Germans. General Maitland Wilson who spent most of the Greek campaign in 'mufti', at the strange request of the Greek government had now been told that the Polish brigade and 7th Australian Division were badly needed in the North African campaign to try to stem Rommel's advance eastwards from Tripoli into Cyrenaica. The New Zealand Division were deployed to defend the Katerini railhead, the Olympus pass and the coastal strip. On their left was 6th Australian Division placed astride the Verria gap. The 3rd RTR positions were reinforced – with a troop of 2nd RHA 25-pdrs, a troop of medium guns, an MG company and an A/Tk gun battery.

On 6 April Brigadier Charrington called a COs' conference on Asphodel Hill. As Lieutenant-Colonel Keller arrived back at his HQ with specific orders, he was met by the Corps Commander Royal Artillery Brigadier A. Lee with conflicting orders to move the battalion *north* of the pass. Shades of Calais again! Keller sent Lieutenant Tom Eeley and the scout car troop to the frontier, first to Monastir and on to Skopje, where contact was made at a blown-up bridge with German recce troops. Eeley kept his troop in Monastir for two days and was greeted with terrific enthusiasm by the local inhabitants. However, orders on the 6th were for a withdrawal back to battalion. By 8 April 1st Armoured Brigade was concentrated in the area between Perdika and Amyntaeon. Two days later Major R.H.O. Simpson related. 'On 10 April my "A" Sqn was detached from the regiment to move to the Ptolemais area and came under command of Lieutenant-Colonel S.G. Lillingston's 4th Hussars.' The morning of the 11th brought a typical Balkan storm, with a turbulent north-west 'Vardar' wind and blizzards of snow which kept the Luftwaffe away. At 1400 hrs 'C' Sqn received orders to move to the

Ptolemais area to counter threats of enemy tanks moving south from Kelle. Unfortunately this was a panic rumour emanating from the nervous Greek Dodecanese Regiment guarding the nearby hill villages. Lieutenant Bob Crisp and 'C' Sqn, 'progressed slowly towards the foot of the gorge leaving behind it a trail of broken down tanks like some Olympian paperchase. Under the mountain we closed round the mouth of the defile in a semi-circle, each troop choosing its hull-down position.' Nothing happened during the long cold night except for more snow and sleet. 'The cross country run of about five miles had played havoc with the squadron strength. One tank had failed to start owing to a cracked distributor. Six others had track breakages. The shepherding RAOC personnel patched them up using *every* spare part available.' The next morning the false alarm about enemy armour was revealed and a return ordered to Amyntaeon. On the way back Crisp saw that 'Five tanks were left lying out in the vineyards with hopelessly broken tracks, their crews dejectedly alongside awaiting orders. Two more had fallen by the way with fractured pistons.' Battalion HQ confirmed by wireless that no more spares of any sort were available. In future any broken-down tanks which could not be repaired by the squadron would have to be abandoned and destroyed after the MGs and breechblocks had been removed. 'Seven dense columns of black smoke spread their message of gloom over the Macedonian countryside that evening as the tanks burned in a series of violent detonations caused by exploding ammunition.'

On 12 April German pressure increased, with mortar and infantry attacks. The RAF bombed the German forces in the afternoon – a pleasing sight. But as the COs of 1st Armoured Brigade were in conference on Sotei ridge at 1830 hrs they saw a less pleasing sight. The battalion War Diary relates:

The road south from the Pass was suddenly filled with about half the Dodecanese Division, some on ponies, some on foot – some armed, some not – most carried overcoats and groundsheets. They were followed speedily by Brengun carriers crowded with Australians, then more Australians and Greeks mixed. The Boche had broken through and the 218th Australian Brigade and the Dodecanese Division had just gone. The Australian Brigadier arrived in his car in a state of great excitement. Lieutenant-Colonel Keller ordered a troop of 'B' Sqn to move forward to Amyntaeon to try and stop the rout. . . . The

Australians were re-formed and marched off during the night and so far as 3rd RTR was concerned we never made contact with them again.

The next day, the 13th, 3rd RTR were ordered to be rearguard to hold the Sotei ridge until midday. A mixed force of New Zealand MGs, two batteries of Northumberland Hussar A/Tk guns plus Battalion HQ tanks covered the flanks, road and bridge. 'B' Sqn was on the forward slope in the centre and 'C' Sqn on the eastern end with 2nd RHA 25-pdrs in clefts behind the ridge. Behind the Sotei ridge was the huge supply dump with thousands of gallons of petrol, oil and food. The attack started at dawn covered by mortars and rifle fire. The noise was terrific. 2nd RHA fired intermittently as the German infantry infiltrated. 'B' Sqn took full advantage, as Jim Caswell related:

The Germans arrived at first light, it was Easter Sunday. I was reserve driver and front gunner. In the turret were the Commander Sergeant Macintosh, the wireless/gun loader and the gunner. We had been told to hold our fire until the enemy were 500 yards away. The usual German blitzkrieg methods were used, first the motorcyclist outriders, then the armoured cars and lorried infantry with the tanks, artillery and Stukas following. At 500 yards Sergeant Mac said: 'Immediately to our front, German infantry, 500 yards, gunners open fire.' I and the turret gunner had a good shoot at the still quite exposed German infantry. In about an hour they had called up their anti-tank guns and their tanks were beginning to arrive. Our RHA joined in and we were giving the Germans a very hot time. We were now firing our armour-piercing shells at the German tanks and nearly all our MG ammunition was fired. Some German shells were ranging on us and after about two hours of battle one hit our front and shot off one of our tracks. So Mac ordered the breech-blocks to be removed from the guns and to bale out. We all got out safely but by this time the enemy was firing heavily all sorts of gun fire amongst us. More Stukas had also arrived. We dodged behind tanks still in action and eventually found shelter in a big shell hole.

Lieutenant Bob Crisp was furious because it was clear to him that the experienced sergeant tank commander of 'Collected' had broken its nearside track in two places, with one end wrapped round the driving sprocket. By studying the marks on the ground it was clear that the wreck was deliberate. "You certainly made a good job of it. Now you can finish off what you started. Remove the machine-gun and breechblock and set the tank alight. Then take your crew and report to Major Warren." The last I saw of that crew in Greece was four heavy laden figures, lurid and unreal in the light of the blazing tank, moving along the crest of the ridge.'

The remains of 'C' Sqn were bombed by a little 'Storch' German Army recce plane. Crisp fired on some enemy transport and watched huge fleets of Messerschmitt, Stukas and yellow-nosed Heinkels passing overhead southwards. 'C' and 'B' and HQ Sqns had only ten serviceable tanks when they withdrew to where 'A' Sqn and 4th Hussars held the pass at Ptolemais.

Captain George Witheridge's tank was hit by gunfire and momentarily caught fire. The crew found themselves in enemy territory with most of them wounded or unconscious. Witheridge was the first to return to consciousness, but the driver was violently sick and was relieved by the second driver. They were now alone. A drill was worked out for speed in starting and moving off. The tank moved forwards to the steepest part of the ridge, the only way to avoid anti-tank fire. It fell rather than ran over the ridge edge and roared, out of gear, to the plain below. Lieutenant-Colonel Keller, alerted by a wireless message, came back in his staff car through shellfire to help the tank and crew which managed to join the tail end of the regiment shortly before Ptolemais was reached.

'My "B" Squadron had a four hour battle in the Amyntaeon plain with German infantry, but we were soon outflanked. Then followed a terrible withdrawal with no sleep for approximately 8 days and nights. I (Major W.R. Reeves DSO) personally was slightly wounded by a bomb splinter in my left arm; the splinter was removed in hospital in Athens. Eventually I got on a ship *Thirland Castle* with an Australian infantry unit and joined the remnant of the 3rd (Battalion) at Suda Bay in Crete." George Witheridge took command of 'B' Sqn after Reeves's wound.

Lieutenant Denis Bartlett, 'A' Sqn, recalled:

The scattered units of the Armoured Brigade rush to the Veve Pass overlooking Florina plain. As night falls a lost column of pathetic Italian prisoners from Albania limp through the pass and the brigade moves into position. The night is quiet – broken only by the roar of the tanks engines reverberating round the snow and ice capped peaks. With dawn comes the knowledge that the Germans are at the foot of the pass, with their armour moving across the Florina plain. A Greek Division with antiquated equipment is holding our right flank. The German drive checks as they meet the opposing British forces from Salonika to Veve. For a week the battle rages at Veve and we have been flown out of the skies. Greece becomes the Stukas' playground. Our gunners take deadly toll of the attacking Germans but now two divisions are facing us on the Florina plain. The BEF is falling back.

Major R.H.O. Simpson OC 'A' Sqn remembered:

After the Amyntain (*sic*) battle, the remaining tanks of 'B' and 'C' Sqn withdrew through Ptolemais position on Easter Sunday. At mid-day the enemy attacked with motorcyclists and a couple of tanks. They were all knocked out by No.1 Troop OC Denis Bartlett who won the MC in this action. They (the enemy) gave up and tried to cut us off by getting round our left flank. At 1730 hrs in evening 40 enemy tanks got within 400 yards. We opened fire with the whole squadron from hulldown positions assisted by A/Tk guns of Northumberland Hussars and a 25-pdr of 2nd RHA firing over open sights. Tanks of 4th Hussars on our left flank withdrew under cover of a smokescreen from my Sqn HQ tanks assisted by 'Bimbo' Warren with his one remaining smoke mortar tank. As it got dark the enemy tanks withdrew, and we also to the Aliakman river. 'A' Sqn lost only one tank evacuated by crew owing to track troubles

And Trooper Fred Dale wrote, ' "A" Sqn and two Sqns of 4th Hussars were moved over to the Veve slopes and opened heavy fire on the tanks and infantry of 33rd Panzer Regt as they attempted to turn the position. There were approximately 30 to 40 Mk III. We did inflict a lot of casualties.' Later, 'The enemy were only 600 yards from HQ. "A" Sqn and a Tp (troop) of 2 pdr A/Tk guns were left as rear guard. We knocked out 4 or 5 tanks, lorries and a couple of guns.' Major R.H.O. Simpson was awarded the DSO for 'A' Sqn's battle.

The Brigade HQ near Manopege was attacked and Germans with Mausers got within 600 yards. The War Diary reports, 'a counter-attack and the attempt was driven off with considerable loss (estimated 20 tanks destroyed) to the enemy. The action was like a Crystal Palace fireworks display in the gathering dusk.' 'A' Sqn had had a field day, and in the evening 'C' Sqn joined in as well. The Adjutant, Captain String got a message through on the wireless to Bob Crisp that 'C' Sqn was to re-form at Komanos. Major 'Bimbo' Warren his OC laughed bitterly, 'and explained that "C" Sqn now consisted of four tanks – his, my two and one of 12 Tp. Four more had packed up during the night and morning with broken tracks and one with broken steering.' At 1800 hrs Major Warren gave urgent orders over the air that 'C' Sqn was to protect Brigade HQ from enemy armour. So Crisp worked his two A-10s towards the Veve ridge with his friend Harry Maegraith: 'I could identify the column quite clearly, a line of about 20 Gerry light tanks coming along in single file, ten yards between each vehicle. . . . The light was failing fast; I said to my Tp Sergeant, "we'll have a bash at them from here" and gave my gunner his fire orders.' The range was 800 yards; after ranging shots and tracer fire, 'Two columns of smoke rose black against the afterglow.' Major Warren recorded in his diary: 'Second Lieutenant Crisp knocked out two enemy light tanks.' 'Bimbo's tank had stuck in a swampy patch. The track had filled with mud and had snapped as it went over the driving sprocket, so Warren took the remaining 12 Troop tank; 'We were now three.' Crisp volunteered to form a roadblock to cover the withdrawal of Brigade HQ. Brigadier Charrington told him that, 'everything was going according to plan. "A" Sqn had given the Gerries a very rough time.' At one in the morning Crisp thought he had done his duty. Unfortunately a petrol stoppage defied his driver 'Skipper' West's efforts, and then 'C' Sqn were down to two.

In the two-day battle near Florina, Corporal G.R. Basford's troop was ordered across the bridge at Ptolemais to cover the withdrawal of General Mackay's 'Imperial' forces. The RAF alerted the defence that a column of about 2,000 vehicles was approaching Ptolemais. As they approached the blown bridge they presented an unbelievable target to the British and NZ field gunners and of course 3rd RTR tanks, though Stukas and Messerschmitts harassed the defences. At dusk forty German tanks under cover of a smoke-screen started to work their way round the British positions. The field gun batteries were ordered back and a fierce fight developed between the opposing tanks. Lieutenant-Colonel Reggie Keller led the regiment skilfully and in the Ptolemais battle 3rd RTR knocked out twelve enemy tanks in various scattered actions for the loss of only three aged A-10s.

The remaining tanks and many tank crews in lorries now took part in the general withdrawal. By dawn on 14 April the battalion had moved 60 miles, fought two actions in 24 hours, and was along the road at Musmei Grevena, on a crater-shaped hill with excellent cover. All available MGs were sited for AA defence as Stuka dive-bombing was heavy. A Ju 88 was shot down. The tank brigade workshops had been sent further back and no wireless contact could be made. During the 15th, various conferences took place. The first order was for 3rd RTR to hold their position in the top Mullah, a crater-shaped small hill at Grevena. The next order said 3rd RTR would withdraw over the River Venetikos at 1700 hrs. Finally General Wilson ordered the brigade – what was left of it – to continue to withdraw to Kalabaka where an Australian brigade was holding a position.

Lieutenant-Colonel Keller went off in a scout car to find Brigade HQ.

Crossing the Mullah, a scene of indescribable confusion met the eye. The (German) bombing had caught transport, guns – ammo lorries and infantry in the narrow defile. The road was blocked except for a narrow lane through the debris. Horses or bits of the mules were hanging in trees – lorries were blown to bits all over the place and the road was filled with a crawling mass of troops and transport. The Boche dive-bombers and Ju 88s were flying up and down the column which was continually halted by drivers abandoning their lorries as the bombers flew over.

The twelve surviving tanks were now grouped into a composite squadron under 'A' Sqn OC, Major Simpson. The CO rode in the Squadron Commander's tank and Bob Crisp took over the only 'C' Sqn tank left from 12th Troop. He ensured that he was the last tank in the 3rd RTR convoy and posted his gunner on the back of the tank to give warning of air attack. When this happened the A-10 was moved into hiding under the olive trees.

The 16 April was spent in cold drizzle with low clouds, marching southwards, skirting the bomb craters and the debris of the retreating army: ammo, equipment, derelict vehicles, dead men and horses. When Crisp reached the torrential River Venetikos, after negotiating three hairpin bends with a 1,000-foot drop, he found his OC 'Bimbo' Warren and Captain Plews the

RAOC officer waiting for him. 'The CO wants you to form a roadblock with your tank.' The tall burly South African took this in his stride, but his tank didn't. It broke the nearside track, but Captain Plews winched Crisp's tank by cable to a clump of low trees where the one-tank rearguard could hide. 'Skipper' West, his faithful driver, refused to leave him. A barricade of timber left over from the bridge construction was laid two deep between the tank and the bank of the river, where the enemy would soon appear. But a 'C' Sqn NCO later appeared to bring Crisp's crew to temporary safety. The next day Crisp borrowed a tank from Major Simpson; he persuaded Captain Plews and a fitter to ride on the back of *his* cruiser tank. The town of Kalambaka was the next objective. In heavy rain half the remaining tanks broke down, victims not of the Luftwaffe but of mud, worn-out tracks and lack of spares. One of the survivors was Major Basil Carey the 2 i/c. The indomitable Crisp shot down a Heinkel 111 at almost point-blank range beside the River Pinios. From a NAAFI store in the centre of Kalambaka the battered 3rd RTR column obtained cans of fruit, milk, breakfast cereals, bars of chocolate and sweets. The trek to Trikkala continued, as Fred Dale of 'A' Sqn related:

On the 27th we only had five tanks left. We had been bombed and machine gunned day after day and after five days our last action was an ambush. After a struggle we were lined up overlooking a valley. As two of the tanks had broken tracks, my tank being the first in line was to be the front of the column, the other four tanks the middle and rear of the column so that the valley was blocked. While this was going on all spare tank crews were taken back to Athens. When the Germans came we did what we had to do. I took the first three motor bikes with machine gun sidecars and three troop carriers full of infantry, the other four tanks did the rest. After all our ammunition was finished the valley was truly blocked.

The remains of the column ran through Larissa in a sorry state after further bombing, although the road bridge was still intact. On the 18th the retreat continued from Larissa to Altautle. By midnight the remaining tanks had broken down and 3rd RTR was no longer a fighting unit.

Trooper Jim Caswell of 'B' Sqn recalled:

The remainder of April was spent in withdrawal. There were no replacement tanks so all knocked out/baled out crew survivors were told to make their best way back to Athens. Sometimes we attached ourselves to Australian or New Zealand rear-guard actions, but the only arms we had were our revolvers which were issued to all tank crews. At least we got a lift in their trucks when they were ordered to withdraw. The Luftwaffe was now in full flight and a score of Stukas or so would attack us about ten times a day. We would take it in turns to act as aircraft lookout. As soon as a warning was given the driver would drive off the road undercover if possible. We would scamper down the mountain slopes hoping to find rocks for protection. It was surprising the few casualties we received from these attacks. One trooper claimed he had shot down a Stuka with his revolver. Thank goodness they did not operate at night. Passing one of our airfields we saw about 20 Hurricanes shot up on the ground. We knew then what had happened to the RAF and our air protection.

The Army blamed the RAF for lack of support. But it was impossible to protect the few limited aerodromes from Luftwaffe attack. AA support could not stave off the hordes of fighter-bombers and bombers. The RAF could not keep their planes in the air for any length of time.

Corporal G.R. Basford was a lucky wireless operator. A tank shell hit the auxiliary petrol tank on the back of his tank and set it ablaze. The crew jettisoned it quickly but the A-10 thundered down the narrow road with its gun broadside on: the muzzle crushed against a telegraph pole which sent the gun and turret spinning and rocked the tank. And it then hit two more poles. Despite this the gunner did some fine shooting, scoring hits on several enemy tanks, one going up in flames on the opposite ridge. When 3rd RTR eventually reached the River Aliakman they were down to eight battleworthy tanks. Basford's tank column was under attack from five Dorniers, often bombing (ineffectively) from only 50 feet. When his 3rd RTR group eventually crossed the Corinth Canal south to Argos, they lay hidden, later embarking in a gale in a caique which was run down and sunk. HMS *Isis* rescued them and on the way to Crete was dive-bombed all the way. After a few days among the olive groves near Malene airfield his group embarked for Alexandria.

There were a few comforts on the retreat. A foraging party

found welcome stores, petrol, oil, lubricant and a jorum of rum at Trikkala. Trooper Fred Dale of 'A' Sqn found a NAAFI warehouse near Larissa about to be blown up by the Military Police. Apart from tinned foods and cigarettes Dale related, 'After a few bottles of whisky and gin the bombing didn't seem to bother us.'

Captain Bartram the LAD officer was in charge of a 'B' Echelon convoy of which SQMS Bill Close and his 15-cwt truck was a part. There were fourteen 3-tonners crammed with 250 members of 3rd RTR: weary tankies, two or three young troop officers, baled-out crews and echelon personnel huddled on piles of bedrolls, stores and ammo. Besa machine-guns were mounted on the cabs of the Bedfords. One man was the observer/loader, the other fired the gun. They trekked for days amid files of worn-out Greek infantry in khaki and puttees, with their cannon and limbers pulled by shaggy ponies. Their ambulances were buses, other transport included mules and donkeys. Lieutenant Bob Crisp and his crew, with Captain Plews 'maintaining' the old cruiser, had an epic journey from Trikkala where they were out of wireless range of the CO. 'We left the metalled surface and the chaotic transport and ambled sedately along over the fields, only coming back to the road to cross a bridge or culvert.' He fired the Bren and then the 2-pdr gun at a Heinkel. At the bridge outside Kastrida, Private Macallum, of the ANZACS threatened to shoot Crisp until the tank gunner trained the 2-pdr on him. 'It was the last British tank in Greece. I was going to get it back to Athens. With every abandoned 3rd Battalion cruiser we passed that intention crystallised into an obsession, held unspoken by every individual in our little party.' A lieutenant-colonel in the Military Police ordered them not to cross the last pass as the tank would block the main road if it broke down. They persevered by night, mixed up in a convoy. At the top of the pass the track plates went. Eight Stukas dive-bombed the convoy. 'We could see that the tank was now in a hell of a mess, a bomb burst right under the front track and suspension.' They then acquired a big New Zealand Division 3-tonner, an officers' mess lorry crammed with Christmas hampers, crates of beer and whisky. Captain Plews sat on the bonnet filling up the damaged radiator as they made their way to Lamia singing bawdy songs. The next stop was in a hot-spring hydro spa where they all wallowed in hot sulphur medicinal waters. On through the defile of Thermopylae until their 'borrowed' 3-tonner was reunited with

Colonel Page, the NZ CO (who of course was a friend of Crisp's!) A 15-cwt truck then took them along the coast road to Thebes, and into Athens where they rejoined 'C' Sqn officers sleeping in the glades of Glyphada at midnight on the 23rd.

Jim Caswell of 'B' Sqn recalled: 'Athens was reached and 3rd RTR were ordered to re-assemble at Glyphada. At the main RAF HQ, the main airport for Athens, evacuated in a hurry; we loaded up with scores of crates of bully, sausages, biscuits, tea, tins of fruit and milk. We threw some bully out to the local population. In the main streets groups of people stood and clapped us, perhaps because our small force did our best or whether they were glad to see us go and hoped for a better life under the Germans. I don't know.'

Corporal H.T. Jarvis joined the RTC in January 1927, and had fought at Calais. Now in Greece and retreating again, he concealed his tank in a wood fringing a vineyard and watched light tanks of 4th Hussars return from the Veve pass and drop down into the plain. He heard the German guns open up on them. The country was so rough they could not get off the road. 'Very soon a large number of the little tanks were flaming wrecks.' A few days later he was wounded in the leg. The field ambulance taking him to safety was bombed by Stukas. Then he watched Grevena being dive-bombed. An RTR truck took him to Larissa. Outside the burning town the truck overturned. Righting it the escape party drove in the snow and rain over the Lamia pass and Jarvis and others ended up in the Grande Bretagne Hotel in Athens which had been converted into a hospital. On being evacuated his Greek steamer was bombed as it left Piraeus, burned and sank. Large numbers of Imperial and British troops were trapped below with no chance of escape. Jarvis in pyjamas got away in a lighter, was taken to a Greek hospital, and thence to the Glades of Daphne, the deserted 3rd RTR camp. Rescued first by Australians, then by Maoris, he eventually reached the Corinth Canal. By ambulance, whaler, then motor launch to HMS *Calcutta*, which fought off Stukas to Crete, and from Maleme, he was eventually transported back to Alexandria.

Sergeant John Maskell's tank eventually came to a grinding halt. It was worn out, and had to be destroyed with a 30-gallon drum of petrol poured over a camouflage net stuffed into the turret and set alight. The gunner Jock Ogilvie carried away his Besa and hauled out a couple of boxes of ammunition. The crew got a lift in a NZ lorry and later rejoined their unit, climbing up through the steep Kozani pass. While 'A' Sqn covered their retreat, Maskell met an RTR lorry heading back towards the front driven by Sergeant Webber taking spare parts. Driving 15 miles they found a disabled tank and between them repaired it.

On 19 April 1941 most of the 3rd RTR survivors reached Atlante and the next day Thermopylae, where with Vickers guns drawn from the docks they were formed into four squadrons as armed infantry in an anti-parachutist role behind the New Zealand Division. 'A' Sqn was near Malakasa on a road north of Marathon; 'B' Sqn between Magoula and Mandra; 'C' Sqn in two suburbs in the hills near Kriekouki; 'D' Sqn was at Khalandrian. All were within 20 miles of Athens. The remainder of 3rd RTR personnel were sent back across the Corinth Canal to Argos. 'Luck was with us, we (Trooper Fred Dale, 'A' Sqn) had just gone over the Corinth Canal when the German paras started to drop. The New Zealanders were defending the port (Argos). It was just like another Dunkirk with guns and lorries and everything being destroyed.'

Captain Dennis Bartlett spoke of the experience: 'The evacuation begins. Co-ordination no longer exists. Personnel and equipment of an Australian base hospital land as base troops embark on the waiting ships. Days drag on – the British Forces are hunted from harbour to harbour but on the 29th April, the last intact force surrenders to the Germans (2nd Panzer Division occupied Athens). Greece is finished. A few hours before capture, I speak to a Greek. He is smiling. "The British will come back", he says, with that funny little beckoning movement of the hand, he walked away to the hills saying his "Goodbye".' Bartlett later spent nearly four years in a POW camp:

On 25 April, while Lieutenant-Colonel Keller was visiting the 'C' Sqn position, a despatch rider appeared with orders for the battalion to move to Nauplion in the Peloponnese, south of the Corinth Canal for embarkation. The 2 i/c Major Carey with most of the transport was sent to Kalamata to provide lifts back and forth from Corinth. On the 26th the battalion set off towards Corinth via Megara. The road was a shambles with huge bomb craters, dozens of dead mules, horses and men all over the road. The bridge at Corinth was still intact but the town was on fire. By dawn on 27 April the RTR column was clear and moving south towards Argos. In nearby Nauplion the battalion were ordered to get under cover 4 miles east of Argos. Captain Norman Scranton and about 100 ORs had two days earlier been evacuated by train from Athens and now rejoined. Embarkation of 12 officers and 180 men took place on a small Greek lighter which transferred them to the destroyers HMS *Hotspur* and *Isis*. During the night they sailed for Crete and were landed at Suda Bay near Candia. RHQ and half of 'C' Sqn moved independently via Sparta to the southernmost part of Monemvasia. Captain Cyril Joly who had joined the battalion after Calais was rescued here by HMS *Ajax*. The Navy sailed on the 28th and landed this RTR party at Alexandria on the 30th. Major 'Bimbo' Warren, Lieutenant Bob Crisp, Lieutenant Harry Maegraith and thirty-three members of 'C' Sqn escaped on HMS *Hotspur*, then to the *Cumblebank*. Bob Crisp and Maegraith shared the first officer's cabin all the way to Port Said. Crisp's remarkable odyssey through Greece was over. He thoroughly deserved his DSO. 'The Greek adventure had removed two thirds of the officers. And of the 60 odd tanks 3rd RTR had taken to Greece at the beginning of 1941, not half a dozen were casualties of *direct* enemy action. All the others had been abandoned with broken tracks or other mechanical breakdowns. They littered the passes and defiles of Macedonia and Thessaly, stripped of their machine guns but otherwise intact. They were of no help to the enemy. No other army would have contemplated using them', Crisp wrote. Nevertheless the LAD fitters had tried very hard to keep the A-10s on the road. On his return to the Delta, the CO issued a special order of the day commending Corporal Ribbins, Troopers Woodgate, Parfitt, Rawlins, Kernahan and Ridpath for 'the courage, determination and devotion' they had shown in maintaining the RTR cruiser tanks, often under air attack.

There were many individual stories of the last tragic days. Major Carey, Captain Bartrum, Captain Bartlett, and Captain Scrafton's party of 100 ORs were captured. Private Bert Jobson, wireless operator, recalled:

Corporal Sammy Crook and I were put in the bag. We spent over four years as guests of Hitler. When we were taken to a PoW camp at Corinth we met quite a number of other well-known Tankies. Major 'Shufti' Carey and RSM Tiny White with whom I shared a same hole behind a rock in Death Valley on the withdrawal when our soft vehicles were ripped to shreds by Junker bombers. We were marched to Salonika, starving except for potato soup and 3 oz of bread.

In the long retreat Lieutenant Dick Shattock acted as officer despatch rider on a BSA motorcycle with Major 'Dicker' Wilson's HQ Sqn, which was attacked every day by Stukas and Messerschmitt 109s. Shattock got the four Bren guns and crews set up to try to defer the Luftwaffe. Wounded in the head by a Stuka bomb fragment he was taken by ambulance back to Kalabaka via Trikkala, thence to Athens and back to Egypt via a hospital ship. The next hospital ship to leave Piraeus harbour was sunk by Stukas.

After getting off the beaches near Argos most of the 200 officers and men might have thought that most of their Grecian ordeal was over. They were wrong. Jim Caswell of 'B' Sqn recollected:

The Navy would come for us about 1 am and leave 3 am prompt to reach Suda Bay in Crete before daylight. There were two Greek whalers waiting to pick us up (from the Monemvasia beaches) in groups of 30s. HMS *Hotspur* was anchored about half a mile out. We reached Suda Bay before daybreak and marched to an olive grove a mile or so from the port now being heavily bombed during the day. There was only a squadron (of 7th RTR) tanks on Crete (two Matildas in defence of the airfields at Herakleon, Retimo and Maleme). As they had crews it was decided that as Rommel had arrived in Africa and was forcing our troops to retreat, as many 3rd RTR tank crews as possible should return to Egypt. Our commanding officer (Major Bill Reeves DSO, recovered from his wound and hospitalization in Athens) was told of a convoy leaving Suda Bay. He commandeered a Greek merchantman *Popi Vernicos* (christened Pop-eye). We embarked, about 200 RTR and 20 German PoW. The ship had not been at sea for 27 years, had no food aboard and was unable to exceed four knots speed, lagged behind the convoy bound for Alexandria. The daily ration was a tin of bully between two, a packet of biscuits plus a pint of water for all purposes.

Fred Dale, 'A' Sqn recalled: 'After 3 days we could still see land, as we were only doing 3 knots per hour. We found the captain and crew asleep at the wheel and it was just running under its own steam. After that our officer Lieutenant Upjohn-Gill took over the boat. When the coal ran out we all had to take a spell in sieving the coal dust. We looked like black minstrels and after that we started to burn all the wood we could find, doors, the wheelhouse, everything.' Major Bill Reeves continued the story. 'Our JO (Junior Officer) managed to read the charts on the bridge and so steer towards Alex. When the destroyer HMS *Grimsby* signalled us to stop, no one knew how to stop the ship! I think we were in danger of being sunk but did manage to stop in the end.' Captain George Witheridge was hurriedly brought to the bridge and read, late at night, lamp signals that spelt 'Stop or we will sink you'; to this, by use of a hand torch, he signalled back, 'Have stopped'. The ship was told to prepare for boarders. 'It was like meeting an old friend (reported Fred Dale). They offered to send us some rations which we refused, so they decided to escort us. It was a lovely feeling to arrive with all the fleet and freighters blowing their sirens full blast.'

Adolf Hitler's diary for 17 February 1945 noted: 'The shameful defeats they (the Italians) suffered caused certain of the Balkan states to regard us with scorn and contempt . . . this compelled us, contrary to all our plans, to intervene in the Balkans; *and that in its turn led to a catastrophic delay in the launching of our attack on Russia*. We were compelled to expend some of our finest divisions there (Greece and Crete). I would have preferred to launch our paratroopers against Gibraltar than against Corinth or Crete.' Perhaps the sixty beat-up 3rd RTR cruiser tanks in their fighting withdrawal of nearly 300 miles helped upset the Fuehrer's Operation 'Barbarossa': the invasion of Russia.

Colonel-General Alfred Jodl, Chief-of-Staff of the German Army told Field Marshal Smuts in 1946, 'Jodl stated that Germany had lost the war because she had been obliged to divert divisions to meet the British landings in Greece. This meant she lost six weeks. She lost time – and with time she lost Moscow, Stalingrad and the war.'

Nearly 12,000 Army troops were lost in Greece including 6,600 British, though over 50,000 were safely brought out, about 80 per cent of the original forces sent there. Battered, nursing their wounds and tankless, 3rd RTR left Greece for the battles still to come in North Africa.

5

THE DESERT WAR –
PREPARATION FOR OPERATION
'CRUSADER'

By one means or another the remnants of 3rd RTR arrived back in Egypt at the beginning of May 1941. It was a tank batalion without tanks and without many tank crews. After seven days' local leave – some had recuperation leave in Palestine – 'We were taken to a camp near Alexandria, but as we were on nobody's ration strength, we were given some bully stew – quite a change from cold bully' recalled Trooper Jim Caswell of 'B' Sqn. 'All the tanks in Egypt were with fighting units in the desert so we awaited a delivery of tanks. Fortunately Rommel was running out of steam and was halted on the Egyptian Frontier, a huge barbed wire fence stretching from the coast miles into the desert.' Operation 'Battleaxe' which started on 15 June was a near disaster for the 2nd, 4th, 6th and 7th RTR battalions. They suffered 91 disabled tanks, of which 64 were Matildas. Rommel's superior tank recovery operation rescued the majority of his tanks from the battlefield. 'Battleaxe' became a byword for blundering. During 'Battleaxe' the Afrika Korps developed a new method of attack. With a dozen or so A/Tk guns they leapfrogged from one vantage point to another, while the panzers, stationary and hulled-down, if possible, provided protective fire. Then the screen of panzers and A/Tk guns alternated in waves of attack.

Guarding the RAF station at Heliopolis airport north of Cairo was the first task given to the tankless battalion. Trooper Caswell recollected: 'We were in barracks and able to have hot showers, as we awaited some American tanks due to arrive soon. Upon arrival at Heliopolis Captain Peter Williams who had gained an MC at Calais, was the senior "B" Sqn officer left: he asked me to list names, initials and religions of those of "B" Sqn who had survived Greece and Crete. They numbered 80 but as the days went by another dozen rejoined us; some had rowed from Greece to Crete and had been evacuated from there with other troops.' The day after 200 3rd RTR officers and men escaped from Crete, the German parachutists dropped and despite a ferocious defence the island was soon captured. Caswell was soon promoted to corporal, bypassing lance-corporal.

Fred Dale, 'A' Sqn remembered: 'We only had one parade a day, for one hour, the rest of the time was taken up with sport and swimming. We could go out after 2 p.m. After a couple of weeks we were fit and rested. We then started drill parades and guard duties. After a few weeks of guard duties we were on the move again to Abbassia Base Depot (the Royal Armoured Corps Depot) where we started individual training again, gunnery and driving courses. I was sent on an NCO course for two weeks to take in military law, star navigation and night marches, also squadron drills and guard Commander's duty, including compass.' Fred Dale duly became a lance-corporal (*unpaid*).

Bob Crisp with his well-deserved DSO was now a captain and 2 i/c 'C' Sqn. He was also bored stiff with the need to stand-to at first light and again at last light, and with days filled with drill and kit inspections. But his great cricketing skills were much in demand at the Gezira Sporting Club; he was popular indeed at Groppi's Continental Shepherds bar, and Tommy's; drinking John Collins and the local beer beside the swimming pool of the Heliopolis Club were also 'lotus-eating' attractions.

The next move at the end of August was to a tented camp about 25 miles from Cairo by the Sweet Water Canal at Beni Yusef. Sergeant Jock Watt with many others visited and appreciated the sights, noises and smells of Cairo: the crowds of people milling about in 'night gowns' breathing garlic over everyone; the noisy tram car wheels screeching and rattling on their rails; the wailing interminable Egyptian music; the horse-drawn garys; bullock carts loaded with women dressed in black; the know-all shoeshine boys and street urchins fluent in the basics of four or five languages; the street vendors and conmen who would sell you anything or anyone; and the aroma of myriad foods being cooked. Bill Close was promoted to 'B' Sqn Sergeant-Major, under Major George Witheridge, who was also promoted after the return from Greece. Bill Close and his OC had both been sergeants together in Warminster in 1938.

Lieutenant-Colonel Reggie Keller, after bravely leading the battalion into two savage doomed expeditions at Calais and in

Greece, went to a staff posting. The new CO was Lieutenant-Colonel 'Bunny' Ewins, a cavalry man who had been RTR instructor at the Indian staff college. Paddy Hehir became RSM instead of 'Tiny' White who had been captured in Greece. The Australian Harry Maegraith was troop commander in 'C' Sqn, and had survived Greece alongside Bob Crisp. The RMO was still 'Doc' MacMillan – another survivor from Greece. Major Wilson, a tough North-West Frontier regular, commanded 'A' Sqn and 'Bimbo' Warren 'C' Sqn. The Royal Armoured Corps pool supplied most of the many reinforcements needed, quite a few from the 8th Hussars. SSM Bill Close recalled: 'They had to be made welcome and given confidence. It was on record that 3rd RTR had lost every tank, every vehicle and at least half its personnel in both campaigns – Calais and Greece.'

3rd RTR was now part of Brigadier Alec Gatehouse's 4th Light Armoured Brigade, along with 5th RTR and 8th Hussars, 'light' because they were equipped with brand new light American tanks, described by Bob Crisp:

> The (M3) Stuart was a strange-looking contraption, straight from Texas; tall in the saddle and with the Western flavour accentuated by a couple of Browning machine guns. The main armament (a 37-mm gun) was similar to the peashooter that all British tanks carried at that time (the 2-pdr), but the frontal armour was much thicker than in our own light tanks and cruisers. The really intriguing things about the M3 were its engine and the tracks. It was simply an aeroplane engine stuck in a tank with radial cylinders and a fan that looked like a propeller. The engine ran efficiently – only – on high octane aviation spirit (speed up to 40 mph).

The main reason why the vast majority of 3rd RTR A-10 cruiser tanks were left in Greece was not due to enemy fire, but to track failure. Each track link of the Stuart was mounted in solid rubber blocks on which the vehicle moved. Driver Whaley was ordered to test a 'C' Sqn Stuart in the open sandy desert out of Heliopolis. He made some fast turns. No 'bang-clatter' and the swerving halt that meant a broken track. Captain Crisp then put the new tank through a variety of turns and manoeuvres, spurting up great fountains of sand and dust behind the tracks. A group of US Army technicians were watching the manoeuvres with great interest. In front of Lieutenant-Colonel 'Bunny' Ewins and others, Whaley was asked for his opinion of the Stuart. He answered, 'Its a honey' and the name stuck.

Two negative points were the short tank mileage and the 37-mm gun that could only fire AP and not HE shells. But its minimal mechanical complexity and ease of maintenance were to be a great plus in the desert warfare ahead, although British tank 'experts' demanded fourteen modifications. Trooper Reay and all the 3rd RTR gunners were soon pounding away at panzer hulks at a dusty battle camp on the desert side of the Cairo–Fayoum road. 'Geordie' Reay said to SSM Bill Close, 'They're my favourite, Germans they are: I could spend the rest of the war firing at them.' Close reckoned Geordie was one of the best tank gunners in the battalion. They needed to be good because the Germans' 88-mm dual purpose AA/A/Tk and new 50-mm Pak 38 anti-tank guns had blasted the British Matildas at Halfaya in Operation 'Battleaxe' – and would probably take out the new Stuarts too.

The Stuart had a crew of four with no co-driver. Trooper Jim Caswell, 'B' Sqn recollected: 'We regarded them generally as better than our previous British tanks but still under-gunned compared with the German Mk III and IV. One day Captain Peter Williams came up to me. "Trooper Caswell, you have done a fine job as squadron clerk, but after all, you are a tank crewman, will you be my driver?"' So, Caswell went on, 'we then learnt about our new tanks, carried out a lot of training and moved up the desert in August. The Germans and Italians were still on the Libyan–Egyptian borders and we still held Tobruk.'

After a successful boxing tournament at Madia camp against the New Zealanders, Lance Corporal Fred Dale of 'A' Sqn was made a *fully paid* lance corporal. He was paid as a wireless operator as well. He thought the Honey was very fast and very reliable though the high octane petrol had to be refuelled every 40 miles. The Browning machine-gun had to be got used to, 'By now all crews had to be able to take over each other's job on the tank (within reason).'

SSM Close and the other squadron sergeant-majors went off into the desert to study navigation. 'Space was the most awesome thing about the Western Desert. The variety of terrain was infinite – soft dunes, stony flats, salt marsh, sand with boulders, sand with pebbles, pebbles with pebbles, miles and miles of flat plain, tortuous ravines or wadis, towering limestone escarpments. Hardly a sign that human beings had ever passed

that way. War relics apart, once the Delta had been left behind,
there were few stone cairns, perhaps a ruined mud-walled fort,
rare clusters of Bedouin tents, even rarer palms around an
oasis.' The squadron sergeant-majors learned to use the
primitive sun compass, a vital instrument in the desert
wastelands. The Arab saying goes: 'The desert is a fortress to
him who knows it, but a grave to him who does not.' The ability
of 'B' Echelon to track down the fighting squadrons at the end of
the day was always taken for granted. Sergeant Jock Watt 'driving
a lorry crammed with 700 gallons of high octane fuel for the
Honeys and the four gallon cans leaked badly (and wasted
perhaps 50 per cent of all fuel en route from docks to tanks) or
a load of high explosive ammunition. (The 'B' Echelon) drivers,
they were the brave ones, we did have the protection of armour
plate.' Watt recalled a bizarre tactic whereby after General
Wavell's withdrawal many of the freshwater wells in the desert
were salted to deny them to the enemy. The problems remained
when the wells were recaptured. Freshly brewed tea made of salt
water tasted grim, the milk curdled and in washing one's person
or clothes with salted water the soap would not lather.

In September 1941 3rd RTR and the brigade returned to the
desert and continued training near Bir Kenayis, south-west of
Matruh. As part of 7th Armoured Division, the famous 'Desert
Rats', 4th Light Armoured Brigade was wearing the emblem of
the Black Desert Rat – the Jerboa. At the end of October the
division was now fully trained and re-equipped and posted
between 'Piccadilly' and Maddalena.

The object of Operation 'Crusader' was to seek out and destroy
the Axis forces of 65,000 Germans and 54,000 Italians around
Gabr Saleh and relieve Tobruk. The Eighth Army had a similar
strength and was composed of 'XXX' Corps (7th Armoured
Division with 4th, 7th and 22nd Armoured Brigades; 1st South
African Division and 22nd Guards Brigade), plus 'XIII' Corps (4th
Indian, 2nd New Zealand Division plus 1st Army Tank Brigade
with slow, heavy Matildas and Valentine tanks). The Eighth Army
had a numerical superiority in tanks – 850 to about 560. Most of
the panzers were superior, but the Italian tanks were inferior to
the mixture of new Grants and Crusaders, Matildas, A-10s and the
166 Honeys of 4th Light Armoured Brigade. However, the 280
German medium tanks were the core of Rommel's armoured
forces – some 242 Panzer IIIs (including 19 of the new Panzer
III(J) Specials) and 38 Panzer IVs. All these now had additional

plates that doubled their 30-mm armour on the hull front. The advent of the new British 6-pdr A/Tk gun with which the motor battalions and motorized infantry brigades were equipped, was balanced by the undoubted deadly accuracy and penetration of the German 88-mm A/Tk guns. These could knock out most British tanks at 3,000 yards range. Brigadier Alec Gatehouse DSO, MC commanded 4th Armoured Brigade and Captain Crisp said of him: 'He was a tank officer as distinct from a cavalry officer and was probably the best handler of armour in the desert at the time.' According to Gatehouse's own records, 'the brigade during "Crusader" was in action continuously for the first fourteen days without rest or maintenance with an average of two battles a day'. The brigade centre line covered 1,700 miles and many unit tanks travelled over 3,000 miles. In five weeks of 'Crusader', the First and Second Battles of Sidi Rezegh, 172 Honeys were knocked out by the enemy (the total strength was 166).

To try to counter the threat posed by the formidable 88-mm A/Tk gun (which in theory would be dealt with by the British 25-pdr field guns with indirect fire), Crisp worked out a system in his 'C' Sqn Honey troop. After the target had been located, and indicated, the first order to the Honey driver would be 'Driver, advance, flat out'. The gunner would do his best to keep the crosswires of his telescopic sight on his target all the time the Honey was moving. The next order heard by gunner, driver and loader would be 'Driver Halt'. As soon as the tank stopped, the gunner would fire *without* command from the tank commander. The sound of the shot was the signal for the driver to let in the clutch and be off again. From stop to start it took about 4 seconds. All the commander did was to control movement and direction of the tank. Mobility was essential for survival for tanks that were outgunned and out-armoured. The best solution of course was a good hull-down defensive position with the enemy vehicles advancing into your chosen field of fire.

The preliminary tactic to the battle was at Abar Kenayis, and consisted of the temporary transformation of 3rd RTR into a large 'convoy' of 3-ton lorries, achieved by rolls of hessian and metal tubing camouflage. In the first week of November the disguised Honeys moved up to Hallequat, south of the Sollum–Sidi Barrani road. On the 80-mile journey over hard limestone outcrop the rubber blocks of the tracks of most of the Honeys had been chewed to bits. Brigadier Gatehouse flew to Cairo with an appropriate exhibit. Within three days Honeys in rear areas were stripped of their tracks, which were sent up by rail to 4th Armoured Brigade.

On 13 November Lieutenant-Colonel 'Bunny' Ewins of 3rd RTR had been briefed about 'Crusader'. All three armoured brigades of 7th Armoured Division were to be passed through the frontier border fencing with support troops, backed by the South African and New Zealand divisions. The Afrika Korps were in the coastal area south-east of Tobruk. The battleground selected was between their forces, their lines of communication and Benghazi. That was the theory anyway! On the night of 17 November the long columns formed nose to tail up to the wire. 'We had a violent thunderstorm. We had to get into the tanks and with the rain dripping through the turret it wasn't very comfortable, believe me,' recalled Corporal Fred Dale of 'A' Sqn. 'The sun came out the next morning. By the time we got to the frontier and in position for the attack our clothes and bedding were dry.' The 4th Armoured Brigade were to make for Sidi Rezegh and 22nd Armoured Brigade for El Adem. The 3rd RTR were the leading regiment and 'A' Sqn was in the lead. SSM Bill Close reported: 'We passed without incident through the gaps blown in Graziani's border wire and queued up at fuel dumps for the high octane aviation spirit. The rain had laid the dust and we rolled on deep into enemy territory without raising the usual clouds. Not a single hostile aircraft appeared.'

6

OPERATION 'CRUSADER' – '40 DAYS IN THE WILDERNESS'

The CO Lieutenant-Colonel 'Bunny' Ewins detached a squadron to investigate a sight of enemy tanks. Corporal Jim Caswell, 'B' Sqn recollected: 'It was only a mirage, the tanks were camels.' SSM Bill Close recalled: 'Mile after mile went by and by mid-afternoon after refuelling again and shedding its camouflage, the brigade was advancing in battle formation, the Honeys in line abreast, 100 yards apart, 200 yards between waves. It was a stirring sight . . . The sandy coloured paintwork barely scratched, each turret bearing its squadron marking – a triangle for "A", square for "B", circle for "C" and diamond for "HQ" – in 3rd RTR green like our shoulder flash. Above us fluttered little yellow pennants, picturesque but dangerous. It hadn't taken long for the enemy to work out that the more pennants there were on the wireless antenna, the more important the target.'

Jock Watt was promoted to SQM, then SSM in the light 'A' Sqn. On one recce he positioned his Honey near a high mound with a pile of stones on top, with just the turret showing: an ideal vantage point for observation. The only problem was that it was an obvious map point for German artillery and a salvo of 105-mm shells immediately straddled the Honey, prompting a rapid exit.

The brigade turned north and at Bir Sciafsciuf had the first brush with the enemy – indecisive, as the enemy withdrew during the night. But the following day, 19 November, the whole of 15th Panzer Division were encountered at Gabr Taieb el Essem, north-west of Scheferzen, some 65 miles from their startpoint. 'B' Sqn were sent off on a mission to support armoured cars of the King's Dragoon Guards and met with seven enemy tanks and armoured cars. Corporal Jim Caswell, 'B' Sqn reported:

At about 4 p.m. we ran into the 15th and 21st Panzer Divisions to our west. We faced that direction with the disadvantage of the setting sun in our eyes. I counted about 200 vehicles to our front most of them tanks and a tank battle commenced. We were outgunned but used our speed and manoeuvrability to some advantage. Advancing quickly in a naval 'tacking' method, we would stop, fire a few shells and retire. Tanks on both sides were hit and many were brewing up. We survived despite being hit six times. I had difficulty in steering our tank, however we reached Leaguer safely. Here the tanks formed a square with their turret guns facing outwards. Our supply trucks would then join us and we would start refuelling, taking on ammunition, petrol, rations and carry out any repairs. Captain Peter Williams surveyed the damage to our tank and summoned the squadron fitters. Our crew had already extracted the pins to break the track. The damaged sprocket was repaired during the night.

Captain Bob Crisp was way ahead of the rest of the battalion with 'C' Sqn. A long column of 200 Military Enemy Transport (MET) had been spotted on the Trigh Capuzzo highway. 'I saw my other three tanks ready and waiting and there was Harry (Maegraith) alongside me grinning. We came over that crest 16 abreast and roared down the slope flat out, the wind catching the trailers of dust. We were all caught up in the exhilaration of that first charge . . . we were compelled to divert our attention from the fleeing transport to several hostile armoured cars. Two small Mark IIs were bustling about like terriers with their teeth showing. We got two armoured cars and one of the light tanks. A third hurriedly abandoned with petrol pouring out. My gunner put a burst of tracer in and the whole thing roared up in orange flame and black smoke.' By mistake his surviving seven tanks reached Bardia, a village harbour on the Mediterranean coast. At dusk on their return back to rally they ran out of the precious high-octane petrol, but the replenishment officer with the petrol lorry arrived during the night. The CO later broke the news that 8th Hussars had lost twenty tanks, 5th RTR three tanks during the day while the Italian Ariete armoured division had severely mauled 22nd Armoured Brigade at Bir-el-Gubi.

The battle continued on 20 November with 15th Panzer being reinforced later in the day by 21st Panzer Division. The battered 22nd Armoured Brigade were ordered east from Bir-el-Gobi to support 4th Armoured Brigade. The Battle Group Stephan was a formidable composite force: part of 21st Panzer with 85 mixed Mk III and IV tanks, 35 Mk IIs, plus 12 105-mm howitzers and 4 deadly 88-mm A/Tk guns. Of this formidable formation Bob Crisp wrote:

> Sneaking through the battalions on our side were disturbing stories that the Honeys and Crusaders were no match at all for the Mark IIIs and Mark IVs in equal combat. It was a simple proposition: our little cannons could not knock them out, and they could knock us out easily. Within the week we were reckoning that it needed three Honeys to destroy one Mark IV. During the entire campaign we were to find no effective answer to the enemy's use of anti-tank weapons well forward with his panzers.

The battle on the 20th was ferocious. SSM Bill Close of 'B' Sqn reported: 'a furious battle flared up during which we were driven back somewhere around our starting point at Gabr Saleh and were reinforced by 5th RTR. Quite a few Honeys were knocked out reducing the Brigade strength to around 100 tanks. Many hits were claimed on Panzers but as we were falling back most of the time there was little evidence of knockouts.' The German tank recovery teams were superb and every night they roamed the battlefields, retrieving wrecked panzers (and quite a few KO'd British tanks as well) and repairing them to fight another day.

Corporal Fred Dale of 'A' Sqn had an unusual day. 'When the battle started we were firing at MK3 and MK4 German tanks. We were outgunned and losing tanks. We were told to fall back to the other squadrons; our tank was now firing over the engine then there was a big bang, we had been hit in the engine.' If it had been the turret Dale would have been killed. 'The order came to bale out. We all escaped unhurt and lay very still since shells were still hitting our tank. The troop officer had been hit in the head. He was lying part across my face and blood from the wound was by now dripping over my face, the crew were all lying face down, not moving.' A German Mk IV tank, 150 yards away had been knocked out and their crew came over to inspect Dale's battered Honey. On the way the Mk IV burst into flames and their ammunition exploded. 'In a short time their recovery vehicle arrived, they loaded up and left.' Dale's tank crew walked as instructed, north-north-east, and were rescued by troops of 4th Indian Division.

Corporal Jim Caswell of 'B' Sqn led a charmed life. Captain Peter Williams spotted a large convoy of enemy vehicles 2 miles away at first light. 'The gunner started firing. The lorries were scattering in all directions and several were immobilised.' Williams ordered Caswell to ram a command truck with a pennant flying. 'Then we were hit, an AP shell had gone through the tank killing Trooper Eastwood, the wireless operator and seriously wounding the gunner, Trooper James and Captain Williams (who later died of wounds). With no crew I decided to reverse out of action to safety.'

Captain Bob Crisp, 'C' Sqn recalled: 'We were startled into reality by a frantic call for help from "B" Sqn who screamed that they were being attacked by over 100 tanks.' Crisp could see forty to sixty panzers clearly coming down a broad depression in line abreast. He led his troop on to the flank, 'of the advancing juggernauts and getting out of the direct line of fire.' In the mêlée that followed his Honey crashed into another Honey: 'out of the turret popped the ferocious face of the "A" Sqn commander (Major Wilson)'.

During the night of 20/21 November the enemy moved west and contact was made with them early on the 21st at Gabr Saleh. Another fierce battle followed until the enemy began to withdraw north-west towards Sidi Rezegh where 7th Armoured Brigade and Support Group were holding the aerodrome. 4th Armoured Brigade pursued but the need to refuel every 40 miles caused delays. The next day their arrival helped relieve pressure on the elements of 7th Armoured Division who had been facing the combined onslaught of both panzer divisions alone.

Captain Bob Crisp, 'had several duels with enemy tanks, knocked out two and learnt a great deal – which of their armoured fighting vehicles I could take on and beat with the Honey and which of them I had to avoid. We were always prepared to take on any number of Italian tanks and any of the German Mark IIs and armoured cars. The Mark III and IV had to be dealt with by subterfuge and the grace of God, rather than by superior fighting qualities.'

Most battles in the desert were a haphazard fracas. Corporal Fred Dale, 'A' Sqn recollected: 'For the next few days the battle was very confusing, first we were helping one lot of infantry (South Africans) being attacked by Panzer Mk IVs; next day we were off to another wireless bearing to help somebody else in trouble. Sometimes we had trouble with replenishing petrol and ammunition. If we were being hard pressed and being attacked we would have to back out of action one by one.' On the night of 22 November: 'That night we had just got back into Leaguer and starting to do our chores when all hell broke loose. Lorries, staff cars, guns, infantry all passing through us in confusion and then shellfire was landing amongst us, some lorries were set on fire. We mounted the tanks to go on a compass bearing for about six miles and meet the rest of the regiment. We could see vehicles on fire for miles around.' Brigadier Alec Gatehouse's Brigade HQ was attacked by Cramer's Regiment 8 of 15th Panzer Division and virtually destroyed. The brigade 2 i/c, 17 officers and 150 ORs were taken prisoner. No less than 35 Honeys, armoured cars, guns and self-propelled (SP) guns were captured. It was a disaster. Gatehouse, who was away from this confusion, drove to 3rd RTR HQ to try to organize a rescue attempt. Only four Honeys were available, so he drove to 5th RTR and organized a counter-attack which in turn received a bloody nose. Nevertheless the indomitable Gatehouse collected the remaining seventy-seven Honeys of his brigade and moved north of Gabr Saleh early on the 23rd to join General Freyberg's NZ Division and relieve the battered 7th Armoured Division formations on Sidi Rezegh aerodrome.

The Afrika Korps had a field day on the 23rd. They overran the 5th South African Brigade; they reduced 7th Armoured Brigade to one squadron of tanks and the Support Group also suffered heavy casualties. All hopes of relieving the Tobruk garrison had now almost vanished. Rommel's instructions were 'to destroy the enemy forces at Sidi Rezegh'.

SSM Bill Close, 'B' Sqn remembered:

It was not until mid-afternoon that we drew within striking distance of Sidi Rezegh which was hidden by a low mushroom cloud from the base of which came thumps, booms, rumblings and streaks of lightning. Gradually we arrived at the top of the escarpment and looked down on a scene which bewildered as much as it shocked . . . motionless wrecks some hundreds of yards apart, others in groups facing in all directions. Some were black and silent, others smouldering and cracking and a few blazing brightly, black smoke curling busily up into the dirty sky. Geysers of dirt shot haphazardly among this flotsam.

Close had just lost two friends – Sergeants Knight and Blackshaw. Now with Trooper Trott his solid Yorkshire gunner, his wireless operator Lance Corporal Gibson and driver Lance

Corporal Colclough, he looked down on the hellish scene below. Sergeant Wollaston commented: 'I was navigator for "C" Sqn, situated up on a ridge and the battle was raging in the wadi. On the other side of the wadi was the El Adem airfield on which there were German tanks, and infantry down in the wadi, guns, gunnery, artillery. I drove down into the mêlée and engaged some arty (artillery) and infantry who were dug in, in the trenches, and came back very fast up the side of the wadi where I met the CO (Lieutenant-Colonel A.A. Ewins), and Captain Crisp and we finished up with about 9 tanks.'

Crisp's troop of Honeys now numbered two – his and Lieutenant Tony Beynon's, the latter acting as troop sergeant. What they both now saw straight ahead and below, in middle distance, was the square, clean pattern of a desert airfield, its boundaries marked by neat lines of wrecked German and Italian fighter planes, its centre littered with limp and shattered tanks, from some of which the smoke was rising black into the blue sky. They also saw at the bottom of the escarpment dark figures of men digging slit trenches, putting down mines, clustering around anti-tank and field guns or, unbelievably, cooking meals. Crisp asked the CO on the wireless for instructions and was then immediately ordered by Brigadier Jock Campbell in a pennanted small open tourer car to follow him into the 'Valley of Death' to fend off a German attack coming from the west. Crisp and Beynon then bravely charged down into and through the valley charnel house, following the Brigadier, who pointed vigorously to the west; 1,200 yards ahead Crisp said they could see 'the array of dark brown shapes, 60 or 70 monsters in solid line abreast coming steadily towards the landing ground . . . towards *me*. The vicious flashes at the end of their gun muzzles stood out in fearful contrast against their sombre camouflage.'

For some time the intrepid 'C' Sqn Honeys played hide-and-seek, sheltering behind the wrecked Crusader tanks of 7th Armoured Brigade. The CO had arrived and told Major Witheridge of 'C' Sqn, 'We are going in with 5th RTR on our right. The 22nd Armoured Brigade are also attacking. Enemy believed to be 21st Panzer Division.' Soon both the RTR regiments of Honeys were inextricably mixed. Having different radio frequencies they could not coordinate the attack. So everyone fired on everyone else. In the distance the Yeomanry regiments of 22nd Armoured Brigade fired at what they assumed were Mk IIIs, but were busy, speeding Honeys also playing hide-and-seek.

Corporal Fred Dale, 'A' Sqn saw that the New Zealand infantry had been overrun by German tanks.

It really was heartbreaking. When we went down to the airfield to attack the German tanks who had also gone through the South African infantry brigade, we had to go through what was left of them. When we did get at close quarters it was bedlam, guns firing all over the place, we were going up one end and down the other. Our tanks came under fire from the anti-tank guns located on the ridge and we were losing tanks. We pulled back to replenish with petrol, 37-mm shells and machine-gun ammunition. Looking over the ridge I saw a line of tanks charge right through the aerodrome towards the anti-tank guns. With that we also started to fire at the German guns. There must have been a lot of casualties.

Remarked Captain Cyril Joly: 'We rallied to the burning tank which the CO had chosen as his landmark. More and more arrived and I was amazed when the total reached thirty.' The regiment had started with about twenty tanks but just before moving off to the airfield the 2 i/c arrived with fifteen more found all over the desert, into which he had put the spare crews.

Soon afterwards we moved into Leaguer. The CO took the regiment SW from the airfield into a quieter area. The long slow tedious march with the billowing clouds of dust and the acrid fumes of the exhausts clogging our eyes and scorching our throats, was the usual last trying ordeal to be endured. When at length we were settled and had sorted the crews and re-arranged the squadrons for the morrow, we waited for the supply echelon to reach us with the evening stew and replenishments of fuel and ammunition. My crew and I and the others who had lost their tanks waited with special anxiety to get more blankets.

Eventually Brigadier Gatehouse sorted out the shambles and 3rd RTR withdrew to the south-west. The baffled enemy who saw this furious battle going on – not much of their making – also withdrew, clearly short of fuel and ammunition. Crisp's Honey caught fire and the crew baled out. Tom Beynon's tank driver was killed by a shell. His foot was jammed on the controls and Beynon tried to release him, only to be run over by the tank.

Captured by the Germans he spent three years in hospital and POW camps.

The situation the next day – 24 November – was that 3rd RTR was still in various survivor groups. Battalion HQ with the CO and Adjutant and two troops of 'C' Sqn totalled only seven Honeys. There was no sign of Brigade HQ or 'A' and 'B' Sqns. But the aggressive Major R.N. Wilson, 'A' Sqn OC, near Bir el Grasa and Gabr Meliha wrote:

Separated from Bn so formed a composite Sqn with five of my Sqn tanks and five of 5th RTR and moved to take position right of 2nd RHA at about 0700 hrs. Very large columns of tanks and guns seen on the right flank. We were ordered to stop the head of column but were shelled heavily and accurately. Informed our A15 Sqn of 'cavalry' on the way, of the position. Engaged enemy tanks on their left flank but was shelled out of it and had to withdraw. Now only about four miles of petrol left. Then we were chased by 12–15 German MkIV tanks and shelled heavily from three sides withdrew being shelled and chased. Four of 'my' 5th RTR tanks did not follow. Was joined by some of Major Witheridge's 'C' Sqn composite Sqn. Three tanks fell out with no petrol. As soon as the enemy tanks stopped two more of our tanks ran out of petrol. Came on a 'B' Sqn tank with Lieutenant Dening, Second Lieutenant Deer and SSM Dean in their party. Sergeant Blackwell was badly wounded in their tank. Approximately 10.45. Total strength now 8 tanks. Completely surrounded, no petrol, limited ammo, decided to try and save tanks and personnel if possible. Plan was to *leave* the tanks to look like derelicts and the crews to lie down about 600–800 yards from their tanks and to remain *still*. This was done. The Germans then set up an armoured OP (Observation Post) which came within 300 yards and we were very heavily shelled, but no damage was done. Shelled again in about ¾ hour – no damage. Lay still until dark. German patrols and artillery were within 800 yards of us all day but must have considered tanks to be derelict. At darkness I called up Bn HQ on wireless and got a reply from Sergeant Ward, Bn Signal Sergeant, that we wanted petrol, then talked to Lieutenant Johnson. He brought it up to us – all of 25 miles – guided by Verey lights.

So far among the many 3rd RTR casualties were Captain Peter Williams, Trooper Eastwood, Trooper Gordon killed in action,

Lieutenant H. Owens, seriously wounded, and Second Lieutenant C.J.E. Oxberry, accidentally shot by a Browning MG.

Captain Cyril Joly remarked: 'There were few moments when the officers could meet and exchange news and comments. It was natural that certain men – the doctor, the padre, the technical adjutant – who during the day ranged far and wide over the battle area in the course of their duties should in Leaguer become the clearing house of news and views and each in his way a focus for certain other officers. . . . In battle the doctor's first-aid post was an oasis of reason and sanity whatever the scale of the casualties or the nature of the wounds he had to treat. He never appeared to be flustered although his feelings had been bruised by the endless stream of torn and tortured bodies which it was his duty to tend.'

The nightly action drill of 3rd RTR was for the three main squadrons to form up in line making three sides of square, HQ Sqn tanks etc., making the fourth side. Guns traversed outwards, all the thin skins formed up inside the square. It became a drill so that everyone knew where everyone else could be found. 'After a meal in my HQ truck, the MQMS (Mechanic Quartermaster) and myself (Dick Shattock, Technical Adjutant) would make a tour of the tanks starting at one point and working round the whole square. I made a record of all tank numbers, drivers names, etc., and any trouble reported. Assessing what could be done and between us giving details to the respective Sqn Fitter Sergeants. That first night there were many stragglers from 8th Hussars, some from 5th RTR and of course many of our tanks missing from the morning's battle. For Mr Chapman and me sleep was out of the question, and so it went on day after day.'

On 24 November Rommel advanced east from Bir Gobi along the Trigh el Abd and south-east from Sidi Rezegh. The Afrika Korps move avoided 1st South African Brigade and 7th Armoured Division but drove Corps HQ before it. Each day skirmishes took place as Sergeant Wollaston, 'C' Sqn related: '(After the airfield battle) we finished up with about 9 tanks. We withdrew from Sidi Rezegh and leaguered up at night. We moved to new positions in the desert and the 9 tanks were put under command of Captain Bob Crisp who ordered us to attack a heavy enemy column flanked by field guns. It became a cavalry charge. The Troop officer took up point position. Visibility was poor, he veered across my front and our tanks crashed. We baled out, the Tp Leader killed, his gunner seriously wounded, my crew evacuated. We sheltered in the V formed by the two tanks. The enemy guns moved and knocked out three more of our tanks which were no more than 150 yards away. Eventually a young German soldier from a battery of heavy field guns came and took us prisoner.' Later, Wollaston, and Troopers Davis, Long and Rupitch escaped.

Bob Crisp described the chaos in Operation 'Crusader':

> None of us had more than the vaguest idea where we were from day to day and hour to hour or what was happening either to our own forces or the enemy's. The campaign swung violently from one end of the desert to the other. One morning we would be SW of Sidi Rezegh, the next afternoon we would be well east of the point where we crossed the wire. There was no such thing as advance or retreat. We roared off to areas of threat or engagement depending on the urgency of the information. We chased mirages and were chased by mirages.

The tank crews had little sleep, little food, and were up well before dawn to get out of Leaguer into battle positions before first light. The unlucky 8th Hussars had been almost destroyed at dawn in their Leaguer – a warning to 3rd and 5th RTR! The combined strength of 4th and 22nd Armoured Brigades on 25 November was about fifty assorted Crusader and Stuart tanks. 7th Armoured Brigade had ceased to exist. So concentrated under Gatehouse's 4th Armoured Brigade, the combined force moved to protect 1st South African Brigade under threat from enemy armour at Bir Taieb el Essem. Rommel's fierce dash south to the frontier, presumably to cut off General Cunningham's forces, had achieved nothing. Nothing that is except for the magnificent retreat by 'XXX' Corps HQ (and the journalists with them). Alan Moorehead wrote: 'All day for 9 hours we ran. It was the contagion of bewilderment and fear, and ignorance. We did not know who was pursuing us or how many or how long they would be able to keep up the pursuit.' The British tank workshops and recovery had done their stuff and by the 26th, 22nd Armoured Brigade had 42 Crusaders and 4th had 77 Stuarts (less than 50 per cent of nominal strength of 166).

The Second Battle of Sidi Rezegh started on 27 November and the Afrika Korps headed north to Sidi Azeiz and west along the Trigh Capuzzo. In the meantime the New Zealand Division had linked up with the Tobruk garrison at Belhamed. For three days a fierce running battle went on near Bir el Chleta trying to prevent German forces under General von Ravenstein linking up with Rommel's panzer divisions and 90th Light Infantry Division. 15th Panzer was the target and 'Strafer' Gott sent 22nd Armoured Brigade to bar their path and 4th Armoured Brigade to attack its flank and tail near Gasr el Arid. The 15th Panzer only had 40 fighting tanks to be tackled by 120 British cruisers and Stuarts. In the afternoon's fighting, although the German column was badly cut up, the British lost 19 tanks, while 3rd RTR lost 9 out of the 22 Stuarts deployed.

Just before this action Captain Crisp noted: 'The CO's orders were at 1.30. There we were delighted to see again the familiar face and figure of Doc MacMillan, the Medical Officer who had disappeared with the CO's staff car in the general confusion. Mac after Calais and Greece was something of a regimental institution. We did not want to lose him.' Captain Cyril Joly commanding 'B' Echelon brought up twelve new Honeys and 3rd RTR was re-organized, HQ Troop receiving 3, 'A' Sqn 9, 'C' Sqn 10, 'and "C" Sqn', said Lieutenant-Colonel Ewins, 'will be commanded by Captain Crisp'. The technical sergeant and his men inspected the new Stuarts and the new crews checked guns and equipment.

In the attack 'C' Sqn suffered heavily from the guns of German Artillery Regiment 33 with *Batterie* 6 destroying 3rd RTR's ten Stuarts at point-blank range. In 17 minutes Crisp saw, 'four of my tanks were blazing infernos: three others just sat there, sad and abandoned. A line of (German) anti-tank guns with their crews still manning them expectantly, lined the edge of the drop (into the wadi below).' The survivors included two young officers in their first action who were made prisoners. Crisp and his gunner were both wounded; his Honey had six holes in various parts of the armour-plating. The next day 'C' Sqn was only five tanks strong, including Lieutenant Harry Maegraith's, but 3rd RTR lost four more Honeys in a tank battle. 'C' Sqn knocked out four anti-tank guns mounted on the backs of trucks and, in front of Brigadier Alec Gatehouse, destroyed three Mk II tanks. Peppered by Mk IVs and Mk IIs firing 50-mm AP shells, Crisp's little force lost one Honey with the crew captured. Again Crisp's tank received six hits, *long range* from Mk IVs, which he showed to Gatehouse.

For several days 3rd RTR rallied at Bir Berraneb with a tank strength increased to forty. Major R.N. Wilson, previously OC 'A' Sqn, was posted to 'B' Echelon as a result of various differences of opinion with the CO. Bob Crisp became 2 i/c to Major

Witheridge's 'C' Sqn. On 30 November 5th RTR had a 'turkey shoot', destroying thirteen M-13s and five light tanks of the Italian Ariete Division. At dawn on 1 December the brigade drove north to rescue 6th NZ Brigade at Sidi Rezegh. Two hours later, climbing down the escarpment in single file, they linked up with the New Zealanders and planned an attack on the forty or so enemy tanks of 15th Panzer ensconced at the far end of the valley, 5 miles in length. Sergeant 'Buck' Kite recalled: 'We were told to "swan across" the airfield and back. We were to draw Jerry's fire while other tanks went in to get the SA or NZ infantry out on the back of them. It seemed an impossibility to me. It was a complete shambles. We were zigzagging among the wrecks. Blazing tanks (ours mostly), casualties and vehicles were scattered everywhere. You couldn't fire at anything as we were on the airfield and Jerry was on the high ground on both sides as we went in. Tanks were pretty useless in my view, except as a diversion.' The Ariete and 21st Panzer were on the ridge facing south and an Axis battle group were on heights facing north. 8th Hussars and 5th RTR led the 'Balaclava Charge'. Ironically the beleaguered New Zealanders declined to return through the valley, exposed to every form of fire, perched on the back of 4th Armoured Brigade tanks, who had reached Belhamed. Kite, who was awarded the MM that day, had his tank disabled as a shot smashed a sprocket. 'The only thing to do was to bale out and hope you'd be picked up. I came out on the back of someone else's tank.'

Tobruk was once again cut off; 3rd RTR and the brigade withdrew to the Trigh el Abd for a week's support of 4th Indian Division around Bir Gobi. Bob Crisp's tank was hit twice by an A/Tk gun hidden in a little white-washed house, probably Bir Gobi itself. His gunner was badly wounded and not even Doc MacMillan could save his leg. Rommel still had part of the Afrika Korps locked up at Halfaya and Bardia. Supporting 11th Indian Brigade's attacks around Bir-el-Gobi, each attempt by 3rd RTR and 4th Armoured Brigade was invariably met by a screen of anti-tank guns backed up by tanks.

On 6 December four Honeys of 'A' and 'B' Sqns were knocked out. The enemy were very aggressive but although their panzers were static their transport was moving back to the north-west. The CO was ordered by Gatehouse to make a 'demonstration' against the enemy. Nobody in 3rd RTR thought it was a good idea! Bob Crisp hated two tactical phrases – one was 'make a demonstration' and the other was 'do a reconnaissance-in-force', i.e. the commander wanted a success without risking casualties! 'C' Sqn therefore moved to make contact on the battalion left flank, and in exchange for two enemy Mk IIIs set on fire, Crisp lost a Honey but rescued their crew. The brigade then moved to take up a battle position at Bir Hatiet Genadel and Crisp discovered two isolated tanks, counted their six bogie wheels, and sure they were Mk IIs, opened fire. He destroyed a County of London Yeomanry Crusader.

On 7 December Rommel started withdrawing north-west and contact was made with 70th Division in Tobruk. Seven new Honeys were delivered and the CO reorganized the battalion once again into three squadrons each of twelve tanks. The good news was that 4th Armoured Brigade was to return to the Delta in three days' time. The bad news was that 3rd RTR would take over 8th Hussar's Honeys and as many as were needed from 5th RTR; 3rd RTR were to stay in the desert.

The brigade was now launched on a wide outflanking movement round the enemy at Bir Haleigh el Eleba and Bir Temrad. So 3rd RTR moved west some 35 miles at a speed of 15 mph. The brigade took up its battle position in a great square, 3rd RTR to the north, 5th RTR to the east and the newcomers, the Gloucester Hussars, facing west. 'B' Sqn was sent off to a brief long-range engagement with enemy transport. On 16 December Brigadier Gatehouse ordered a reconnaissance-in-force to relieve pressure on the Indian Division 30 miles to the east. His Brigade Major, David Silvertop, would command the reconnaissance with a squadron of Royal Armoured Cars, Bob Crisp's 'C' Sqn and a troop of A/Tk guns with one petrol lorry. The whole brigade was grounded by lack of fuel, hence this step. At 0630 hrs on the 17th they set off past the rubble of Bir Temrad. At 1015 hrs they had sneaked up to within 2 miles of Rommel's forces: men, vehicles, field guns, tanks and an occasional Mk IV. Just as Crisp was planning a quick charge in line abreast towards the middle of the rear of the enemy column, three enemy Mk IVs and a Mk III came 'sauntering through the scrub' towards 'C' Sqn. So the whole squadron of Honeys went into action, with the result that two enemy tanks fled, but two remained behind, still and silent. Crisp was badly wounded and brought back to meet the RMO Doc MacMillan, sent up with an armoured car escort. He later recovered but his friend Harry Maegraith was killed in the same action.

Captain Cyril Joly took over command of 'C' Sqn. His report stated:

After making contact with enemy 'C' Sqn formed line for an attack which destroyed four enemy tanks. The track of Lieutenant H.G. Maegraith's tank was shot away. Captain Crisp went to his assistance. The crew of the disabled tank climbed on the back of his tank. The Sqn was then being encircled and it became a race to beat the closing of the circle. The whole Sqn was successfully extricated but a direct hit on the back of Captain Crisp's tank killed Lieutenant Maegraith and wounded Captain Crisp, Troopers Rogan and Beach. Last seen of the main enemy column was a general withdrawal NW covered by approximately 23 tanks.

The brigade and 3rd RTR pursued the enemy to Mechili and then lost touch, but followed up again to Msus and Agedabia; 3rd RTR remained for a time with 7th Support Group (part of 7th Armoured Division), losing six tanks near Antelat, deep in what was called the Cyrenaican Bulge. 'We (Corporal Fred Dale, 3rd Troop 'A' Sqn) had our last action there and lost a couple of tanks but also did a lot of damage to the A/Tk guns. We were then told we were going back to Egypt and handed our tanks over to Ordnance. We were transported by road on Boxing Day, to Tel Aqqaqir about 60 miles from Cairo. We were now looking forward to rest and leave.' And Corporal Jim Caswell, 'B' Sqn commented: 'Fortunately for the Afrika Korps we had unusually heavy storms in the desert and we got bogged down whereas they had better going on the coast road and most of them got away. On our tank radios we could receive the BBC World Service, it reported Germans digging in near Derna. We were 50 miles in front of them – it was a nasty thought if they had cut off our supply lorries. However, later they surrendered, we were refuelled and were able to resume the chase. We bypassed Benghazi and captured Fort Msus.' 'A' Sqn acquired a great deal of freshly baked bread and Italian wines. Fred Dale recalled: 'The Axis fought rearguard actions and put down mines to delay us but eventually made a stand at El Agheila. We found that our log noted we were drinking Italian wine on Christmas 1941! 'Crusader' was over, "forty days in the desert".'

The battalion Padre mysteriously borrowed two 3-ton lorries for two weeks in mid-December and returned on Christmas Eve from an RAF supply base. One lorry was full of bread, the other full of tinned meat and veg; 'like manna from Heaven' was Sergeant Jock Watt's comment. The Christmas dinner was turned into a banquet, a rich stew of meat, veg, bully and crushed oatmeal biscuits. The Christmas pudding was a thick slice of bread coated with jam fried until the jam soaked through to the cooking fat. The Padre also brought from NAAFI a large stock of English cigarettes (Victory V's made in India), producing a ration of five per day.

7

THE BATTLE OF GAZALA – OPERATION 'BUCKSHOT'

If Operation 'Battleaxe' had been a near disaster, 'Crusader' was certainly a near victory. Tobruk had been relieved. The Afrika Korps had quit the battlefields of Sidi Rezegh and Rommel only had 40 out of 300 panzers in fighting condition. The Eighth Army had lost 2,900 killed, 7,300 wounded and 7,300 taken prisoner. The Axis forces had 2,300 killed, 6,100 wounded and nearly 30,000 POWs taken (mostly Italian). For the time being Cyrenaica had been cleared.

The New Zealand Division had been sorely battered, a South African brigade had been demolished and 7th and 22nd Armoured Brigades were not battleworthy. 4th Armoured Brigade returned to Cairo fit, tanned, desert-trained but disorganized. The Crusader and Matilda tanks of 22nd and 1st Army Tank Brigades had been proved unreliable. The Stuarts had been shown to be fast, reliable and capable of dealing with Italian and Panzer Mk II tanks. However, in straight combat with Mk IIIs and the Mk IVs the advantage was nearly always with the German tanks.

Trooper Geordie Reay, 'C' Sqn recalled: 'You had to get into about 1,000 yards to stand a chance of doing any damage, and I'm talking about damage to the side of their tanks not the front. We used our speed. We were like a lot of flyweights fighting hulking heavyweights. We had to run round them and tackle them broadside on. You learned that by trial and error.' SSM Bill Close wrote, 'Sidi Rezegh was a severe battle for 3rd RTR and casualties were heavy. The cream of the battalion went west and it was never quite the same. Too many friendships were cut short.' Close and others were afflicted with desert sores, partly caused by minor grazes and cuts that failed to heal, and partly by the lack of fresh food and vegetables.

For the first three months of 1942, 3rd RTR enjoyed the fleshpots of Cairo while refitting with new tanks and receiving replacement tank crews. There were decorations too for

Lieutenants Ross and Thompson, who received MCs, while there was also an MC for Bob Crisp when he came out of hospital to add to the DSO won in Greece. Corporal Geordie Reay was awarded the MM, and in February more decorations were announced. MCs were awarded to Major Upcott-Gill, Second Lieutenant Edwards, Captain Hamil, and MMs to Sergeants Filer, 'Buck' Kite, Rowlands, Stubbs and Trooper Dudley. Lieutenant-Colonel 'Bunny' Ewins had had a very difficult month of continuous battle in 'Crusader', made perhaps harder by the strong characters of some of his officers. He went on sick leave and was posted to a staff appointment.

Rommel's riposte started on 21 January. He struck against the inexperienced 1st Armoured Division at El Agheila and by 4 February the revitalized Afrika Korps was back at Gazala. The pendulum of the Desert War had swung back vigorously. The Eighth Army had by now created a defensive 'Gazala Line' of defended 'boxes' or strongpoints running south into the desert from Gazala on the eastern side of the Jebel Akhdar mountains. Each box was defended by a full brigade and surrounded by minefields and thick belts of wire. The gaps were patrolled by armoured car units. In the south was the French-manned Bir Hacheim under General Koenig. Sixteen miles away to the north was another box held by 150th (British) Infantry Brigade. North again lay 'Knightsbridge' box held by 201st Guards Brigade. Other boxes continued the 45-mile Gazala Line north to the sea and were manned by South African and British units. As usual Rommel was outnumbered in men and tanks. His seven tank regiments (four panzer, three Italian) faced the Eighth Army's 700 tanks. Some of these were the new General Grants, made in America.

Jim Caswell, now promoted to full sergeant, was in command of a Grant tank:

They had a 37-mm and machine-guns in the turret and a 75-mm gun at the side of the tank – a match for German guns, but because it was not in the turret, it only had a 25 per cent traverse. We also had the luxury of a front machine-gun. The new tanks (Grant and Lee) were also quite high and not squat like the Germans, thereby presenting a better target for the enemy. The 75-mm could fire high explosive shells as well as armour piercing. The Americans trained us in these tanks and we learnt the bracketing system to target high explosive shells.

The Americans were anxious to come back up the desert with us 'to that damned, darn shooting gallery'. Some engines were diesel, some petrol. There was always a fight for the diesels because they did not catch fire as easily as the petrol ones did.

3rd RTR carried out training and firing exercises in the desert just a couple of miles from the Mena Hotel near the Pyramids. 'B' and 'C' Sqns – the heavy squadrons – were equipped with twelve Grants each. 'A' Sqn, the recce squadron had sixteen of the fast, light Stuart (Honey) tanks. RHQ had two Grants and two Honeys. The Grant was a British-sponsored version of the American M-3 medium tank, the General Lee. It weighed nearly 29 tons and had 57 mm of front turret armour. SSM Bill Close recalled: 'This was to be the first tank fitted with a 75-mm gun and capable of firing both HE and AP, most welcome news to the tank crews. It was fairly fast with a possible road speed of about 25 mph, well armoured and considered capable of out shooting an enemy tank or anti-tank gun except the 88-mm. We looked forward to meeting the panzers more or less on even terms.' Sergeant Jock Watt noted that the power was supplied to some Grants by a nine-cylinder air-cooled radial engine (a petrol guzzler), and to others by an unusual engine of five six-cylinder blocks mounted on one crankshaft, located fanwise through 180 degrees. This ex-Chrysler bus six-cylinder engine had its own ignition system and carburettor.

Brigadier Alec Gatehouse, who had commanded 4th Armoured Brigade with so much skill, was promoted to Major-General, commanding 10th Armoured Division. In his place came Brigadier G.W. (Ricky) Richards DSO, MC, having been GSO1 to the Desert Rats throughout 'Crusader' and then 2 i/c of 22nd Armoured Brigade.

When Sergeant Fred Dale, now a fully qualified gunnery instructor, finished his course, his leave and a spell in hospital with a jaw problem, he returned to 'A' Sqn. 'When I got back I found we had a new Colonel (G.P. Roberts) and very good he was. We also had a lot of promotions. I was still in 3rd troop and still with Sergeant Dean. We had about 75 per cent of the same faces and they were a lovely bunch of lads, always so cheerful. They always worked together, if one crew had finished their maintenance, they would help the other crews finish their maintenance. We now had TEWTs (Tactical Exercise Without Tanks) for about a week. We had Sergeant Major B. Close and

Sergeant Harned DCM made up to 2nd Lieutenants in the field at the end of April. Close to "A" Sqn. Harned to "B" Sqn.' Dale examined the Grant. 'It had a crew of six men. With the limited 75-mm gun traverse you had to turn the tank in the direction of the enemy which wasn't very convenient under fire. The engine was very reliable, Radial Aero, it could do 120 miles under good conditions. The only thing wrong was the height (9 feet 4 inches). It was hard to hide behind any ridge without showing the top turret. Anyway the crews were overjoyed to be able to fire a large 14 pound shell at the Panzer tanks.'

Many of the replacement crews came from 4th and 8th Hussars and other cavalry regiments. Lieutenant Bill Close noted, 'they were all tank trained and very soon fitted in with us tankies. Also my two corporal tank commanders (both with MMs) by this time were veterans. Following a last exercise deep in the Wadi Natrum area we were at last considered to be ready for our next trip "up the blue".'

Before he became a squadron commander Captain Cyril Joly described some of the problems encountered by a young troop commander, as he was, in the campaigns of 1942.

The great handicap which we all had to overcome was that there were too many things to think about at the same time. A course had to be set either by the troop commander or, more usually, by his conforming to the movements of the squadron or regimental navigator. The enemy had to be found and identified. The other two tanks had to be instructed about their formation or chivvied if they failed to keep in place. The driver had to be given his orders about his direction and speed, the gunner warned about the target and which gun to use, the loader-operator told to load the gun. The correct information had to be passed over the wireless to the squadron commander. If these things were not done properly, or if they were done at the wrong time, the whole manoeuvre or battle was liable to fail at the crucial moment, with men's lives lost and valuable tanks destroyed. It was a matter of practice and more practice and practice whenever possible. It was a question of lengthy discussion about the action that each tank would take in certain eventualities, of careful planning of the use of ground or the mutual support that might be given by other troops or even other arms, such as the infantry and guns.

Gradually one gained more confidence. Navigation or map-reading became less of a problem. We evolved certain simple drills which covered most of the troop's tactics. One learnt where to look for the enemy and quick methods of identifying him. Orders and information, which earlier I had hesitated in passing, I now gave out almost unconsciously. I soon had no difficulty in remembering the correct wireless procedure and, in fact, learnt also new, abbreviated and simplified methods. We all acquired a great deal of confidence in each other, and so made ourselves into a really effective fighting machine.

At the same time the training within the crew improved. Though the tank broke down just as frequently, we mended it more quickly. As my ability to judge the distance to each target – always difficult in the peculiar condition of light and ground in the desert – improved, so, with the improvement of the gunner's shooting, we were able to hit our targets sooner in each action.

Several of 3rd RTR's commanding officers and squadron commanders were destined to become divisional commanders – often at a very young age. Lieutenant-Colonel 'Pip' Roberts had been Assistant Quarter Master General (AQMG) at HQ 'XXX' Corps during 'Crusader' but had always been a regular RTR officer since the late 1930s. As Brigade Major in the early desert campaigns of 4th Armoured Brigade, he had plenty of staff experience. At the end of January 1942 he wrote: 'Here was I, never having fired a gun of any sort in anger and there was 3rd RTR having been through Calais, Greece and the Western Desert and quite a large proportion of the Regt had survived through it all. . . . How I enjoyed my arrival at 3rd RTR. I had left 6th RTR as Adjutant and I was returning (aged thirty-five) to a regiment as CO barely two years later.' RSM Paddy Hehir had been a trumpeter in 3rd RTR in 1927. Dicker Wilson the 2 i/c had been in 2nd RTR in England. Major Jim Hutton, newly arrived 'A' Sqn OC, had been with 3rd Armoured Car Company with 'Pip' Roberts in 1931. Cyril Joly, now commanding 'C' Sqn, was the youngest major, in his mid-twenties. The Adjutant was Captain Peter Burr, ex-Westminster Dragoons, 'he was a meticulous organiser, a most conscientious worker and got on well with everyone. The RMO MacMillan was a contemporary of mine at Marlborough,' noted 'Pip' Roberts. Major George Witheridge, a great gunnery expert and former instructor at Lulworth, commanded 'B' Sqn. He wrote at the time:

The Bn was busy behind Bir Hacheim preparing for battle. The 75-mm gun on the General Grant, the new American lend-lease tank was the first time in WWII that a tank gun would enable tank crews to destroy their greatest enemy at that time, the enemy A/Tank gun (5-cm PAK 88 and 8.8 cm FLAK 18 or 36). These were often sited between the German Panzers and went too often unobserved so causing much damage to our armour. Psychologically crew members felt they should engage the enemy *tank*, a similar beast, a larger and apparently more dangerous target. They did to their detriment, for the *ground* gun was the more effective and being unobserved took its toll of British armour. We prepared behind the southern flank of the Gazala line. Alternative positions were reconnoitred, navigation using sun compass was brushed up. Everyone believed our new punch would be more than a surprise to the crews of the Panzers MkIII and IV. Our tank guns were zeroed out to 1,000 yards range.

4th Armoured Brigade, with 3rd RTR, 8th Hussars, 5th RTR, plus 1st RHA and 1st KRRC (as motorized infantry), were part of 7th Armoured Division, commanded by 'Jock' Campbell VC. He was killed in a car accident on 23 February and his place was taken by Major-General F.W. Messervy. The re-equipping of 3rd RTR with tanks, vehicles and spares was too slow for Roberts who promptly bypassed channels 'by ringing up the headman of HQ Middle East to get things moving at once, surprising my Adjutant and Quartermaster'. Major Dicker Wilson the 2 i/c was called back to Cairo to organize a new training school.

After his head wound from a Stuka in Greece, Lieutenant Dick Shattock was graded 'B' (non-combat for six months), went on a REME course in Cairo, then to Palestine and the Staffordshire Yeomanry. He and Lieutenant Guy Barker (also 3rd RTR) rejoined the battalion in March 1942. Lieutenant-Colonel Roberts explained that the 2 i/c Major 'Bill' Reeves would soon be promoted and Colin Franklin the Technical Adjutant would also 'move up'. So Shattock, 'took over a troop in "C" Sqn commanded by Cyril Joly. My troop sergeant J.M. Harned had won the MM recently. Later the CO told me that Jim was getting an immediate field commission and would be taking over a troop. At this time Bill Close was also commissioned.' So Shattock became Technical Adjutant to help with the training in the new Grant tanks, and was promoted to Captain with the highly experienced MQMS Chapman as his 2 i/c. He had a jeep and towed a 3-tonner. Captain Ivan Payne, the REME officer with his Scammell, towed a captured Panzer Mk III into the desert for Lieutenant-Colonel Roberts's new Grant tank to practise on with the 75-mm side gun. The results were not impressive. Colonel 'Pip' felt that the HE shell might be more effective than AP at close quarters. Major George Witheridge commanding 'B' Sqn noted:

The main 75-mm gun had no range scale or clinometer, so we file-marked the elevator wheel for range setting. We marked the traversing wheel in the same way. We developed a successful bore and vane sight which was used by all tanks as being essential. Hoods were developed and made in unit workshops in the desert for the periscopes, preventing sun rays entering the gunner's slot and blinding his vision of enemy and targets. Unfortunately the HE shell issued came from old WWI stocks, some had not been reworked and exuded. A shell fired could be premature, cause death and damage – to two of my crews. In one, the gun was destroyed, the gunner killed; in the other the gun was wrecked and the gunner wounded.

In April the brigade was training south of Sidi Azeiz. Lieutenant Bill Close recalled:

It was a most trying time in most uncomfortable circumstances. Temperatures at midday were in excess of 110° and life in the tank was almost unbearable, even the flies dropped dead inside. One could fry an egg on the back of the tank. It was the Kahmsin season, the hot wind that comes up from southern Sahara, which blows up in a matter of moments and can last for two or three days. No movement was possible, visibility was down to about ten yards. It affected the enemy in exactly the same way.

At Menphia in March the battalion Padre organized tortoise races. In one particular spot hundreds were discovered and adopted. The races were for tortoises 2, 3 or 4 fingers high. Entrants were marked on their shell by their proud owners and placed in the centre of a circle. The Padre ran a tote and the first tortoise to cross the outer circle line in the sand won that race. Besides football and snakes and ladders, a bizarre fighting black ant competition was devised. An artificial swimming pool was constructed by laying a large tarpaulin inside a stripped lorry, 3 feet high, with its four corners jacked up. Filled to the brim from a nearby pool every man in SSM John Watt's 'A' Sqn had a splash.

Lieutenant-Colonel Roberts wrote: 'Early in May we moved to an area 8 miles NE of Bir Hacheim. The Germans had two alternatives – one was to make a sweep south of the minefields at Hacheim and then swing NE, in which case his lines of communication would be long. The other was to make a gap and break through the minefields in the north with shorter Ls of C. Our brigade as a whole carried out a great many reccies to counter either of these moves. In the south (where 3rd RTR were based) a particularly good battle position was selected three miles SE of Bir Hacheim where the whole brigade could take up hull-down positions. A mile east of the Hacheim defences an Indian motor brigade prepared and later occupied a defended area.' Every squadron had its miniature range so that when field firing was not possible, every tank gunner kept his hand and eye in. Squadron cookhouses and officers' messes were up, games pitches made and bathing parties organized to the Tobruk area beaches. Roberts continued: 'Our battle position was 9 miles away to the SW. 8th Hussars were two miles to the east, and 5th RTR 4 miles to the NE. Brigade HQ and 1st RHA were centrally placed with 1st KRRC further away to the east.'

Major George Witheridge recalled: 'Stand to, Stand down were at first light and last light, became a drill with great meaning for us. All my soldiers slept beside their tanks while lying under the tank sheet. The other end of the sheet was tied to the tank, at sand guard height and formed a sort of sloping roof over them. We dug down for protection, in the sometimes sandy or rocky ground. The command "Alert" sent all concerned to their battle stations before first light. We went into the desert, fighting fit and pleased with our new tanks when compared with past mounts. We knew that we could wallop the Hun harder than ever before. We felt that Providence had come to our aid.'

The Bletchley 'Ultra' Intelligence had alerted the high command to a probable attack by Rommel between 25 and 28 May. The CO organized a large-scale outing and bathing party to Tobruk on the 23rd. At 0430 hrs on the 27th the Adjutant, Captain Peter Burr woke the CO to inform him that 3rd RTR were at half an hour's notice to move. His 60-lb tent was struck and a large breakfast ordered for 0600 hrs. 3rd RTR were in position

'Skylark' with Major Cyril Joly's Grant squadron on the left, Major George Witheridge's 'C' Sqn on the right and Major Jim Hutton's 'A' Sqn of Stuarts 2,000 yards ahead.

The Eighth Army's Operation 'Buckshot' was designed to recapture Benghazi. In the event, Rommel moved up and attacked and, it was hoped, thereby run his head into the trap.

On 26 May a large enemy column had moved east from Segnali heading down the Trigh Capuzzo. During the night of 26/27 May the Afrika Korps, main body turned south and by first light had refuelled *south* of Bir Hacheim. By 0800 hrs on the 27th, 4th Armoured Brigade with one regiment still not in position, faced the *whole* of the 15th and 21st Panzer Divisions. The CO had told all his officers on the night of the 26th: 'I have a gut feeling that Jerry will attack tomorrow. Everyone will be up at one hour before first light and we'll take up battle formation I have reconnoitred. Get a good night's sleep. That's all.' Captain Dick Shattock recollected: 'Sure enough the Colonel had been right. The distant sound of engines grew louder to an ominous rumble . . . on my headphones at last came Pip's calm voice. "Do not open fire until they are one zero zero zero yards." A moment later came Jim Hutton's order. "'A' Sqn get cracking and stop fiddling with your knickers." Then the immense volume of firing started. The "thin skins" (part of HQ Sqn) under Captain Dave Tomlin waited in the comparative safety of the protecting sandhill.'

'We had been going about ten minutes', wrote the CO Lieutenant-Colonel 'Pip' Roberts:

the light Sqn was about 2,000 yards ahead when they reported a lot of dust and unidentified movement three miles to their front, perhaps the 8th Hussars. Then a report from Brigade came through that the Indian Motor Brigade just east of Hacheim had been over-run by tanks about three or four hours before. (Jim Hutton reported) 'large numbers of tanks to our front, about 3,000 yards away coming towards us – 'can they be friends?' 'No *not* friends.' 'But their crews are sitting outside them.' 'Well when they get a little closer open fire on them with your Brownings.' Peter (Burr, the Adjutant) report to Brigade about 100 enemy tanks moving NW. Their position now about four miles SE of our original leaguer area. We continue to move forward slowly, closing up on the light squadron and looking for a suitable hull-down position. There they are – there are more than 100! Yes, 20 in the first line, then there are six, no eight lines, and more behind that in the distance. A whole ruddy Panzer division is quite obviously in front of us!

Roberts noted ruefully that the carefully worked out defensive hull-down positions for 3rd RTR and the brigade had been abandoned. He gave fresh orders: 'Hello. Regimental orders. "B" and "C" Squadrons (Grants) take up battle line on the ridge 300 yards to our front. "B" Sqn right, "C" Sqn left. "A" Sqn (Honeys) protect the right flank. Try to get in on the enemy's flank. Keep in touch with 8th Hussars who should be coming up on our left at any moment.' (One troop of 'A' Sqn were sent to the left flank). The 'Chestnut' troop 1st RHA 25-pdr field guns arrived. One troop went into action with their 'quads', in line with 3rd RTR tanks, in an anti-tank role.

Lieutenant Bill Close, 'A' Sqn recalled: 'I realised that the Afrika Korps was going about its business. After Jim Hutton reported the enemy strength, "I say again 200 tanks", I started to count them myself. They were coming on faster than I had thought at first glance.' Corporal Buck Kite MM was sitting in his turret, the drivers had their flaps open, the crews were passing round biscuits plastered with jam or bully beef. He saw the ninety or so enemy vehicles ahead coming towards him. 'When they were about 1,000 yards away, Jerry must have received their order to open fire. There were flashes all along their front rank and a hail of shells all going one way screamed around us. We still hadn't received the order to open fire and waiting for it was pure agony. We were still moving slowly forward and at least three of our number had been hit and were in flames, by the time the order came.'

Major George Witheridge of 'B' Sqn on the right, heard:

'Hello Cambrai – Cambrai calling – Fire now! Cambrai out.' This was the order for all 75-mm guns to open fire, the enemy being within 1,000 yards range. Immediately my small world seemed to vanish in the madness of the moment. We caused chaos in the German ranks. Plain to see, Panzers turning to the right and to the left trying desperately to avoid the hail of death-dealing 75-mm solid shot from the Grants, soon to be augmented with shot from the higher velocity 37 mm guns. Some German tanks appeared to run into each other and the infantry clinging to their hulls were being thrown off their backs. Three German Panzers were on fire, crews bailing out and great indecision seeming to reign. They were brought to a halt at about 900 yards. The famous Chestnut troop of 25-pdrs joined in the slaughter. Coloured tracer from several guns criss-crossed the space, the air was full of flying metal, noise and confusion and brave men were dying.

The 8th Hussars had been caught before they could get into battle formation and sustained heavy losses; 5th RTR were ordered to advance into the area between 3rd RTR and 8th Hussars. Lieutenant Bill Close, with 'A' Sqn Honeys remembered: 'I gave my gunner Trotter, gun control and concentrated on looking for 5th RTR and keeping us in one piece. The Grants were big enough to stand and slug it out but a Honey had to make it as difficult as possible for the opposition. Every few minutes I ordered "Driver advance right a few yards" or "Driver reverse left" and sent up prayers for the early arrival of 5th RTR.'

15th Panzer Division facing 4th Armoured Brigade received a severe shock with the ferocity of fire from the new Grants, but as the CO 'Pip' Roberts noted: 'Further tank casualties had been inflicted on both sides but as far as the Boche were concerned as soon as one tank was knocked out another took its place. They merely used their rear lines of tanks to replace casualties in the front line and attempted no manoeuvres.' But 15th Panzer had moved some tanks and anti-tank guns very wide round the 3rd RTR right flank. The CO said: 'Peter (Burr the Adjutant) tell Brigade "we cannot hang on here much longer, either there will be nothing left or we will be cut off, or both". But "C" Sqn on the left are going back.' Major Cyril Joly, the OC had twenty-five hits on his Grant, and his periscopes were smashed. He was wounded with blood streaming into his eyes, and his squadron were out of ammunition. The CO again: 'The situation was now serious. "C" Sqn on the left were in trouble. The RHA troop were still in action. On the right "B" Sqn seemed to have three tanks still firing but obviously had little ammunition left. No sight of 5th RTR coming up either on our right or left. There were certainly twenty Boche tanks knocked out in front of us, if not more. If we are to re-organize at all, we must go – and pretty quickly.' 5th RTR were, meanwhile, equally heavily engaged with 21st Panzer Division, inflicting some losses.

Corporal 'Buck' Kite of 'B' Sqn gives this account of the ferocity of the engagement:

My troop officer's tank on my left began to back out of the line in some sort of trouble. The tank on the other side was burning furiously. We were being hit by all sorts of things and though it was suicide to put your head outside, it was impossible to see anything inside. The air was stinking and thick with cordite fumes from the two guns going hammer and tongs and our eyes were red rimmed and streaming. You could taste the explosive. Now and again there would be a terrific thud and the interior filled with dust and sparks as the tank rocked on its bogies. Despite the noise and the smoke we were scoring hits. We were using ammo at a tremendous rate and I was relieved when the CO came on the air and ordered us to reverse slowly while continuing to engage.

Kite picked up a baled-out crew. 'There was a heavier than usual crash and the 75 gunner said he couldn't fire any more as the gun was damaged. We hadn't gone another 50 yards before there was an absolutely terrific thump and bits of metal and sparks flew about inside and the tank stalled.' The driver was badly wounded but the 75-mm gunner took over the sticks and restarted the Grant. 'We'd barely backed another 50 yards when a solid shot hurtled in and crashed into the engine at the rear without touching anyone.' The two crews baled out dragging two wounded men with them and were rescued by a 5th RTR Honey. Kite looked back at the battle. 'The enemy tanks were slowly moving forward again and our six remaining tanks were still engaging them with every gun fit to fire. The rest of the Grants were either burning or standing abandoned.' The newly commissioned Jim Harned, Kite's troop leader, had his head blown off by a shell at the beginning of the action. Kite back at the echelon was told by the motor transport officer: 'There's a fit tank there, Corporal Kite, will you take it over?' It was driven by Lance Corporal Stubbs who was destined to be one of 3rd RTR's most determined heroes. Over the hill came a Grant, the driver through open visor saying to Dick Shattock: 'It's Mr Harned, sir, he's been killed.' A group of men helped to lift Jim down. The RMO MacMillan arrived. A shell fragment had hit the base of the head. 'Doc said he would have died instantly. The shallow grave was dug at once, grim faces but no time for ceremony.' Corporal Jim Jolly in 'A' Sqn was taking his disabled Honey slowly back into Tobruk for repairs. Driving through the minefields near his destination he pulled the tank off the track to let an ambulance through and ran over an Italian box mine that blew a hole in the bottom of the tank, smashed the driver's legs and blinded poor Jim Jolly. Lieutenant Bill Close's Honey received five hits during the battle but Lance Corporal Trotter told him that he had scored direct hits on two panzers at point-blank range and seen their crews bale out.

The CO gave orders for the battalion to rally on the high ground to the north-east. He took his command Grant slowly back with at least two baled-out tank crews sheltering behind. Two wounded men on the back were given morphine. In reverse for 400 yards, then a dash, flat out for the rallying point, leaving a cloud of dust behind. Seven Grants were still battleworthy, another three had guns out of action. Major George Witheridge OC 'B' Sqn was unhorsed but found himself another charger. Lieutenant-Colonel Roberts was anxious for the ammo lorries to replenish his surviving tanks. A Grant with two guns of 75-mm and 37-mm got through their 'stock' of shells at a very quick rate. A recce Honey reported that six enemy tanks were stalking the rallying point, so the Grants, ammunition-less, retired a further 4 miles to the north-east.

Ammunition and petrol lorries eventually linked up as 3rd RTR survivors drove through the French Foreign Legion force holding the Bir Hacheim 'box'. Brigade HQ then ordered 3rd RTR to join them 3 miles south-east of El Adem. Roberts now only had battleworthy 6 Grants, 10 Honeys and the RHQ of 1 Grant and 1 Honey. Major Witheridge took over the Grants and Captain Upcott-Gill the Honeys. Captain Dick Shattock wrote: 'We heard during this incredible day that some of our thin skins (echelons) had been put in the bag including Doctor Mac! The news had thrown the whole of the 3rd into gloom. But out of the dark came about 30 or 40 figures, our own people who had been captured by the Germans earlier in the day and had slipped away from their captor's vehicles. When the Doc appeared that night amongst these ghostly figures the joy was immense.' Rommel wrote in his journal: 'The advent of the new American tank had torn great holes in our ranks. Our entire force stood in heavy and destructive combat with a superior enemy.' But it was three batteries of 88-mm A/Tk guns that caused 3rd RTR most trouble and loss.

From El Adem the battered 4th Armoured Brigade fell back a further 15 miles east to Hareifet-el-Nbeidat. The next morning, 28 May, Major Shan Hackett, 8th Hussars, plus six Honeys linked up. He was promptly made OC Light Sqn which was now up to full strength. Two more Grants turned up too. At 1400 hrs Brigade launched a counter-attack with 5th RTR almost at full strength. The target was a column of tanks, A/Tk guns and lorries moving west. The combined 3rd RTR/8th Hussars force moved on a second unarmed convoy. The Light Sqn led on a frontage of 1,000 yards with RHQ (two tanks) and the Grant squadron five abreast (actually a total of five and four). Major Charles Armitage and the RHA battery joined in the task force. Some 8 miles ahead on top of a sheer escarpment were ensconced three enemy 88-mm guns. Roberts sent the Light Sqn flanking right while the Grants took on the A/Tk guns with success. Armitage's RHA guns produced a smokescreen and in the fracas that followed the CO's tank was knocked out, but Major George Witheridge and Second Lieutenant Carp destroyed the remaining 88s.

The French Foreign Legion held Hacheim, having repulsed the Italian Ariete Division, the Guards held 'Knightsbridge' box and 2nd Armoured Brigade were reasonably intact south-west of El Adem. But 7th Armoured Division HQ had been overrun, with the GOC, Major-General Messervy and GSO1 'Pete' Pyman briefly captured but later making an escape. The 3rd Indian Motor Brigade had been demolished.

For the next few days the sorely battered brigade received, as the CO put it, 'a series of orders, counter-orders and at times disorders'. Major Shan Hackett took his Honeys back, and with reinforcements 3rd RTR's strength was seven Grants and twelve Honeys. Brigadier Bill Carr now ordered support for 22nd Armoured Brigade. 'Since the enemy were clearly visible I suggested that the Grants HE would knock out their anti-tank guns. We took up station, with the Grants and Honeys in rear, selected targets for each tank. We were in line myself in the centre. For about 20 minutes we had some good shooting. 3rd County of London Yeomanry on our right were some way ahead. As we advanced Grants in line, Honeys behind . . . we were now very close to the enemy. Two tanks on my right were hit and one was burning . . . so I halted everyone, retired in reverse gear and then rallied to our start point. The Doctor's (Captain MacMillan's) white scout car went up to deal with the two killed, one wounded.' The indomitable Major George Witheridge had survived Calais, Greece and Sidi Rezegh and now had splinters of metal and perspex in his eye and had to go back to hospital. Another 88-mm gun shelled the survivors, killing instantly

Second Lieutenant Carp. 'During the day up drove (Second Lieutenant) Vic Carp's Grant, his left hand track and drive sprocket tangled with barbed wire. Did I (Dick Shattock) think it was all right.' Shattock thought that the Grant could perform for a few hours and then be cleared up in Leaguer that night. 'Honestly Vic, I cannot keep you back on account of this. I am certain it will not let you down.' An hour or so later the CO 'Pip' Roberts sent for Johnny Dunlop and Dick Shattock. On arrival at the CO's command tank, Peter Burr, the Adjutant told them, 'an 88's just got poor Vic's tank and it blew up'.

On 2 June, the remains of 4th Armoured Brigade stuck in a Khamsin sandstorm encountered 21st Panzer Division again. 'Pip' Roberts's orders were with his 12 Grants, 14 Honeys plus RHQ of 1 Grant and 2 Honeys, to move south and establish itself on the Trigh Capuzzo, the wide east to west track.

After only 12 minutes – about midday – visibility reduced to 20 yards and a bit later to 10 yards. Officers in scout cars were sent in various directions to collect all the lost sheep! When it cleared the next hazard was a steep escarpment up which the Honeys, RHA guns and Grants laboriously climbed by two narrow tracks. Once on top a battle ensued for several hours with 15 enemy tanks and A/Tk guns. After some time the Grants ran out of 75-mm ammunition and the RHA gunners were getting casualties from direct HE fire. Brigade gave permission to withdraw. Route: by the track up which we had just come; rally, a mile NE from the bottom of the track; order of withdrawal, gunners, Honey Squadron, Grant Squadron. It all went off without a hitch. The Boche had failed to follow us up. We moved off towards Brigade. Our losses – one Honey destroyed, three Grants damaged and a dozen RHA gunner casualties.

Sergeant Jock Stewart was rearguard in the clifftop battle and came up on the airwaves to report that he had knocked out two German tanks. Not far away 5th RTR came up against a much stronger force of tanks of 21st Panzer Division, losing eighteen tanks out of twenty-seven, their CO, Lieutenant-Colonel Robie Uniacke being killed by machine-gun bullets. Nothing much happened, but orders and counter-orders. On 6 June another similar tank battle ensued with Captain Granton OC Grant Sqn with ten tanks, plus the Light Sqn ordered off to the left flank.

After a few minutes the CO's tank was hit badly. 'There was a terrific bang and flash and all hell seemed to have been let loose.' The CO and Adjutant Captain Peter Burr were wounded. The wireless operator later died of wounds, as did the 37-mm gunner who was scorched all over with the flash. The RMO Doc MacMillan appeared and took charge. Corporal 'Buck' Kite in a Grant saw the CO's tank but, 'We remained firing in line until last light.' He then looked into the damaged command tank. 'The inside was full of bits of flesh and spattered with blood.' Kite towed the CO's tank back for three miles into Leaguer, 'where we buried the gunner, Sergeant Burn and the driver Topper Brown.'

Wrote Dick Shattock: 'I was called up to the tanks. The Colonel's tank and another had been hit. On arrival the scene was quite horrifying, the side turret 75-mm gun loaded with HE shell had blown up in the breech. The Command Grant had a 7 man crew. The Brigade link radio operator fitted into the space left of, and beside the driver. The adjutant occupied the space behind the 75-mm and acted as loader in action. The Colonel was in the turret with wireless operator on the Bn net and the 37-mm gunner. The Sergeant gunner of the 75-mm was killed instantly, his facial flesh burnt and torn exposing the skull beneath, the gun breech jagged and torn apart beside him. The driver and radio operator also got the blast and were both seriously injured and had been lifted out of the tank by the front hatch screaming in agony. Miraculously Peter Burr was unhurt but very shocked, the Colonel and turret crew had blast injuries but were all still alive. . . . From there on we lost all officers down to Captain and were so depleted that we were no longer functioning as a fighting battalion.' SSM Jock Watt 'A' Sqn recalled sadly after the CO's wounding that since the war began the battalion must have lost at least two regiments in dead, wounded and POW. He remembered 'Pip' Roberts's calm radio comments such as, 'Come on now, don't be shy, get up into line with me.'

Lance Sergeant Fred Dale, 'A' Sqn recalled. 'That day we now have only two regiments left in the brigade, 3rd and 5th Tanks. We took up position on the ridge as the leading German tank patrol appeared probing. "B" Sqn was sent out to meet them. A small tank battle started but it was short and sharp. They lost five MkIII tanks and three (Grants) were lost from "B" Sqn but they were directly below us.' Later, Dale and six men of 'A' Sqn were sent down in a 15-cwt truck and under fire buried their dead in very hard ground, having collected their identity discs.

The next day Dale's Grant was hit and the bogies shot away. He and the crew baled out and were picked up. On 8 June the remnants of the Stuart Sqn went to 6th RTR who had joined the brigade to replace 8th Hussars, and the few remaining Grants went to 5th RTR. For a few days the regiment did not exist. Four days later a combined 3rd/5th RTR was created under Major Archer-Shee (ex-10th Hussars). Regiments were amalgamated and re-formed every day. 1st Armoured Brigade – brought up to Capuzzo – was split up and distributed to other units. On 11 June the remnants of four armoured brigades (1st, 2nd, 4th and 22nd) were merged under the command of 4th Armoured Brigade. Two Grants under Lieutenant Dick Seed and Corporal 'Buck' Kite took part in another terrible action on 13 June. The enemy had dug-in his anti-tank guns on the edge of a wadi near Hagget Sciaaban, south-west from El Adem.

The mixed bag of survivors under command of 4th Armoured Brigade were ordered to advance and engage the enemy concentration. Using hardly any of his tanks but fighting almost entirely with his A/Tk guns he reduced the brigade to a handful of tanks. It was a disaster. Corporal Buck Kite recounted:

> We trekked through the Tobruk perimeter defences and out the other side to the Sidi Rezegh area. The next day (13th) we were told we had to delay the advance of the enemy's armour. We took up a position on a ridge with the 3rd RTR contingent on the right and RHA guns to the right of us . . . late afternoon about 50 enemy tanks appeared over a ridge about 800 yards to our front. For an hour the air was thick with shells. My own Grant was hit repeatedly but though it shuddered and shook nothing went through the armour. With the RHA 25-pounders firing solid shot over open sights and us blazing away with our AP we inflicted enough damage to make Jerry stop and think. Down the line on my left, one or two of our tanks were burning and "others" had ceased firing, obviously hulks.

In the end the surviving six Grants backed away slowly, then faster and finally escaped. All three 3rd RTR tanks had been hit – Lieutenant Seed's and Kite's more than twenty times. After an epic journey they eventually reached the remains of 4th Armoured Brigade a mile or so beyond El Alamein railway station. Other survivors were Fred Dale, Geordie Reay, Sergeant Smithhurst, Jock Watt the RSM, Bill Close and many others, nearly all of them rudely unhorsed who 'rallied' once again. Tobruk fell at 0630 hrs on 21 June. Major-General Klopper, 19,000 British soldiers (including most of 4th RTR) 10,000 South Africans, and 2,500 Indians were taken prisoners. Operation 'Buckshot' was one of the worst disasters of the war. The Guards Brigade were pushed out of the 'Knightsbridge' box. The whole army withdrew eastwards. General Ritchie admitted defeat and abandoned the Gazala Line. Wrote Dick Shattock: 'We were by then in complete chaos. What was left of the whole unit, tanks, trucks etc. were scattered having been ordered as small groups into all sorts of different tasks. A route had been cleared through the Tobruk perimeter minefields as the Germans had very nearly surrounded us. A force was desperately holding an escape gap east of Tobruk. The entire remaining "Army" converged on this one small escape channel. Hundreds, maybe thousands of vehicles trying to converge onto a single line bordered by stakes and wires marking the edge of the minefields. Everyone was exhausted from more than twenty days and nights of action.'

By the night of 25 June Rommel's tired but victorious panzers had advanced a hundred miles up to the Mersa Matruh position. Well might the Battle of Gazala go down in history as a carefully planned defensive battle, well thought out, well conceived, but it was a battle which turned into a bewildering defeat.

Captain John Dunlop, having survived all the desert battles of 'Crusader' and 'Buckshot' composed the following epic lines to be sung to the tune of the old sea shanty 'Wrap Me Up in my Tarpaulin Jacket'.

> Well Rommel got ruder and ruder
> And so did the Ninetieth Light
> But the Gunners got warm at El Duda
> So we all got away in the night.
>
> Now at Knightsbridge, I suffered a Trauma
> At Harmet I learned how to brew
> And I walked home again at Acroma
> and sang with the rest of the crew.
>
> As we motored the minefields by moonlight
> in the area south of Tobruk
> Although I knew friend Rommel soon might
> attack, I did not bother to look.

Then at Sidi Rezegh in the sunlight
They all looked like 'Honeys' to me,
Yet it turned out an 88 gun fight
And the 'Honeys' were Mk IV and III.

At length we drew back to Imayd
And the rest we were glad to receive
As we sat there we dreamed and we sighed
For Alex and Cairo and leave.

8

OPERATION 'GAMEBIRDS' – BATTLE OF ALAM HALFA

The British soldier needs to be resilient in the face of defeat. At the beginning of the Battle of the Gazala Line confidence in 3rd RTR was very high: an excellent new tank, the General Grant; capable new CO, Lieutenant-Colonel 'Pip' Roberts; time for leave, better food and conditions; extensive training; and well-reconnoitred hull-down battle positions. Four weeks later 3rd RTR was back where it all started, without any Grant tanks, and with casualties among their commanders and tank crews. Two highly experienced squadron commanders were wounded and in hospital: Jim Hutton, 'A' Sqn, and George Witheridge, 'B' Sqn. Cyril Joly, 'C' Sqn had a face wound and Alec Doig a troop commander was also wounded. The newly commissioned Second Lieutenant Jim Harned and Second Lieutenant Carp had both been killed. The Adjutant Peter Burr had been wounded too. Decorations arrived – an MC for Captain Barker and MMs for Troopers Cunningham and Trotter.

Dick Shattock recalled: 'A composite Bn was to be formed from one squadron of 3rd Tanks, one from 5th RTR, the third from another unit. A cavalry Major arrived to take command. I went with him to inspect a pool of tanks in rather poor condition.' The cavalry officer did not realize that a petrol-filling funnel was needed to fill up a Grant tank. 'Jim Hutton arrived soon afterwards and took command of the Comp Bn, and Dick Steed also joined them.' This composite battalion was involved in fierce fighting, along with other hastily organized units rushed up to delay the German advance. What remained of the 3rd Tanks finally got back to Alexandria: Reggie de Vere as Lieutenant and Quartermaster, George Upcott-Gill, Bill Close, Dudley Easterbrook, and Bob Crisp. There was now a need for a new RSM. One who arrived from Blighty failed to impress the desert veterans. So, to his surprise, Jock Watt, aged twenty-three was made up to become Regimental Sergeant-Major, probably the youngest in the British Army. In his Crusader tank he was responsible for helping to guard Battalion HQ and 'B1' Echelon supply column when it was on the move. He also had an old Buick truck fitted with a radio, an operator/driver and two tank replacement crew. By now the Sherman tanks were beginning to arrive, two squadrons of them, though 'A' Sqn were assigned Crusaders, which was not very popular news. The four HQ tanks were to be Grants.

Early in July 1942 the unit was called 3rd/5th RTR. Major W.M.M. Hutton MC was promoted to Lieutenant-Colonel and CO and on 4 July 3rd/5th RTR 'battlegroup' left for 'XXX' Corps, except for Major Granton's 'B' Sqn which were waiting for replacement Grant tanks at Amiriya. Two days later 3rd RTR was once again its old self under Major C.B. Franklin and moved to Khatatba. 'B' Sqn collected twelve assorted Grant and Lee tanks from the Tank Depot Service. The wounded Lieutenant-Colonel 'Pip' Roberts was visited in a Cairo hospital by Major Franklin and Captain Barker. The large desert camp at Tel el Quabir, 20 miles from the Bitter Lakes was tented (huts for officers), but had an open-air cinema, fresh water supply and regular cooked meals.

The Axis forces kept up their strong offensive but eventually on 4 July Rommel called it a day. The German General von Mellenthin wrote in his *Panzer Battles 1939–45*: 'On 4 July the position of Panzer Armee Afrika was perilous, only 36 tanks in running order and a few hundred infantry in the last stages of exhaustion. There is no doubt that we could not have resisted a determined attack by the Eighth Army.' During July desultory fighting continued on the limited front around Alamein. On the 9th 'B' Sqn in support of 'Bobcol' threatened sixteen Mk IIIs, IVs and M-13s but were not in action. Two days later 'B' Sqn moved to Quassasin to report to the 8th Armoured Brigade Group with which the battalion were to spend the next year of campaigning. On 11 July, the Afrika Korps sent a force of thirty Mk IIIs and Mk IVs against the 8th Armoured Brigade Group, and under heavy shelling 'C' Sqn lost four tanks but claimed in turn four tanks, an armoured car and a troop carrier. The next day 'C' Sqn moved to Tahag Camp 30 at Quassasin where Major H.M. Strange rejoined the regiment. 'B' Sqn stayed in action under heavy shelling by 105-mm guns on the New Zealanders' front.

On the 13th, 'Pip' Roberts, now with a DSO and MC, rejoined from sick leave and assumed command. Major Cyril Joly and Captain P.F. Burr also returned from hospital. Brigadier E.C.N.

Custance, CO 8th Armoured Brigade visited the battalion and explained their role in a counter-attack to relieve pressure on the Australian and South African forces in the north which were now being heavily attacked.

It was an amazing war. On 4 July both the Axis and the Allied forces were in a state of exhaustion. With new equipment and reinforcements they were at each other's throats a week or so later.

On 15 July Major Granton was wounded in Operation 'Bacon' when 'B' and 'C' Sqns were in action fending off the counter-attack on the New Zealand Division. Captain J.C. Balharrie took over from Granton in 'B'. The next day in Operation 'Bright' 'B' and 'C' Sqns were attacked early in the morning by a force of twenty Mk III and IV tanks and were forced to withdraw to a new position 2,000 yards to the east, losing six tanks in the process. In turn they destroyed three, and damaged two Mk IIIs. These actions so depleted the battalion that 3rd and 5th RTR were merged again. 'B' Sqn had only 5 tanks, HQ 2 and 6th Troop 3. The battle continued on the 18th and 19th as 'B' Sqn, again commanded by Major Granton with six tanks, had an evening action. They supported 9th Indian Infantry Brigade against thirteen Panzer Mk III and IVs, destroying two and damaging four of them. The Luftwaffe were very active and thirty Stukas dive-bombed at 1030 hrs on the 19th, while ten attacked again at 1600 hrs. The following day no less than 137 reinforcements arrived. 'B' Sqn took up a position called 'Death Valley' near Point 564 where heavy shelling and constant Stuka attacks caused 3rd/5th RTR to withdraw. Corporal Ogilvie and Trooper Riddle were killed and four ORs wounded. It had been an unpleasant fortnight and 3rd/5th were withdrawn on 24 July into 10th Armoured Division Reserve. Sixty-four more reinforcements arrived that day including Lieutenants E.M. Phelan and J.R.D. Hudswell. On the 26th Lieutenant-Colonel Roberts took command of 22nd Armoured Brigade; Major H.M. Strange assumed command of the battalion, and Major Granton went to hospital. Captain Balharrie, 2 i/c 'B' Sqn, supported the South Africans on the evening of the 27th. At the end of the month Brigadier Custance inspected his brigade: 3rd RTR, Nottinghamshire (Sherwood Rangers) Yeomanry and the Staffordshire Yeomanry. Both had been in the Middle East for some time, stationed in Palestine, but still had their horses. Captain Bill Close went to Palestine with a team of NCOs to help them with their tank training.

Major Cyril Joly described the July actions:

For a fortnight day in and day out, sometimes north of it, sometimes south, occasionally on the summit of its crest, we contested the vital ground of the Ruweisat Ridge against what remained of the Panzer divisions and 90th Light. The battle ebbed and eddied on the bare slopes of the rocky ridge – every yard of ground daily bitterly contested. At the western end of the Ruweisat Ridge there was a small valley area (Death Valley) over which so many battles had been fought. Its floor was littered with the bodies of the dead, neither side prepared to grant the truce to enable them to be buried. During those two weeks of July we were followed by the sickly sweet, pungent, musty odour of decomposing bodies.

Dick Shattock wrote: 'One night during my rounds of inspection of tanks and vehicles, talking to my friend "Squirrel" Oxberry who was commanding a troop of "A" Squadron Stuarts. He said, "Dick my number's up, I will be killed tomorrow, I know it." I replied, "We are all tired beyond normal limits, you are imagining it, you will be OK." But he was adamant. That night in laager Squirrel's tank was missing.' Many weeks later Shattock and the MO set off by jeep to search the battlefields. Eventually they found the very light sand-coloured camouflaged Stuart with Oxberry's skeleton lying on the floor of the tank, its 37-mm gun barrel hit by an HE shell.

On 'Pip' Roberts's promotion, Lieutenant-Colonel 'Pete' Pyman took command of 3rd RTR while refitting at the end of July in the Canal Zone. He had been GSO1 in 7th Armoured Division, and he and Major-General Frank Messervy had been briefly captured during Operation 'Crusader'. He was a very experienced staff officer, but like 'Pip' Roberts, 3rd RTR became his first command at regimental level. Lieutenant Bill Close, 'A' Sqn recalled: 'We were somewhat apprehensive as to how he would compare with our well-loved 'Pip' Roberts. We need not have worried. He became one of our best and trusted COs, an excellent commander, a skilled tank tactician and most considerate in his use of tank crews.' Lieutenant Peter Ross joined 3rd RTR in their training area west of the Wadi Natrun where he met the Adjutant, Captain Guy Barker and the CO. 'Lieutenant-Colonel H.E. Pyman. Dark, short, supremely self-assured, full of dynamic energy, in profile and stature not unlike Napoleon. "There are three things I will not tolerate in my officers. Drunkenness – idleness – and stupidity" he said to me.' Ross joined 'A' Sqn and was given command of the Recce Troop of Daimler 'Dingo' scout cars, which were well suited to desert surfaces, heavily armoured with one Bren gun. Only one in two cars had a wireless. The establishment was ten cars, five patrols of two each, though Ross rarely had more than seven cars.

The resilient Bob Crisp after his severe head wounds received during Operation 'Crusader' returned to 3rd RTR. He took command of 'A' Sqn and almost immediately persuaded 'Pete' Pyman to allow him to form a 'Jock' Column. 'For about eight weeks we (Crisp and Lieutenant Bill Close) swanned about in the desert with very little success. We did have one or two minor actions capturing a couple of armoured cars and half tracks with 75-mm A/Tk guns. We also shot up an enemy airfield not far from El Adem.' At one stage Trooper Gillespie, Crisp's Crusader tank driver refused to carry on. He had already baled out of three or four tanks knocked out in battle while driving Crisp. Lieutenant Close noted: 'Sooner or later the bank of courage does give out.' In one action Close's Crusader was hit by an AP shell and set on fire. The gunner, wireless operator and Bill Close were caught by the flames and badly burned. They were evacuated to hospital, 'a nice one outside Cairo for four pleasant weeks, followed by two weeks rehabilitation at Lady Lampson's hospice on the banks of the Nile'. Close had soldiered in Calais, in Greece, during Operations 'Crusader' and 'Buckshot' and fully deserved the excellent food and special dinner-dances attended by chosen Egyptian lovelies, the talk of Cairo.

Sergeant Jim Caswell had two unusual experiences in the immediate post 'Buckshot' period. In mid-May he attended a gunnery course in Cairo with both hands covered with desert sores and heavily bandaged. Ten days later at the end of the course he travelled up to the front on a train carrying replacement tanks. Just before dawn the tanks on the first twenty 'flats' concertina'd together crushing fourteen ORs. With twenty other tank troopers he hitched truck rides up towards the front line. This was the time of the 'Gazala Gallop', the full disorganized retreat. On the coast road Caswell spotted sixteen Grant tanks parked near the sea, deserted and abandoned by a Tank Transporter Unit. They had fuel rations but no ammunition. As the senior soldier, Caswell organized a Grant tank convoy and decided to drive it towards Egypt rather than leave the tanks to be captured. After twenty miles, 'a cavalry Brigadier called us to halt, drew his revolver to shoot me on the spot – for desertion'. It took some time to convince the irate Brigadier: 'You ought to be going the other way. I've been looking for these tanks for two days.' Indeed, twenty new Grants might have saved the day at the end of 'Buckshot'.

Trooper Geordie Reay became a corporal. 'It was a simple process of elimination. As long as you survived you would get your promotion. They had to have someone to do the job!' Bill Close was promoted to Captain, as 2 i/c 'A' Sqn, but was still Commander of 3rd Troop. Lieutenant-Colonel 'Pete' Pyman wrote in his *Call to Arms*: '3rd RTR were short of about fifty per cent of their officers and about the same proportion of their men. They had already fought through Calais, Corinth and Capuzzo and knew a great deal about active fighting.'

During August 1942 many fundamental changes took place in Eighth Army management. General Alexander took over from General Auchinleck as Commander-in-Chief Middle East. General Bernard Montgomery came out from the UK to command Eighth Army, succeeding General 'Strafer' Gott who had been tragically killed in an aircraft accident. The fall of Tobruk had so appalled Prime Minister Winston Churchill that he had caused 300 brand new Sherman tanks to be diverted to the Eighth Army. The 44th Infantry and 51st Highland Divisions also arrived in the Delta from the UK. Rommel had also heavily reinforced and re-equipped his three key units, 15th and 21st Panzer plus 90th Light Infantry Divisions. He now had seventy-three Panzer Mk IIIs with long 50-mm guns and twenty-seven new Mk IVs with 75-mm guns. The Italian 'XX' Corps had the Ariete and Littorio Armoured Divisions, the Trieste Motor Division and Trento, Bologna and Brescia Infantry Divisions.

The appearance on 13 August of 'Monty' as General Bernard Montgomery was swiftly nicknamed, galvanized the Eighth Army at all levels. Brigadier 'Pip' Roberts met a group of senior officers: General Horrocks, Bobby Erskine (GSO1 'XIII' Corps), Freddie de Guingand, Chief-of-Staff, Eighth Army and several other characters, 'including a little man with white knobbly knees, an Australian hat, no badges of rank, whom I took to be a newly arrived war correspondent.'

Montgomery soon realized that the Alam el Halfa Ridge was the cornerstone of the closely woven strongpoints devised by Brigadier Kisch, the Chief Engineer of the Eighth Army. Three main ridges ran east and west, south-east of the much-fought-over Ruweisat Ridge. Operation 'Gamebirds' was the plan for a defensive battle described by Lieutenant-Colonel Pyman: 'News of the enemy approach – Rommel's last bid for Cairo – brought 3rd RTR racing from their temporary home near Cairo to Alam el Halfa to join 10th Armoured Division under Alec Gatehouse.' Rommel struck suddenly on the night of 30/31 August through the minefields on the southern flank and turned north in a brilliant right hook. 'A classic defensive battle. Montgomery grouped all his armour under one command and his artillery also and occupied the decisive ground with his infantry, sappers and other support troops, with a defensive minefield well out in front of him. The reconnaissance troops were to draw the enemy back through the minefield towards his main grouping. All developed as planned and while the enemy sat looking at him, licking their wounds, Montgomery ordered down a heavy air and artillery attack. From that moment the battle was won.'

The armoured brigades were still relying on Grant tanks, many of which were reconditioned. First the enemy fell upon the 22nd Armoured Brigade, backed up by Stuka dive-bombers, and worked their way eastwards. The 1st KRRC with their new 6-pdr A/Tk guns had a field day around Heimeimat, knocking out a dozen tanks. When 15th Panzer reached the Deir el Agram depression the main attack fell on the Sherwood Rangers and then the Staffordshire Yeomanry, supported by the 25-pdrs of the Kent Yeomanry; 3rd RTR had a minor role losing four tanks but claiming at least three enemy. Major Cyril Joly was told by the CO: 'Its like the Gazala battles over again except that this time we shall be sitting in the path of the Panzer Divisions not by ourselves but with the whole brigade around us. Just to our east another armoured brigade and behind them a complete infantry division.'

Joly recollected:

Late in the afternoon from our dug-in positions on the ridge we glimpsed through a sandstorm our own light tanks and beyond them the menacing squat slopes of the German armour. By nightfall they had driven in our light screen. All night the Air Force bombed and machine-gunned the enemy leaguers giving them no rest or respite to fuel. At dawn we could see the mass of the German divisions lying dispersed and stationary to our south, pounded by waves of formations of bombers and by our own long range artillery. The Germans attacked again with little enthusiasm. They withdrew when we had knocked out about ten of their tanks though they had some successes against us. One tank of my squadron was holed and the tank commander killed. Away to the left I could see three more of our tanks on fire.' The German panzers kept up attack after attack. 'In the afternoon their tanks attacked once more. Again they were driven back harried by swarms of fighter-bombers. All through that night and the following day, in perfect weather and skies, the enemy columns were bombed, machine-gunned and shelled . . . the enemy was seen to be withdrawing during the afternoon of the 3 September.

General Montgomery with marvellous support from the air forces had won a decisive defensive victory. Certainly at least thirty-eight panzer tanks were left behind on the battlefield. On 4 September Major Bob Crisp of 'A' Sqn and Major Christopherson, Sherwood Rangers, led columns to harry the enemy retreating through the Heimeimat–Munassib minefield.

'Cairo was wonderful, no shortages of anything, marvellous food and drink in an atmosphere of feverish war gaiety, women and night clubs galore, all tremendously exciting after wartime Britain.' Lieutenant George Morris had arrived via the *Windsor Castle* to Cape Town, thence by the *Scythia* to Suez and Port Tewfik. An elegant 7th Hussar colonel interviewed him at the Royal Armoured Corps barracks at Abbasiya and decided he should join 3rd RTR. 'All very hectic, playgrounds such as Groppis, Shepherds Hotel, the Pyramids Auberge, Ghazira Island, wine, women and song.' In late September on a full brigade exercise his Grant broke down. By themselves he and his crew waited – as the radio had a maximum range of 20 miles – for four days; then they marched for three days and by good luck found an abandoned 3-ton lorry – a cook's truck with food and water. With his gunner, Lieutenant Morris then walked due north and both were eventually rescued. He took part in the Operation 'Gamebirds' pursuit, 'Under the command of one of the Squadron leaders, a very distinguished soldier (Bob Crisp), a composite force, consisting of elements of 3rd RTR and the Notts and Staffs Yeomanry through the sand sea at Alam Halfa. Some eight wheeled armoured cars did get through the sand sea, however, ineffectively. So many officers went into action straight off the boat and were killed the first day.'

By 8 September Rommel was back where he started. When

General Montgomery inspected 8th Armoured Brigade on 10 September he must have been well pleased. 3rd RTR had exchanged their Black Rat (Jerboa) emblem for the Red Fox's mask. Four days later the brigade moved to a new training area 45 miles west of Wadi Natrum. The 2nd RHA then took over from the Kent Yeomanry.

9

OPERATION 'LIGHTFOOT' – 'A MOST DESPERATE DAY'

'During the six weeks left to us after Alam Halfa', Lieutenant-Colonel Pyman wrote, 'we trained very hard. Gunnery and physical fitness absorbed most of our time.' And Lieutenant Peter Ross, 'A' Sqn noted:

Exercise after exercise, day in, day out, practising the same things all the time until we could do them in our sleep. Yet it was never good enough for the CO. Peter was a perfectionist, determined that his Bn would perform as a machine-like weapon, making the maximum contribution and cutting casualties to a minimum. Our main exercise was to learn how to go through a minefield at night and fan out into battle positions at dawn. The sappers cleared the gaps and lighted the verges putting empty petrol-tins with a tiny cross-shaped slit on one side, on stakes 3 feet high, the light inside visible to us but not to the enemy. Then the fighting vehicles crossed followed by the echelon. The whole regimental group had to pass through. As the 25-pdrs and their 'quads' and the infantry vehicles were underpowered, Peter insisted that the column must keep going. A drill was devised whereby tanks towed 25-pdrs and anti-tank guns. Later, the sweat, tedium and fatigue of those weeks resulted in the enemy's shock at our speed in crossing his minefields.

Sergeant Jim Caswell, 'B' Sqn recalled:

The lanes through the dummy minefields were about three tanks wide and were marked by white tapes and hurricane lamps. The tanks threw up a lot of sand and dust so it was almost impossible to see the tank in front. If one tank lost the way the others would follow into the minefield! We were promised a moonlit night for the operation and hoped it would be alright on the night. . . . What a change to the other battles we had fought (Churchill had promised all the supplies and equipment that Montgomery wanted), always being out-tanked and out-gunned. The American Sherman tank had arrived. It had a 75-mm gun in the turret and was reliable mechanically, again some had petrol, some diesel engines.

The Sherman's 75-mm gun was in the turret, not in a sponson and could fire AP capped ammunition. It weighed 30 tons and stood (the Mks I and II) 10 feet 4 inches high. Corporal Geordie Reay stated: 'It was too big for my liking. Jerry wouldn't have much trouble hitting it.' New two-way wireless sets and better armour plating with the all-round gun traverse were definite advantages. Sergeant Fred Dale of 'A' Sqn was quite enthusiastic about the recce tank now being the Crusader instead of the Honey: 'The new A-15 Crusader was a very low tank (2 feet lower than the Sherman) with an all round power traverse. It had A and B wireless; "A" set for receive and send, "B" set to talk directly to the crew, not like the other tanks we had where you had to kick the gunner on his left or right shoulder to make him turn the turret in the required direction, and to fire the gun you had to kick him in the *middle* of his back or shout as *loud* as you could! The main gun in the Crusader was a 6-pdr which fired solid shot and HE shells. The machine-gun was the Besa, which had two rates of fire, high and low. The engine was a Rolls Royce Merlin, very fast and had to be governed down to a moderate speed. Overall a very good tank, but the armour on the front was not thick enough.' Dale's crew for Alamein was Scully, Willis, Redpath and Killick. Dale was now a full sergeant with his own troop in 'A' Sqn. His friend Sergeant Dean was now SQMS.

General Bernard Montgomery visited 8th Armoured Brigade on two occasions, briefed all officers and then addressed all ranks. He told them in his brisk, common-sense manner how he (and the Eighth Army) were going to win the forthcoming battle. His confidence was magnificent and percolated throughout his army.

After brigade training was finished, 3rd RTR moved up into the 'Blue', as part of 10th Armoured Division under Major-General Alec Gatehouse. In turn they belonged to 'X' Corps, the *Corps de Chasse* under General Herbert Lumsden. The CO noted:

Already Montgomery was working to his well known technique. No commander went into battle without knowing Montgomery's plan. He never upset his Corps or Divisional Commanders unnecessarily and he helped us junior commanders immeasurably. He was so clear, so concise and so confident. Previously he had made sure that he knew us all and we never felt that he was unapproachable. 'Let your soldiers know what you mean them to do and give them the means with which to do it. They will make mistakes of course, but so will the enemy. It is the side who makes the fewest mistakes which wins in war.'

'Pete' Pyman lectured his officers on 10 October on 'Staff duties and sequence of tactical thought'. The next day Captain Dennis, the Divisional Field Security Officer lectured them on 'Security', followed by Major H.M. Strange on 'Navigation'. Then Captain J.C. Balharrie on 'Gunnery', and a staff captain from Brigade on 'Military Law'. On 16/17th Operation 'Harridan' took place. On the 20th the brigade moved from the staging area to the assembly area. The next day was a conference on Operation 'Lightfoot' the first major series of attacks. The main move took place on the 23rd.

Montgomery's plan was for a major attack by night with his infantry and sappers clearing and forcing two lanes through all the protective minefields. Then he would launch the 600 tanks of 10th Armoured Division through them to destroy the enemy armour. He had 200,000 men under his command, 1,500 A/Tk guns (half 6-pdrs, so effective at Alam Halfa), 1,000 field and medium guns and about a thousand heavy and medium tanks. All the old faithfuls were on the other side of the wire – 15th and 21st Panzer, 90th Light and a dozen Italian divisions. Of Rommel's 850 A/Tk guns, nearly 90 were the deadly 88s.

The CO Lieutenant-Colonel 'Pete' Pyman described the tactics. 'The battle of Alamein was certainly the greatest battle we had fought so far in WWII. It was virtually three "break-in" battles and three "pursuits" and 3rd RTR was used in five of these six phases. The "break-in" battles ('Lightfoot') were the phase before 'Supercharge' and the third was the battle for El Aqqaqir. The pursuits can be considered as lasting from the breakout at El Alamein to Agheila.'

Montgomery had several tricks up his sleeve. The most important was the vast attack by night, unheard of in the desert to-date. Another was the number of dummy formations, tanks and lorries, made of rubber but looking the part to the Luftwaffe. Most of the tank regiments had canvas shields fitted to welded brackets to disguise Shermans and Crusaders as 3-ton lorries. When on the move, 'B' Echelon vehicles ran all over the tank tracks in the sand so they could not be identified by air photography.

Lieutenant-Colonel 'Pete' Pyman was fortunate that despite their dreadful casualties in the Western Desert, 3rd RTR had many veteran leaders as they went into Operation 'Lightfoot' – Majors Johnson, Crisp, Franklin, Granton, Strange and Captains Barker (Adjutant), Shattock (Technical Adjutant), Close, Watts, Dunlop, Balharrie and Doig. 'A' Sqn had 16 Crusader Mk IIs (2-pdrs) and Mk IIIs (6-pdrs), 'B' Sqn 10 Mk II Shermans, and 'C' 14 Mk I Grant tanks.

'A tank cannot be properly controlled using the periscope and almost always the commander must have his head outside. The driver may need to close his hatch; in any case he is controlled by the commander. The wireless operator gunner and second driver also have periscopes.' Lieutenant George Morris had just collected eighteen Sherman tanks from Alexandria. 'These particular Shermans have a hydraulically controlled gun-levelling system that was installed for firing on the move. Rarely used as it drained the batteries and was inaccurate. We always fired from a stationary position.' Morris's crew was composed of a gunner from Ireland, a giant blond Norwegian driver, called 'Tiny', a young Jewish co-driver/gunner, a London cockney gun loader/wireless operator, a hairdresser in civvy street and the crew cook.

Captain Dick Shattock, Technical Adjutant, having recovered from glandular fever, rejoined 3rd RTR on the night of 23 October: 'Bob Crisp was now Major O/C "A" Sqn, George Upcott-Gill O/C "B" Sqn, Johnny Johnson commanding HQ Sqn, Colin Franklin commanding "C" Sqn – Guy Barker was Adjutant, Paddy Hehir was now Lieutenant & QM, Tony Viney was Captain commanding the "thin skins". Alamein was so crowded with troops and the miles of thick defensive minefields laid by the Germans.' One Stuka raid dropped a bomb near Dick Shattock's jeep, punctured the radiator with shrapnel, 'two poor chaps were headless, one being the LAD Sergeant under Ivan Payne'.

Lieutenant Peter Ross with the Recce Troop reported to Major Crisp. 'We were shown our route and told that we were to take over a sector in the Alamein line. I was sent forward with the Assistant Adjutant to recce the route and make arrangements with the Bn whose area we were taking over – in "Fly Valley". A fierce battle at the end of August had resulted in heavy casualties on both sides. Swarms of flies infested the place, fed on human corpses. We stayed there overnight, marking on our maps the position of *every* tank and the best routes for our squadrons to approach. Then we returned and led the Bn into the new area by night. Each tank went to a spot evacuated by one of the other Bn.' Ross's driver Trooper Johnston from Liverpool was a pre-war test driver, brown-haired, with the compact build of an athlete, whose object was to win the VC. Two of his armoured car commanders were Lance Corporal Bennett, a north-country townsman and devoted socialist with an agile mind, and Lance Corporal Beck, a regular, intelligent and efficient. 'They made a perfect team.' Much thought went into the preparation of the evening meals. Ross was shown a 'menu' which included Burgoo, Panhaggelty and Scowse.

The final move up, Ross recalled: 'By night through our own minefield gaps we went winding along tortuous tracks, nose to tail, slowly, the recce troops followed by the Crusaders, then RHQ, the Grants and finally the new Shermans followed "Hat" track till we came to our area.' Evidence was clear of the great 'sun-shields' deception plan. Each RTR tank was driven up to each '3-ton lorry shape' which was re-erected by each crew over their tank.

On 22 October the CO, Lieutenant-Colonel Pyman, briefed all his regimental commanders. He told them that 10th Armoured Division in 'X' Corps would penetrate the gaps made by 'XXX' Corps in the north into the open country beyond and in Operation 'Supercharge' engage the enemy's armour. At 2140 hrs on the 23rd the great barrage from 800 guns would fire 100,000 shells into the Axis defensive 'boxes'. The field guns would be 30 yards apart and stretch from the sea to the Qattara Depression. A full-scale attack would be mounted in the southern sector but that would be a feint to draw off the enemy's armour. The real thrust would be in the north. The infantry would go in first, followed by tanks which would fan out to beyond the minefields. Lieutenant Peter Ross observed: 'He stopped talking and looked at each of us for a moment as we sat silent on the sand. Then he lifted his head, and said, as though to himself. "It's a beautiful plan", a semi-smile of appreciation relieving his stern features.'

The 8th Armoured Brigade reached the start line in front of Mitereiya Ridge at midnight in the New Zealanders' 7-mile-wide box. There were six marked tracks through the Allied minefields named 'Boat', 'Hat', 'Bottle', etc. 3rd RTR were on the left (southern) flank with the Nottinghamshire Yeomanry, then Staffordshire Yeomanry in the centre and right flanks respectively.

The 3rd RTR War Diary states for 24 October: 'through enemy minefields, 0615, only halfway through, Crusaders and Grant Sqns battle positions on ridge. 0930 Mk III destroyed by Grant Sqn; Chestnut Troop (1st RHA) do good work. 2130 route through Boat heavy shelling; 2215 bombed by RAF Wellingtons; 2315 occupy position of previous day. *Chaos* sorted out.' On 'Kidney' ridge, RSM Jock Watt's Crusader heaved, moved by an earthquake amid a series of violent explosions. The sky above was lit up while a whole column of echelon trucks and infantry Bren-gun carriers was ablaze and intense fireballs shot up into the air as ammunition lorries exploded. The enemy could see this gigantic fireball, and in front the column of tanks outlined by the blaze, and sent down salvo after salvo. The battalion was very exposed and was ordered to break column and disperse. Rapidly and very hurriedly vehicles spread out in all directions away from the blazing column. At daylight 3rd RTR tanks, stranded but luckily undamaged, drove out of the minefields where they had driven in the night.

Lieutenant-Colonel Pyman remembered:

The first phase in which we had confined fighting by day and one or two very awkward night engagements. All through the first night we passed through minefields and our own gun positions and the noise was terrific. I wondered how any enemy could be left. That was stupid of me; when dawn broke on the first day, we were caught in a minefield but we thrust our way forwards until we were in (hull-down) positions facing very much alive enemy tanks and anti-tank guns. And there we were, firmly halted but it had taken us all our time to get there. We had failed to reach our assigned positions by daylight and any hope of a breakaway was out of the question.

The CO 'Pete' Pyman after his traumatic capture and escape during Operation 'Crusader' now acquired a nervous habit – he needed to know every half hour – *exactly* where Battalion HQ was on the map. The unfortunate new RSM acting as Liasion Officer in the CO's jeep, carrying instructions and orders between HQ and Sqn OCs, was summoned, throughout the battle of El Alamein, dodging 'stonks' and minefields, to Lieutenant-Colonel Pyman's tank to mark on the CO's map, the *exact* location. The radio call to Jock Watt was 'Mope, Mope, come to me and give me my position' – which he did.

'We got the order to advance verbally as wireless silence was being maintained, and despite the dust, drove without much bother through the gun lines where the noise and blast were appalling. We'd been going some time when we reached a wadi where we were forced to halt. Some tanks veered off the paths cleared by the Sappers and their tracks were blown off. Crews jumped out and set off anti-personnel mines and there was *chaos*. We could go neither forward nor back.' Sergeant 'Buck' Kite could hear the sound of the 51st Highland Division bagpipes as they tried to push over the ridge. 'We were ordered to stay in our tanks and stand turret watch. We had to look out for an enemy counter-attack. What with the rum, the noise and the excitement, it was all you could do to keep your eyes open. As it began to get light I could see tanks everywhere, quite a few of them crippled and preventing the movement of others.' Captain Bill Close recollected: 'In the half-light we were nose to tail, unable to move and came under artillery and anti-tank fire, without being able to do much about it. Several tanks in front of mine were hit and I thought it was going to be my turn when somehow we were able to push on and deploy on the ridge though we didn't get very far.' The Sherwood Rangers (Nottinghamshire Yeomanry) lost 16 tanks, the Staffordshire Yeomanry and 3rd RTR about 11 each. But the brigade claimed to have knocked out over 40 enemy tanks and AFVs.

The Luftwaffe dropped flares and then bombs on the echelons of the Nottinghamshire Yeomanry and 1st Buffs and then blazing fuel tankers and exploding ammunition lorries attracted fire from every enemy gun. The Nottinghamshires were in confusion and ordered to withdraw, as was 3rd RTR. This meant the Staffordshire Yeomanry then led.

Sergeant Fred Dale recalled:

The next day (25 October) we did get through to the ridge and stayed there. The battle went on for days. The Engineers lifting minefields and us following through them. There was a lot of excitement amongst the new lads until they dropped a barrage on us, then they quietened down. Mind you, some of the old lads were not very happy with the situation. We were then told the 8th Armoured Brigade were to prepare to attack in bright moonlight (aided by many searchlights) over the ridge to the next one, which we did, and the Infantry dug in all along the ridge. My troop lost one of our Tank Commanders. Corporal Reay came to my troop. There was never a dull moment with him around. As we were going through the next minefield on the forward slopes which the Sappers had cleared, we were to follow the Nottinghamshire Yeomanry. When German bombers came over and bombed them and 1st Buffs Infantry, we had to fall back over the ridge.

Lieutenant Peter Ross took over the wheel of his armoured car as Trooper Johnston was unable to keep awake after driving through the first night. 'Dawn came, we were moving slowly nose to tail in a vast minefield, with another regiment on our right 100 yards away and beyond that another, and yet another – endless streams of armour and the same on our left. We halted wondering what was going on at the head of the column. A ridge in front of us was being criss-crossed by enemy MG fire, but none of our tanks climbed it. Wireless silence was now ended.' Later in the day a guttural voice came up on 3rd RTR frequency: "Ullo Tommy! 'Ullo Tommy! 'ow do you like losing all your nize new tanks?' Ross again:

Word came from the leading tank that there were still fifty yards of gap to be cleared. The sappers were being mown down and couldn't work any faster. Two vehicles blew up on mines in the column to our left. A Crusader tank behind us jumped to one side with its track hanging loose. 'Eighty-eight' whispered Trooper Johnston, 'Christ.' Somehow the gap was cleared and the leading tanks surged ahead and fanned out on the forward slope of the ridge. I was ordered onto the crest with a platoon of lorried infantry (1st Buffs). We spotted several gun positions. The infantry dealt with two of them and we engaged a third with our Brens. Over to the right was a blazing mass of British equipment, a troop of 25-pdrs with their quads and half a squadron of tanks had got through the minefield in the dark and were caught on the skyline by the enemy artillery at first light.'

Paddy Hehir the Lieutenant Quartermaster (Lt QM) came round with rations and rum and the RMO, Captain MacMillan, attended to the 3rd RTR casualties as they came in. 'That day I (Peter Ross) lost another car, Bert's on a mine and the commander, one of my best, was killed. Corporal Bennett guiding the car on foot through a mine "swamp" was badly wounded.' Major Bob Crisp told him: 'Bad luck losing those two cars, but it wasn't your fault.'

The Battalion War Diary noted:

25th move along 'Bottle' behind Staffs followed by Notts. 0530 very heavy shell and A/Tk gunfire. Staffs lose 6 tanks, no hulldown positions available 0700 reach battle positions, with Notts on right, A/Tk guns left and Staffs in reserve. 0715 attack by 40 enemy tanks but they withdraw; 0800–0900 two enemy 88-mm A/Tk guns destroyed. 1100 heavy shelling. REs try again clear and lift mines, 1500 very unpleasant hour, 1700 reports 27 enemy tanks 4,000 yards away. 1915 Division to be withdrawn for 24 hours. Stuka attacks (which caused much damage).

Lieutenant-Colonel 'Pete' Pyman recalled: 'Every time we tried anything our tanks were met by accurate anti-tank gun fire and our troops by deadly machine-gun fire. That day I lost most of my engineers in their gallant attempts to clear the minefields. *It was a most desperate day* for a commanding officer to have to endure. We attacked the enemy positions again during the next night but without much ultimate success. We had been heavily attacked from the air as we left our positions and several of our tanks had been burnt out. These together with the results of the air attacks turned darkness into light. In spite of this we started well and the forward and lighter anti-tank defence soon fell into our hands.' The CO admitted that few of the tank regiments involved in Operation 'Lightfoot' were good at night attacks. 'As soon as dawn came we were involved again in rigorous tank and anti-tank gun battle. The Germans were adept at their use of the anti-tank screen. These screens held us up for as long as a whole day. And in the morning they would be gone.'

The first 'break in' phase for 8th Armoured Brigade had achieved little, but in the attritional fighting of the initial two days had caused almost as much damage as they had received. 3rd RTR were back in the front line again on the 29th losing two Crusaders and a Scout car.

Major Crisp's 'A' Light Sqn was sent out on reconnaissance towards Tel el Aqqaqir, the main objective for the next operation, 'Supercharge'. Several Mk III panzers were operating behind cover of a screen of A/Tk guns. Captain Bill Close and his troop sergeant Geordie Reay crept forward in the early morning of the

29th playing hide-and-seek behind a number of knocked-out derelict tanks. 'We managed to get in the rear of several MkIII Panzers before they spotted us and we knocked out three or four of them,' recalled Close. Sergeant Fred Dale recollected: 'Geordie got into a good firing position and knocked out the MkIV long barrel Panzer which had been doing a lot of damage. He won a well deserved DCM.' 'A' Sqn reported that part of 21st Panzer Division were in a defensive position north of Tel el Aqqaqir. Lieutenant Peter Ross had been sent by the CO to contact the armour with the New Zealanders, which was operating in the north, before getting into battle positions at first light preparatory to 'Supercharge'. Trying to rescue the wounded crew of a Crusader on his recce, Ross's armoured car was hit and burst into flames. Trooper Johnston died of burns. Ross was awarded the MC for rescuing the wounded Crusader crew under heavy MG and A/Tk fire. Stuka raids occurred most days but the Allied air forces were very active too. Major-General Herbert Lumsden issued a warning order on 30 October of an impending attack by 10th Armoured Division.

10

OPERATION 'SUPERCHARGE' – 'DOGGED BY LACK OF NIGHT TRAINING'

Ferocious fighting took place in Montgomery's 'end-game' around the insignificant mound named Tel el Aqqaqir for 48 hours after Operation 'Supercharge' was launched on 2 November 1942. The brigade now attached to 1st Armoured Division was to follow 2nd Armoured Brigade into the battle near the 'Kidney' feature. For over a week the Eighth Army had been slugging it out with the Afrika Korps across the myriad minefields. 15th Panzer Division and the Italian armoured Ariete Division clung to the line of the Rahman track and gave 1st Armoured Division's attack a terrible bloody nose. *Panzer Armee Afrika* was at the end of its tether and only 24 out of 90 tanks were still battleworthy – but they fought on and on. The Battalion War Diary has a few laconic items: '2 Nov, left of 2 A/Bde 1200 try push SW towards Tel el Aqqaqir; 1400 KO'd 1 Mk IV, 1 Mk II, 1600 lost 3 Crusaders trying to observe over the ridge; 3 Nov KO'd 1 Mk III'.

On 2 November the Nottinghamshire Yeomanry moved up at dawn along the main coastal road, then down 'Diamond' track through many minefields, and had some excellent shooting. The Staffordshires were on their left and were heavily shelled by 88-mm guns. 3rd RTR led on the 3rd and 4th trying to bypass Tel el Aqqaqir.

CO Lieutenant-Colonel 'Pete' Pyman's views were that '3rd RTR were not really paying a very good dividend until the breakout at Tel el Aqqaqir for which they were partly responsible (Kellett's Sherwood Rangers played a much more important part). We were dogged by lack of night training. Throughout the night we should have pursued the enemy and cut him off on the coast railway twenty or so miles westwards but instead we kept covering each other's tracks in the dark.

Eventually the Brigadier (Custance) halted us and made us leaguer up and keep quiet.'

After ferrying the CO back to Brigade HQ for a briefing, RSM Jock Watt's Crusader was hit by a shell on the side of the turret and blasted him down inside on top of the operator. With blood running down his neck a little later at the Regimental Aid Post (RAP), Doc MacMillan was scratching and scraping many pieces of metal from the back of Watt's neck.

Sergeant Fred Dale, 'A' Sqn recalled:

The New Zealand infantry broke through the German defence positions. Now it was our turn. We had to do a night march through the slit trenches the Infantry were occupying. First one way, inches from the trench, then the other way – it was a nightmare. You could hear the Infantry personnel shouting at you. We were now through the German defences and starting to run into their armoured divisions, the 15th and 21st Panzer. The big tank battle started. There were very heavy casualties on both sides. The 8th, our Brigade, was hit very badly but it did (help) finish the German Panzers. The following morning 3 November we were through. The chase was now on. We are back to 10th Armoured Division. That night it was raining very heavily. We were told to stop, but our Colonel (Pete Pyman) asked if he could go on.

There was a certain amount of confusion with 1st, 7th and 10th Armoured Divisions simultaneously trying to locate their 'centre lines' on a dark and stormy night. Rommel ordered the Afrika Korps to retreat at 1530 hrs on the 4th. General von Thoma, Rommel's 2 i/c was captured that day. Monty was seen talking to him before he was sent off in an armoured car.

On the evening of 4 November 3rd RTR arrived at a spot 15 miles north-west of Bir el Abd and early the next morning had a field day around Galal. They knocked out a Mk III, took fifteen POWs and at midday spotted a large column of MET headed by twenty enemy tanks (M-13s of the Italian Centauro Armoured Division), moving fast between the battalion and the Nottinghamshire Yeomanry heading south-west. The War Diary continued: 'Terrific party for all. All enemy tanks KO'd and many of the MET burning or taken in charge. Rest of day collecting PoWs 1800 hrs total bag for day 10 tanks destroyed, 323 PoW into the cage, 3 A/Tk guns destroyed: numerous MET destroyed and captured.' In all, 8th Armoured Brigade with negligible loss destroyed 53 Italian tanks and took 1,000 prisoners. The Sherwood Rangers did best with a bag of 26 tanks, the Staffordshire Yeomanry 10, 3rd RTR 10 and the RHA the remainder. Major Franklin was shot in the thigh by an Italian prisoner and went back to base hospital in the same plane as General von Thoma. At 2000 hrs 3rd RTR led the brigade towards Fuka along the line of the railway, covering 11 miles. RSM Jock Watt at Battalion HQ saw the coast road with flat desert on either side crammed with enemy lorries and guns and a few tanks crawling westwards. The tanks were disposed of first and 3rd RTR settled down to a 'pigeon' shoot: a strangely satisfying orgy of destruction and death. The CO became known as 'Pyman of Galal'. He was proud of that accolade. The following day they 'collected' another 280 POWs and leaguered 5 miles west of Fuka. Here Rommel's ADC Captain Voss commanded a spirited rearguard, but 3rd RTR captured an entire Italian battery of guns. The brigade overran the airfields at Fuka on 6 November before a very heavy rainstorm stopped play.

On the coast road west towards Mersa Matruh, the less experienced tank crews were inclined to loot abandoned enemy stores and equipment. But the old hands were reluctant to risk their lives from booby traps for a handful of souvenirs. When a tank was lost, the loot went with it!

Lt George Morris, with the Sherman squadron, recollected:

The barren desert bloomed incredibly with millions of tiny variegated flowers. We were halted outside Mersa Matruh in a dreadful area, heavily contaminated by its previous occupants, Italian troops, some dead and smelly. I thought of that place as Charnel Valley: smell, dirt and flies. We moved on to Halfaya Pass dominated by Fuka ridge where on the approaching plain we were fired on by accurate, Italian heavy artillery commanding from the ridge. Our own gunners returned the fire, still attached to their ammunition limbers, literally on the move. The Italians soon ceased firing and started down the pass, white flags aflying, led by an immaculately uniformed Colonel, around 6,000 men following. . . . Our progress trundling over the desert or on the coast road was inevitably slow. Sometimes we were halted by formidable gun screens of the dreaded 88 mm anti-tank, anti-aircraft cannon. We developed a drill to overcome these deadly barriers. We deluged their guns with HE from out of range, to anti-tank shells, from our own 75s and our own gunner's 25-pdrs, at the same time creeping round their flanks when of course they had to retire.

The battalion stayed beside the seaside for two weeks doing maintenance and swimming every day in the blue Mediterranean beside the waving palm trees. Rather curiously Major Bob Crisp visited the flesh pots of Cairo, ostensibly to see a dentist, and was not seen for some considerable time! Lieutenant George Morris of 'C' Sqn calculated that during the North African campaign, 'our total turnover of personnel was 186 officers and around 2,000 other ranks out of a complement of 700 all ranks. The casualties were usually the newcomers who could not orientate sufficiently quickly to survive.'

Decorations were awarded in November – a well-deserved MC to Captain Bill Close and MMs to SSM Quinn and bar to his MM for RQMS Stewart. 'Buck' Kite and Reay received the MM. The Quartermaster provided rum to celebrate the Close, Reay, and Kite awards. In a wadi near Mersa Matruh, Sergeant Smith, Corporal Whitehouse and Corporal Bill Jordan found ten Germans hiding. After searching them they were handed over to Provost Sergeant Myers to be sent to a new POW pen. Arriving there the captured German officer complained to the cage commandant that he had been relieved of his wristwatch; Lieutenant-Colonel Pyman sent for Bill Jordan and said: 'Take my advice, send it back. If it was to result in a court-martial, although he is in the enemy army, his word (as an officer) would be taken before yours!' Major Alec Doig took over from Bob Crisp as OC 'A' Sqn, a first-class tank commander who had served with the Kenyan Rifles, and a big game hunter in peace-time.

On 30 November 3rd RTR were brought up 650 miles in tank transporters from Matruh to Agheila and temporarily placed under the command of 'Pip' Roberts's 22nd Armoured Brigade. Lieutenant Peter Ross recovered from his burns found 3rd RTR resting near Merduma. 'The land here was flat with clusters of palm trees giving shade. Everyone was in triumphant mood. Colonel Pete met me at the door of his tent with a big grin and a handshake. As ever he was immaculately turned out, his Napoleonic strut even more pronounced. On his chest was the ribbon of the DSO awarded in recognition of his masterly leadership at Alam Halfa.' To his surprise Ross was sent to Brigade for two months as Liasion Officer, where Major Cyril Joly was Brigade Major at the time. Captain Bill Close led his Crusader troop into and over a wadi on the pursuit. A mine exploded throwing the tank on its side. Two of the crew were killed and Bill Close wounded. The RMO Captain MacMillan gave him some 'pep' pills. 'I transferred to another of my tanks and pressed on.' After observation of the 'Charing Cross' road, the battalion moved on 8 November into Matruh and rescued fifty Indian soldiers held prisoner.

On 3 December 8th Armoured Brigade leaguered south of Agedabia and 3rd RTR probed the defences of Suera. For the next three months, the brigade was under the command of 7th Armoured Division, the Desert Rats. For almost two weeks patrols pushed into the Suera position, and on 13 December 3rd RTR led the brigade past the desert end of the salt marshes near el Haseit and made a 6-mile incursion. In dense fog on the 14th, the battalion with brilliant navigation led, followed by the Sherwood Rangers, and bumped the strong El Agheila defences. The next day in a fierce action they met an Italian tank force of fourteen M-13s of the Centauro Armoured Division and knocked out seven of them. Sergeant 'Buck' Kite encountered a German Mk III tank: 'A shell had taken his commander's head off, his trunk remained upright in the hatch, wearing an Iron Cross.' 3rd RTR echelon swanned into an enemy Leaguer by mistake and lost twelve trucks and many personnel. The battalion stayed at Merduma until the end of December. They had travelled 1,000 miles from Alamein.

In "Lightfoot" and "Supercharge" General Montgomery had won a substantial victory. Well might Churchill order the bells of all British churches to ring out merrily. To many who fought at El Alamein it must have seemed that victory was remote, since the Axis forces for nearly ten days had fought tooth and nail. The Eighth Army had 13,500 casualties. The Axis yielded 30,000 POWs of which 20,000 were Italian. Their dead and wounded probably totalled another 10,000. The British lost 500 tanks of which half were repaired while the panzers lost more than 200 and the Italians 130.

The capture of El Agheila by 8th Armoured Brigade opened the road past 'Marble Arch' – Mussolini's triumphant arch marking the Libyan frontier – on to Merduma, Nofilia, Wadi Regel and Wadi el Fachria. The Germans fought many brilliant little rearguard actions. The 90th Light Infantry Division was particularly notable and they also left minefields and booby traps for the

Mk I 'female' tank C-6 (Second Lieutenant J. Allan) named 'Cordon Rouge', Albert Road, Battle of the Somme. (*Tank Museum*)

Lieutenant C.H. Sewell VC. (*Sewell family*)

The action that won the VC for Lieutenant C.H. Sewell, painting by I.S. Appleton. (*Tank Museum*)

Tank Corps review, 1935. (*Author's collection*)

3rd RTC training, 1938. (*Tank Museum*)

Light Section 'A' Squadron before embarkation for Calais. (*A. W. Green*)

A-9 Cruiser Mk I, close support tank, HQ 'A' Squadron, knocked out,
Calais. (*Tank Museum*)

Lieutenant-Colonel
R.C. Keller,
CO 3rd RTR.

Captured 3rd RTR A-10 Cruiser tanks in Piraeus. Armed German guard on the left. (*IWM HU39519*)

Lieutenant Bob Crisp's broken down tank at the bridge over the Ventikos. (*Bob Crisp*)

3rd RTR survivors returning from Crete, including Sergeant Jock Watt, Corporal Jim Jolly, Sergeant Basford, Corporal Hoskins and Sergeant Boris Tordoff. (*Jock Watt*)

Alexandria Camp, June 1941. Left to right, standing: Lieutenant Dick Shattock, Dudley, 'George' Upcott-Gill, Sidley de Burgh; kneeling: 'Squirrel' Oxberry. (*Dick Shattock*)

A-10 tank firing smoke shells, training in the desert east of Matruh, August 1941. (*Dick Shattock*)

Officers before 'Buckshot', May 1942. Left to right: Major Cyril Joly, CO Lieutenant-Colonel 'Pip' Roberts, Major George Witheridge. (*Dick Shattock*)

Lieutenant Dick Shattock (left) and RMO Captain 'Doc' MacMillan.
(*Dick Shattock*)

General Bernard Montgomery's 'intrepid tanky', August 1942. (*IWM*)

LAD fitters working on a Sherman suspension unit, September 1942. (*Dick Shattock*)

Major S. Johnson (left) and Lieutenant 'Paddy' Hehir, quartermaster, October 1942. (*Dick Shattock*)

Sergeant Jim Caswell and 'B' Squadron tank crew with looted swastika flag, El Alamein, November 1942. (*Jim Caswell*)

Lieutenant-Colonel 'Pete' Pyman and 'O' Group, December 1942. (*Dick Shattock*)

Victory parade, Tripoli 1943. *(IWM)*

Shermans and Crusaders being driven to REME main workshops in Tripoli for overhaul, February 1943. (*Dick Shattock*)

3rd RTR officers west of Tripoli, February 1943. Left to right, back row: Lt P. Ross MC, Lt H. Bennett, Lt Hudswell, Lt A. Birkett, Lt H. Kirkham DCM, Lt E. Phelan, Lt W.P. Hughes, Capt J. Dunlop; middle row: Capt M. Gilboy, Capt J. Payne REME, Capt T.A. Viney, Capt W. Close, Lt G. Morris, Lt P. Brookshaw, Lt W. Hall, 2/Lt Farningham MM, Lt and QM P. Hehir, Lt J. Anderson; front row: Capt and Tech Adj R.G. Shattock, Maj S. Johnson, Maj C.B. Franklin, Maj H.L. Upcott-Gill MC, Lt-Col H.E. Pyman DSO MBE, Capt and Adj J. Watts, Maj A.K.R. Doig, Maj G.H. Barker, Capt J.W. MacMillan MC RAMC. (*Dick Shattock*)

'B' Squadron sergeants, Alexandria, November 1943. Left to right, back row: Bob Lawton, Eric Foot, Frank Sheppard, Jim Caswell, Ben Wallinger; front row: SSM Shepherd, Bob Sumner, Peter Toy, Dicky Dickson. (*Jim Caswell*)

3rd RTR officers before D-Day, Beaumont Barracks, Aldershot, May 1944.
Left to right, back row: Lt W.T. Brooks, 2/Lt S. Montgomery, 2/Lt P. Pells,
2/Lt C.T.W. Lindguist, 2/Lt D. Collie, Lt J.H. Thompson, 2/Lt B. Dewick,
Lt R. Goldsmith, 2/Lt R. Lemon, Lt H.O. Bennett; third row: Lt W.F. Yates,
Lt D. Osbaldeston, Lt A. Birkett, Lt R.H. Bates, Lt J.F. Langdon, Lt C.G. Dear,
Lt J.R.D. Hudswell, Lt H.G. Stubbs MM, Lt T.M.E. Maloney; second row: Capt
G.A. Morris, Capt S. Farningham MM, Capt B.J. Hamill MC, Capt F.M.
Dingwall, Capt C.E. Anderson, Capt N.A.F. Kent, Lt H.D. Abercrombie,
Lt A. Carter, Capt A.M. Dixon; front row: Capt the Revd Taylor CF, Capt J. D.
Dunlop, Capt J.C. Balharrie MC, Maj W.H. Close MC, Maj H.L. Upcott-Gill
MC, Lt Col D.A.H. Silvertop MC (CO), Maj R.F. Burr MBE, Maj J.A. Watts,
Maj S.M. Johnson, Lt (QM) V. Hehir, Capt J.W. MacMillan MC RAMC.
(*Bill Morris*)

'B' Squadron 3rd RTR passes 6th Guards Tank Brigade's Churchill tanks
during 'Bluecoat', July 1944. (*IWM*)

Lieutenant H.G. Stubbs leads 'C' Squadron into Boom, outskirts of Antwerp. (*Antwerp Archives*)

Lieutenant-Colonel D.A.H. Silvertop DSO MC, 3rd RTR, September 1943. (*Antwerp Archives*)

3rd Battalion the Monmouthshire Regiment and 3rd RTR take a break during their advance through Holland. This photograph was taken south of Helmond, 24 September 1944. (*Author's collection*)

'Comet' in Operation 'Plunder'. (*Tank Museum*)

'A' Squadron in Operation 'Plunder'. (*Tank Museum*)

Captain Graham Scott 'A' Squadron marking up his map. (*Les Slater*)

unsuspecting. Flat anti-tank Teller mines destroyed or damaged all trucks and most AFVs. The nasty little 'S' mines threw up a canister of large ball-bearings before exploding. The Italians made equally unpleasant explosive thermos flasks. Casualties to mines occurred to the infantry formations with distressing frequency.

The brigade waited for supplies to catch up and spent Christmas astride the Merduma–Nofilia track. Sports competitions took place, impromptu concerts, Church services, an excellent Christmas dinner (turkey, pork, pudding, bottle of beer, fifty fags). The officers' and sergeants' messes fared well and whisky and gin supplies were almost adequate. Monty had visited the brigade on 23 December to watch a battle practice and award decorations won at El Alamein.

FIRST REGIMENTAL ARMOURED GROUP INTO TRIPOLI

For the advance on Tripoli, 3rd RTR was still commanded by Lieutenant-Colonel 'Pete' Pyman DSO, MBE; Major H.L. Upcott-Gill was 2 i/c; Major Alec Doig, OC 'A' Sqn; Major G.H. Barker, OC 'B' Sqn; Major S.M. Johnson, OC 'C' Sqn, and Captain J.A. Watts was Adjutant.

The Battalion War Diary reports: '6 Jan (1943). "B" Sqn to fire new Sherman tanks, "C" Sqn co-operate with an Army film unit. When on the 8th the Corps Commander Lieutenant-General Oliver Leese visited the regiment, "B" Sqn laid on a demonstration. The next day the CO gave a lecture "Deployment of an Armoured Regimental Group". On the 12th in a sandstorm the CO practised night moves involving "snakes" with 80 vehicles to a mile, a speed of 4 miles in the hour with a halt of 15 minutes every hour.' The brigade was now in the Wadi Chebir area defended by 15th Panzer Division.

The advance continued on to Nofilia where the ground was covered in tiny scented flowers, to the well-mined fort of Sirte. The main enemy defences were met at Beurat south of Misurata. The Axis forces now held a line from the sea to Gheddabia and were reputed to have a strength of 100 tanks. The tank strength for each of the three armoured regiments of the brigade was 25 Crusaders and 28 heavies such as Shermans and Grants. The next attack would be to breach the Wadi Zem Zem line. The 33rd German A/Tk Battalion under *Hauptmann* Zahn put up a fierce defence and the brigade lost twenty-four tanks in a late afternoon battle. On 15 January, 3rd RTR near Wadi Raml took on fourteen Panzer Mk IIIs. Although two Shermans were brewed-up, a Mk IV and a Mk III were knocked out and four others hit. The next day on the way to Sedada, Stukas and ME 109s bombed heavily but AA shot down one of each. A hundred Italians with a German officer in charge were taken POW.

On the way to Tripoli Sergeant Jim Caswell's tank was set on fire by a stray shell. The crew baled out but activated levers at the rear which pulled out and set off fire extinguishers, so the fire went out. Fitters came up to replace electrical parts and ignition harnesses. Catching up with the regiment Caswell's crew came across two recent graves with black berets on hand-made crosses. 'One was Trooper Eric Ingram, brother of my gunner Alec Ingram. Naturally Alec and all of us were very upset. When we rejoined the Regiment we were given a flank protection role. We saw two German tanks and a half track emerging from behind a hillock about 300 yards away. I put Alec on the target and ordered him to shoot the one in the rear first and then the other two. He shot up all three. It seemed in some way to avenge the loss of his brother. Alec was mentioned in despatches.'

By 19 January 'A' Sqn Crusaders were within 1,000 yards of the Tarhuna road. The CO regarded this area as 'European country', very difficult for tanks. The elimination of 88-mm A/Tk guns would now be an 'infantry job'. On the 21st Lieutenant E.O. Hall was killed by shrapnel, and Captain Bill Close directed medium artillery onto an enemy column of guns and MET. The divisional commander, Major-General George Erskine, visited the battalion. Mines were a problem and on the 22nd in the battalion area Major Gerrard, Captain Robinson and six sappers were killed by anti-personnel mines. The battalion was now under fire from Castel Benito, near Tarhuna.

Sergeant Buck Kite and his two Crusader recce troops: 'visibility was bad and there were plenty of enemy about. All went well until I turned a corner and saw three self propelled guns and some enemy soft-skinned vehicles.' Corporal 'Jessie' Matthews then stalled the Crusader's engine. Kite shouted at him on the intercom, 'My God, Jessie, what a place to stop for a piss.' As the tank radio was on, the whole regiment heard Kite, including the CO. He reported back the enemy position for supporting gunners to deal with. Kite again: 'When we got to Castel Benito airfield, we were told the Recce Squadron ('A') should go hell for leather down to the road and keep on (to Tripoli) regardless.' Near the town they were halted. The CO wrote in his memoirs: 'We swept on to Tripoli, eight miles east we were ordered to halt apparently to allow a "more famous" regiment to enter Tripoli first. For the honour of 3rd RTR, I must say that we were already there!' Pyman also wrote a citation for Kite, which included 'reported the enemy positions with *good humour*'.

'The Cherry Pickers', 11th Hussars, were under the command of 8th Armoured Brigade and nipped past 'A' Sqn into Tripoli on 23 January, and Monty followed at high speed to savour this great achievement by the Eighth Army. The War Diary states: '23rd Moved behind 11H, 0500 after very fast move, group arrived in Tripoli area L515633, first armoured Regt group to arrive. CO's tank reached 26 mph, 2 i/c was passed going 22 mph.' It was a lovely area of cherry orchards in full bloom, olive groves, date palms, vineyards, eucalyptus trees and Italian colonial whitewashed farms and villas.

Lieutenant Peter Ross rejoined 3rd RTR, 'and took over my troop again. We were leaguered five miles from the city on a flat grassy area which looked like reclaimed marshland. There were several dug-outs built by the Italians which we used as kitchens. Living quarters consisted of tents.' Ross went into the town and bought eggs, cauliflowers, carrots, onions and potatoes, all very popular in the mess that evening. An Irishman, he had just enough Italian, Arabic, French and English, 'to be cheated by the hard-headed Libyans in all four tongues'. Returning from hospital Lieutenant George Morris noted: 'Our Brigade handed over its tanks to an untried Brigade and we settled down in bivouacs. We used the Del Mehari (Racing Camel) as an officers' club. We found an Italian Officers' brothel, fun for a few days until the Military Police closed it down. Gallons of vino, very intoxicating when drunk like beer.'

On 27 January a whole batch of decorations arrived, Mentions in Despatches to the three COs, Lieutenant-Colonels Ewins, Roberts and Pyman, plus Captain Barker, RQMS Turner, Sergeant Sneyd, Lance Corporal Tunney MM, Trooper Prince, Lieutenant G.E. Anderson (WOII), Troopers Partridge and Rogan. In addition eight Commander-in-Chief Middle East Commendation Cards were awarded, to Major P.G. Page (killed in action), Captain Alec Doig, Captain C.B. Joly, Lieutenant F. Adams (POW), Lieutenant H.G. Maegraith (killed in action), Lieutenant A.H.E. Stuart (killed in action), Second Lieutenant B.J. Hamill and Corporal H. Stubbs.

Two days later the first leave party of 100 ORs went into Tripoli, where ENSA, NAAFI, divisional theatre and cinema were now deployed. Brigadier Roscoe Harvey DSO, the new brigadier, inspected the battalion which now included Major C.B. Franklin back from hospital. Major H.M. Strange was posted to 'XXX' Corps HQ.

There was of course considerable 'bull' for the Grand Parade on

4 February for Winston Churchill to inspect his victorious Eighth Army. Alan Moorehead the journalist wrote: 'The Highland pipers went piping into the main square. At last after thirty months of warfare the ragged and dishevelled desert soldier stood with wonderment and emotion beside the playing fountains . . . so many had died or been withdrawn through wounds at a time when the struggle looked futile and endless. . . .' Lieutenant Peter Ross recalled: 'Like other formations we put out a skeleton force with one member appearing for each rank. I was chosen to represent the subalterns. The parade was impressive, lines and lines of troops standing smartly in front of the white, sunlit building; Winston swept past in a staff car returning our cheers and salutes in his usual vulgar manner.' On 8 February further awards were posted. The DSO to Lieutenant-Colonel Pyman, the MC to Major Upcott-Gill and the MM to L/Sgt J.B. Filer.

Lieutenant Peter Ross noted, the next week, 'Pete (Pyman) called us one day to an Orders Group. First he summarised the campaign so far and the lessons to be learnt from it, pointing out there was still some hard fighting ahead particularly when we reached the hilly country and the Mareth Line. He surprised us by expressing thanks for our loyalty and support and telling us that he was leaving the Bn to take up a post as Brigadier in England.' Pyman himself in his memoirs wrote: '3rd RTR was a good regiment . . . they were ordinary, normal men but they were inspired with a great enthusiasm to win. . . . These were the men who won for us.' Pyman left on 17 February and his lecture to a group of very senior officers from England and some Americans (including George Patton who was asleep throughout) is shown as Appendix A at the end of this book. On the 22nd Bob Crisp (in his absence) was awarded an MC and Sergeant F. 'Buck' Kite the MM. RSM Jock Watt, SSMs Stewart, Cresswell and Wood were recommended for commissions; Sergeant Patterson MM, Corporals Fitton and Organ, Troopers Everett, Mills, Keens and Beat were posted as Sherman tank experts to the British First Army battling away in Algeria. Captain E.W. Gilboy became regimental gunnery officer instead of Major Barker. And Lieutenant-Colonel D.A. Silvertop arrived as the new CO.

RSM Jock Watt caught a plane – an old Dakota – from Castel Benito aerodrome to fly back to Cairo to attend an Officers' Selection Board. This was successful and he then went to Palestine for a week's course at Officers' Training College. As Lieutenant Watt he was in charge of £½ million sterling destined to the Field Cashier in Tripoli. With his escort of four sergeants, they guarded the valuable forty packing cases on board the cargo ship *Everley*. Their convoy of five ships was protected by four destroyers and was violently attacked by Luftwaffe fighter-bombers near Tripoli harbour. A Military Police captain met the ship as it docked and checked that the Sudanese dockers did not loot the Eighth Army's pay.

Major Cyril Joly wrote about life in the Western Desert where food and drink was of major importance:

At times, though, we were tired and dispirited, worn out by the heat and the lack of water and the monotony of the food. Fresh meat, milk, bread and vegetables were out of the question; they would never have lasted the four or five day journey from Alexandria or Cairo without adequate refrigeration facilities. The ration consisted of a variety of tinned foods, some more popular than others. Bully beef there was at all times, and in the main it was our favourite, since we could make it quickly into a satisfying and palatable meal, either hot or cold. Tinned bacon was invariably all fat and was rolled in revolting lengths of paper which we took to be bacon, only discovering our error when we could chew the solid lump no longer. Tinned sausages we liked until they were replaced by a substitute variety made, it was alleged, from soya beans which were promptly named 'Soya links' and reviled at all times, except when they came as a novelty to another diet which had begun to pall. There was a tinned stew of meat and vegetables, known shortly as M & V. Biscuits there were in unlimited quantities, thick or thin, hard or soft, some of which tasted of sawdust, others of mud, but always there by the box-full when all else ran out, to be eaten by themselves, with tinned margarine, or with tinned jams or marmalade. Tea, of course, was the main standby, thick and sweet and strong as only the Army made it – a 'brew' as it was known to all and sundry. Mixed with a dash of rum on a cold night or in any depressing circumstances it was a life saver and reviver.

Water, too, was always a problem and, except for those troops who were near the supply points, was limited to never more than three-quarters of a gallon per man per day. Separated as we were from the main waterpoints at Matruh by so great a distance, we were limited to a mere half gallon per man per day. This four pints was all that each man could expect, though in the spring and autumn, after the small amount of rain that fell, we might hope to have the ration augmented a little from the nearest 'Bir' which might have filled up. In the course of time we all evolved a method of allocating the usual four pints in a satisfactory way. One pint we heated and used for washing and shaving. After use it was poured into a crude filter, made of a four gallon petrol tin with holes punched in the bottom and filled with alternate layers of stones and sand. Each day's supply was caught and kept in another petrol tin, which by the end of a week or ten days was sufficiently full to provide a bath of sorts. After the bath, the water was again filtered and used for washing clothes. Finally after another filtering it was used in the radiators of the lorries and trucks.

Another pint we kept in a water bottle as an emergency supply which we could consume each day, though the whole pint was not normally drunk, as most of us preferred to wet the material covering the outside of the bottle, which, when left in the shade, was then cooled by the evaporation of the water.

The two remaining pints were issued to mess or cookhouse, one pint to be used for making tea, the other to be used for cooking.

Meagre though this supply was we soon learned to manage on it and to work out a system of private rationing which satisfied our wants. Some drank little and often, others a lot at certain fixed times. Some men preferred the water by itself, others mixed with fruit juices or lemonade tablets. We were always affected by the quality of the water, which was often the greatest tribulation which had to be endured. Usually it was fairly good and tasted reasonably sweet despite the disinfectant prescribed by the doctors. Sometimes, however, it was brackish, salty and discoloured. At these times life was made distinctly more unpleasant. The milk curdled in the tea, the sugar seemed to have no effect; the water was loathsome by itself and equally vile when mixed with anything else!

12

BREAKING THE MARETH LINE – 'EL HAMMA OR BUST'

On 21 February 1943 the brigade moved out to El Uotia for a week's training with new tanks, new guns and new reinforcements. It was known that Rommel, now an ill man, had assembled 140 tanks of the 10th, 15th and 21st Panzer Divisions at Medenine. By the 25th 3rd RTR had reached the Ben Gardane area, described by Lieutenant Peter Ross. 'We leaguered in a grove of trees, some in blossom, pink and white. There were olive trees too, lovely delicate things all planted in rows. . . . When we left Tripoli the new CO appointed me battalion navigator, needing mathematical ability, converting grid and magnetic bearings, back bearings, checking mileages. The responsibility was great . . . use of protractors, maps and God knows what else.' Eighteen reinforcements arrived; Major O.G.C. Carey-Thomas became the new 2 i/c; Lieutenant H.E. Kirkham was evacuated ill; and awards were announced, the MC to Captain Hamill, and MMs to Sergeants Rowlands, Stubbs and Trooper Dudley. On 5 March the Army Commander visited 3rd RTR and presented medals to Major Upcott-Gill, Captain Hamill, Sergeant 'Buck' Kite and Sergeant Stubbs. The next day the panzers made a serious attack backed by 1,500 infantry on the defensive line held by 51st Highland Division holding the coastal road area, the 201st Guards Brigade in the centre at Metameur, and the New Zealand Division inland on the left flank. Another classic Monty victory followed as the Eighth Army anti-tank screen, well deployed, destroyed fifty-two enemy tanks in a day, some of them Shermans captured at the Kasserine pass battle on the Algerian/Tunisia frontier.

In the Medenine battle, tank commanders of 3rd RTR were asked for their claims of knocked-out tanks. Sergeant Jim Caswell, 'B' Sqn, 'claimed two and another sergeant three. He was awarded the MM but was killed in the left hook around the Mareth Line a few days later.'

Early in March, the tank state of 3rd RTR was 17 Crusaders and 29 heavy tanks. 'B' Sqn had 15 petrol Shermans, 1 General Lee and 'C' Sqn 13 Shermans. Some horse trading went on and four petrol Shermans were swapped for diesel Shermans from the Staffordshire Yeomanry. Lieutenant Peter Ross's armoured cars were unreliable South African vintage. 'Dead cobras' he called them. Rommel left for Germany on 15 March and the appropriately named General Messe took command of the Afrika Korps, now part of the 'First Italian Army'. The 8th Armoured Brigade now came under the command of General Freyberg's 2nd New Zealand Division. One new phenomenon was the 'Triumphant Entry' into villages and towns where the locals cheered and clapped the RTR arrival, and also proffered wines of various strengths and quality. The CO kept coming on the air with 'navigator, are you *sure* you know where we are?' Ross had a sensible answer: 'Yes, yes I'm quite happy about everything!'

Monty's plan, 'Supercharge II', after the Axis troops withdrew from Medenine was to launch a frontal assault on the Mareth Line. This was a fortified defensive barrier similar to the Maginot Line and built by the French to guard Tunisia. The 50th Northumbrian Division backed by 51st Highland and Indian Divisions would make the main attack on 20 March. Freyberg's New Zealanders and 8th Armoured Brigade would make a 150-mile left hook and flanking movement to turn the Mareth Line defences.

On 19 March the brigade formed up in nine columns, 3rd RTR led by Lieutenant Ross. 'Our tanks were loaded onto transporters. It was a dusty march, carried out mainly by night. No lights were allowed and there was wireless silence. We rounded the Matmata massif 22 miles inland to which the Mareth line extended and headed for the narrow gap between the Jebels Melab and Tebaga, leading to El Hamma.' Bill Close, commanding a troop of 'A' Sqn Crusaders, recollected: 'Later on the terrain became impossible, several transporters becoming bogged down and we were forced to unload the tanks. Moving at night with no lights allowed is difficult for any force, but for tanks it is a nightmare; tank commanders peering out of the turret with dust rimmed eyes, straining to maintain station with the tank in front.'

On the way a fitter's lorry suffered a 'near miss' from a bomb causing six casualties, and a Mk III Crusader was knocked out by a 50-mm A/Tk gun causing three more. On the 21st the New Zealand attack went in on the enemy defences on the

Kebili–Gabes road, with minefields in front of the old Roman wall, marked 'RR' on the maps. The Sherwood Rangers on the right, and the Staffordshire Yeomanry on the left tackled the newly arrived Italian Giovani Fascisti Division. At 2200 hrs in full moonlight the 25th Wellington Battalion and 26th South Island Battalion of 6th New Zealand Brigade under Brigadier Gentry, accompanied by Royal Engineers, cleared gaps in the minefield. They were followed by Major G. Barker's 'C' Sqn of Sherman tanks, 3rd RTR, and jointly staged a brilliant attack through the minefields and captured Point 201, taking 1,500 mainly Italian POWs. On the 22nd the New Zealanders tore a gap in the minefields, and the armour in single file moved through. Monty's main frontal attack on the Mareth Line, however, had failed, with 50th Northumbrian Division taking heavy casualties. 21st Panzer Division and 164th Light Afrika Division were being moved westwards to block the left flanking movement now clearly obvious to the enemy. On 23 March Monty rushed up General Horrocks's 'X' Corps (1st Armoured and 4th Indian Divisions) to support the New Zealand flanking movement. Lieutenant-Colonel 'Flash' Kellett, the popular CO of the Sherwood Rangers, was killed by a shellburst on his tank, and the CO 3rd RTR, Lieutenant-Colonel David Silvertop and his 2 i/c Major Carey-Thomas were wounded by accurate enemy shelling and evacuated. The 2 i/c later died of his wounds.

Operation 'Bootleg', the main attack on the Tebaga gap, was an excellent example of cooperation by all arms. The combined air forces 'blitzed' the opposition's defence with tank-busting sorties (including raids by Kittihawks and Hurricanes of the RAF, RAAF, SAAF and USAAF). The gunners put down huge concentrations of fire and at sunset on 24 March, 3rd RTR and the Sherwood Rangers made a brilliant attack to capture the high ground on the left flank defended by 88 mms. 'B' Sqn Shermans were severely handled by hull-down tanks and A/Tk guns. Lieutenant George Morris 'C' Sqn reported: 'We had turned NE towards Gabes on the coast aiming at El Hamma, a gap in the high ground, good going for tanks. We encountered heavy opposition, the enemy obviously had been alerted of our move to outflank Mareth. They were well established on a ridge some 1,000 yards from where we were obliged to take cover. The other heavy squadron was ordered to attack across the intervening valley and met with stiff opposition, losing some tanks and being obliged to retire. I well remember the Squadron leader (Major

Franklin) screaming down the radio "smoke, for fuck's sake, smoke". We put down a barrage of 75-mm smoke shells under cover of which "B" Squadron regained the ridge.' Sergeant Jim Caswell, 'B' Sqn recalled: 'The Kittyhawk fighters were flying only a few feet above the tanks bombing and strafing a few yards in front of us. We were accidentally on the same wavelength and could guide the pilots to targets with coloured smoke. The brave New Zealanders rode on the back of tanks as far as they felt safe to do so. We were driving over German slit trenches, some German survivors were hurling grenades at us. I saw one New Zealander catch one before it exploded and throw it back towards the Germans with devastating effect. We reached our objective, receiving very few casualties. We were helped by a sandstorm which blew up.'

The enemy defences were 6,000 yards deep, covering the 1,500-yard gap between the hills on each side of the valley. The 3rd RTR lodgement on the high ground was crucial for the main attack. Operation 'Plum' was due to start at 1600 hrs on 26 March. Lieutenant-General Horrocks wrote: 'The tanks of 8th Armoured Bde under Roscoe Harvey advanced up the valley in open order. They thought they were being launched on a second Balaclava but there was no hesitation. The New Zealanders emerged from their trenches where they had been lying up all day and swarmed forward.'

The three armoured regiments were formed up in two long lines at 50-yard intervals across the valley, with the Shermans in front, the Crusaders behind and the carriers in the third line. 3rd RTR were on the left (twinned with the 24th NZ Battalion), Staffordshire Yeomanry in the centre (twinned with 23rd NZ Battalion) and Sherwood Rangers on the right (twinned with 28th NZ Battalion). Fifteen minutes before zero hour (1600 hrs) the RAF got to work with sixteen squadrons of Kittihawk fighter-bombers, covered by five squadrons of Spitfires. They did a great deal of harm in the ranks of 164th Light and 21st Panzer (15th Panzer arrived on the scene the next day).

3rd RTR were hidden up in the wadis around Point 201, a little hill, and formed up close to the mined Roman wall. For the first time an RAF observer in a tank would be in wireless contact with the aircraft to direct them on to targets, and presumably off them too! Sergeant 'Buck' Kite, 'A' Sqn recalled: 'We were to charge a line of guns we'd been watching for a couple of days. They were in concrete emplacements . . . gun, gun, gun . . . one about every 200 yards. We had to get through them and open the road to this place El Hamma. It was very worrying to put it mildly.'

General Freyberg, the NZ GOC had not much faith in British tanks before Operation 'Plum'. But he was reassured by the sight of 8th Armoured Brigade's three regiments forming up and coming down the forward slopes behind the tanks of 2nd Armoured Brigade, part of 1st Armoured Division. Lieutenant Peter Ross wrote: 'Throughout the next morning the bombing continued. Under cover of a sandstorm we moved into our position. The tanks of all three brigade regiments lined up on the remains of the Roman Walls, no more than a bank a foot high. Between the hills stretching right across the gap stood 70 tanks, their engines growling, fifty yards apart. Behind them another 70 and behind them infantry on foot and in carriers. On the back of each tank crouched two or three New Zealand infantry. We were to advance in line abreast. There would be no stopping whatever the opposition . . . The sight of the great grey machines lumbering through the semi-darkness was terrifying.'

Lieutenant George Morris's troop was on the extreme left of the line. 'Off we went over good hard desert, little resistance when suddenly my tank hit a mine and simultaneously one of my other tanks blew up. I only lost a track, the mines were Russian wooden box type captured and used by the Germans, not so damaging as their Teller mine. The following NZ infantry platoon passed through us over a short slope which concealed our knocked out tanks. They were cut down by heavy machine gun fire before our eyes and none survived. The next morning our tracks repaired, we carried on. The slaughter among the enemy was astounding, corpses pinned into their slit trenches with bayoneted rifles. We picked up a number of SS Panzer Grenadiers, nasty fellows, but by then very forlorn.' Captain Bill Close, 'A' Sqn recounted: 'Shortly after we had bypassed the first defences the German anti-tank gunners came to life, hitting several Shermans which burst into flames. The crack of 88-mm guns and the chatter of Spandaus added to the noise and chaos. Two Crusaders on my left were hit, then I saw (Sergeant) Geordie Reay's tank on my right hit. It ended up on its side in a concrete emplacement.' The crew baled out. 'Major Alec Doig was some way to my right, in the centre of a line of enemy anti-tank guns. I saw his tank get hit, some of his crew baled out, but Alec had been badly wounded.' Bill Close was now in command of 'A'

Sqn. The RAF observer was in Major Doig's tank and also became a casualty. 'The Kittihawks were coming over us in waves and taking on targets to our immediate front. I (Bill Close) hoped they were good at tank recognition.' Two hours after the attack, the position was still very confused; the tanks of 1st Armoured Division started to move through 8th Armoured Brigade's positions. 3rd RTR had suffered badly: 'A' Sqn had lost seven tanks and 'B' and 'C' at least ten Shermans. The acting CO Major Upcott-Gill ordered 'A' Sqn to reconnoitre out towards the foothills at first light, where panzers in hull-down positions were attacking from a flank the rear units of 1st Armoured Division. Close's troop corporal's tank was hit, bursting into flames with only two crew members bailing out. Two troops of 'B' Sqn came up and had a pitched battle with the dug-in panzers, dealt with them, but not before losing three of their own Shermans. The 3rd RTR War Diary had one brusque comment: '28th fighting all day', but they found eight 105-mm and four 75-mm enemy guns abandoned in a wadi, and many tanks, guns and ninety POWs were captured by the battalion.

Pockets of Germans fought on all day and night particularly around Point 209 held by 433rd Panzer Grenadier Regiment. Eventually the total bag of prisoners was 6,000 of whom 2,500 were Germans. Under cover of dust storms most of the enemy escaped northwards up the coastal road. The Battles of Mareth and the Tebaga gap were over – the Mareth left hook was a formidably successful operation.

General Freyberg of 2nd New Zealand Division sent a long report of the Mareth battles to his Prime Minister in Wellington dated 16 April. Rather surprisingly, but honestly, he made reference to the battalion. These are quotes from 21 March: 'At 10 pm in full moonlight 6th NZ Brigade accompanied by engineers of 8th Field Coy to clear gaps in minefield and followed by squadron of Sherman tanks of 3rd Royal Tank Regiment staged brilliant attack which went through minefield and captured Point 201 capturing 1,500 Italian prisoners.' Later: 'To gain observation and gun positions a series of operations on both flanks were carried out, one of these was a brilliant attack at sunset on 24 March by 3rd Royal Tank Regiment and Nottinghamshire Yeomanry of 8th Armoured Brigade with most effective co-operation from massed artillery and RAF fighter bombers.' And again, 'Our success was due in no small measure to gallant fighting of British armoured units.'

13

MARETH TO TUNIS – 'ONLY THE TWO THIRDS FIGHTING'

From Wadi Metaba, Oudref, Metouia, Fan Fatnassa and Bouman, 8th Armoured Brigade progressed to Wadi Akarit. On 28 March 1943 the rearguard of the retreating 15th Panzer Division counter-attacked from the left flank near the Wadi Metaba and all three armoured regiments were in action and lost tanks. Gabes was captured on the 30th but the German rearguards were getting away into the hills fast. Sergeant Fred Dale, 3rd Troop, 'A' Sqn recalled: 'We went straight for the coast road and sat on the hill overlooking it, hoping to have a turkey shoot. Alas most of them had gone. Again the chase was on making for Hammanlif about 200 miles away.' On 2 April the Army Commander addressed the brigade and the next day Lieutenant-Colonel Ian Spence, ex-Staffordshire Yeomanry, joined as the new CO, described by Lieutenant Peter Ross as 'a brilliant officer with a warm personality'. And the next day the redoubtable Lieutenant-General Sir Bernard Freyberg VC visited the battalion, to thank them for their part in 'Supercharge II'.

Montgomery's plan now was to capture the ports of Sfax and Sousse to land supplies needed for the final push to Tunis. The next set-piece battle took place on 5/6 April, an action to get across the Wadi Akarit and capture the dominant ridges of Jebel Beida, Roumana and Fatnassa. Three infantry divisions took part, 51st Highland on the right, 50th Northumbrian in the centre and 4th Indian on the left. It was a titanic struggle, and late on the 6th the panzers counter-attacked, aided by First Army Shermans, captured in Algeria and known cynically as 'Rommel's Tank Delivery Regiment'. All three armoured regiments were involved in repulsing the panzers. Peter Ross recalled: 'We suffered heavy casualties. At nightfall we withdrew into leaguer on a forward slope, ¼ mile behind the Gabes–Gafsa road. Mac (RMO Captain MacMillan) was recruiting help from able-bodied men to deal with the wounded. As the night progressed more tanks came in, offloading battered men, some savagely torn, some so badly hurt that all Mac could do was give them morphine to help them die as painlessly as possible.' Lieutenant Peter Ross was applying bandages to a wounded corporal and was ordered by Lieutenant-Colonel Spence to make contact with an American unit from First Army approaching along the road from the west. On his return he brought back a badly wounded German officer for Doc MacMillan to treat. 'He'll fucking well have to die. I've too many of our own chaps to deal with' was the answer. Mac had worked for hours, was exhausted and went on working all night. With his head neatly bandaged the German officer went off in the morning into captivity.

3rd RTR, having survived the Wadi Akarit battle, the next day arrived at Point 183, codenamed 'Bluebird', then the Mahares–Mezzouna railway, codenamed 'Gin', going into action at Seskret el Noval. The battalion were on the brigade left flank and were held up by a panzer force of twenty-six tanks on Point 124, which included captured Shermans and eight brand new Mk VI Tiger tanks. These monsters had just arrived and were destined to dominate the battlefields in the future. On 8 April at breakfast time the battalion knocked out two Mk IVs and a Mk III on the high ground of Chebket en Nouges. The Eighth Army entered Sfax on the 10th in a fertile green coastal belt dotted with French settlements. 3rd RTR was in reserve on the 9th but managed to destroy two armoured cars and acquire eight German POWs. The next day they took La Hencha and by 12 April were on the outskirts of Sousse.

The sound of gunfire ahead, Sergeant Rowlands was dressed smartly (by desert standards) in KD slacks, a black pullover and hanging round his neck a long gaudy scarf and a pair of binoculars. He sported a large waxed moustache. Enter left, a staff car with a red-tabbed staff officer standing up with head and shoulders through the observation hole in the roof. The staff officer asked the sergeant what the situation was up at the front. Rowlands saluted. 'Same as usual, Sir. Only the two Thirds fighting.' 'How come?' said the SO. And the answer, 'The Third RTR and the Third Reich.'

The brigade were ordered towards Enfidaville through El Djem and Sousse, a land of milk and honey, olive trees, fields of rich crops and harvests of poppies, rows of trees, banks covered with wild flowers, yellow daisies and lupins. There were also remarkably pretty European women, refugees from the bombed coastal towns. By 16 April the brigade had advanced by Sousse, Sidi Bou Ali to the area south of Enfidaville. The Italian Trieste and Folgore Divisions were defending Takrouna ridge overlooking the town. 3rd RTR were under the command of 6th New Zealand Brigade. Sergeant Jim Caswell, 'B' Sqn recalled: 'We arrived in front of quite a high hill with a fort on top (christened by 51st Highland Division, 'Edinburgh Castle'). We identified an Italian regiment with white suncaps dug in on the steps on the hill, about 500 yards away. We fired HE and MG at them. One of our tanks, OC Sergeant Peter Toye, became ditched. We drove up behind him to fix a tow rope when a sniper shot me through the neck.' Captain MacMillan dressed the wounds, administered morphine and Caswell eventually reached the 2nd British General Hospital in Tripoli. Lieutenant Peter Ross was wounded by a shell fragment on a recce to the New Zealand infantry. Mac emerged from his white scout car with an enormous pair of scissors 'to cut off your leg, you bloody fool', then 'Hm, nice Blighty one'. Via a Kiwi casualty clearing unit Ross went back to hospital in Tripoli, then to Cairo.

The battalion put in an attack under a barrage on 19/20 April but the enemy still held out on Takrouna ridge although Enfidaville was freed. The Recce Sqn patrolled each day; Sergeant Fred Dale, 'A' Sqn remarked: 'Some valleys were mined and some of the hills were vertical, it definitely was infantry country. We were not much use to them only that they knew we were there. We later watched (the German) 90th Light Infantry Division march in under their own officers.' On 23 April Captains Hamill and Dunlop were sent ahead as observation units. 'B' Sqn destroyed three 20-mm guns. Their tanks drew heavy fire. The New Zealand infantry told them they could take the objective by walking on to it without the noisy RTR to attract attention. Long Stop Hill was captured on the 26th, Massicault on 6 May and at long last Tunis and Bizerta fell on 7 May. In the last week of the North African war 56th 'Black Cat' Division fresh from Syria had time to get a bloody nose in an attack on 11/12 May on Takrouna. Later, the 90th Light, 15th and 21st Panzer Divisions – the old foes – and Marshall Messe and Generals von Arnim and von Sponeck and the rest of the Axis forces surrendered on the 13th. The intrepid 90th Light Infantry Division were led by their divisional brass band who a few days later gave a concert to their captors. The first number was 'We're gonna hang out the washing on the Siegfried line'. Afterwards they challenged their captors to a game of football – and won! As Corporal Geordie Reay of 'A' Sqn said at the time: 'It was a bloody good thing the First Army and the Americans landed when they did, otherwise we'd have been going up and down the desert still.'

14

END OF THE DESERT WAR AND A 'WEARING OF THE GREEN'

The battalion stayed in Enfidaville for about six weeks. The first leave party went into Tunis on 13 May and swimming parties started the next day. On the 20th a great Victory Parade with Winston Churchill present took place in Tunis to celebrate the end of the war in North Africa. Lieutenant J.H. Thompson and four ORs took part and the CO, Lieutenant-Colonel Spence, attended. Major C.B. Franklin, a very experienced 3rd RTR squadron commander was given an unusual duty: he and Brigadier 'Ricky' Richards, OC 22nd Armoured Brigade were the two official escorts to take Generals von Arnim and von Cramer by air to London via Algiers. They had a great deal in common. Von Cramer had at one time or another commanded 15th and 21st Panzer Divisions in the desert campaigns. He had a high opinion of the 3rd Tanks. A quarter of a million Germans and Italians of the so-called First Italian Army (the old Afrika Korps) were now POWs. Major Bill Close had a great respect for his three main opponents but ranked them 21st Panzer, 90th Light Infantry and then 15th Panzer Divisions.

3rd RTR moved on 22 May to the Hergla area: an excellent site close by the sea. Leave parties went off to Algeria and feasted off fresh lobster. ENSA shows, cinema and concerts, Tombola and sports meetings were very good for morale. Those suffering from desert sores and skin complaints found sea water and sulphur springs beneficial. A brigade holiday camp was opened at La Goulette and more awards came through – an MC to Major G.H. Barker and MMs to Troopers J. Cunningham and D. Trotter. But amid this garden of Eden a tragedy took place. Lieutenant-Colonel Spence decided to take his senior officers round the battlefield at Enfidaville, which involved driving through the enemy minefields. The CO and Major A.R. Leakey (just arrived to command 'B' Sqn) in their jeep were alerted to danger when a 'jumping jack' anti-personnel mine exploded behind them and wrecked the following truck. 'We were following in close column making our way slowly out of the danger area,' Close recalled. 'There was a tremendous bang, my jeep leapt into the air and choking black smoke blotted out everything as we crashed to earth. A series of violent explosions followed.' Bill Close received wounds to head and stomach and his driver Lance Corporal Williams died of his wounds. Close went to a casualty clearing station in Sfax then played hockey at the Overseas Club. As a punishment he was sent by the senior doctor Major Morgan back to hospital in Tripoli, not by air, but by road. He was in hospital for six weeks and found the battalion at Homs on his return. 3rd RTR had handed their tanks over to 4th RTR for Operation 'Husky' in Sicily.

During June 1943 training continued and seventy-eight battalion tank gunners helped calibrate guns of Sherman tanks and were duly mustered as gunner/operators. The gunnery tests were very thorough: the British 6-pdr gun versus the American 75-mm, at a 4-foot squared target, 1,500 yards away with 20 rounds allotted. There was also a coaxial gun test on the move at 5 mph. Lieutenant George Morris was battalion gunnery officer at the time, and returned from a course in Cairo in July. 'There was plenty of firing which did my hearing little good. It was a pleasant time, good vino and lots of swimming. Fishing with hand grenades kept us well supplied – welcome exchange to bully beef.' It was likely that in the next campaign 3rd RTR would have three heavy squadrons of Sherman tanks. A Recce Troop was formed with six Dingos and ten Bren-gun carriers.

Every six days a hundred ORs were sent to the holiday camp near Tunis, a great success, but the Military Police processed a large number of charges! On 21 June King George VI visited the brigade at Zavia and the battalion duly gave three cheers. Lieutenant-Colonel David Silvertop returned from hospital and Lieutenant-Colonel Ian Spence returned to the Staffordshire Yeomanry. Two days later 3rd RTR moved to Homs 60 miles east of Tripoli and training courses restarted – distance judging, driving and wireless. Sport was almost top of the agenda and brigade sports meetings were held at the Leptis Magna Roman amphitheatre.

Lieutenant Peter Ross, recovered from his leg wound, returned to 3rd RTR at Homs. The CO, David Silvertop, promptly made him Adjutant. Ross said: 'Brigade had organised a race meeting well advertised among all ranks for which most elaborate sweepstakes had been arranged. One sultry afternoon (9 July) we motored out into the desert to the ochre-coloured "course" stretching endlessly away into the heat haze. A bugle call signalled the opening ceremony. The brigade was drawn up on three sides of a square faced on the open side by Brigadier Roscoe Harvey (a near professional steeplechaser) and his staff.' The Brigade Major rotated the drum. The Brigadier won the first prize of £100, the Brigade Major drew the second winning ticket. Indeed the first ten tickets went to officers. 'Fate sometimes moves in a mysterious way. The soldiers however did not interpret it as *fate*!', wrote Ross. 'The jockeys were local Arabs in full regalia with turbans and robes flying in the wind, having "fixed" every race beforehand. With fiendish yells they continued past the winning post for miles into the pink hazy distances of the desert. MPs chased them in jeeps to bring the winner back for his prize.'

A football league started, also rugger, cricket, hockey, boxing, swimming, athletics and for a few, horse racing. Major A.R. Leakey was very athletic; according to Sergeant Bill Jordan, 'he could run like a hare. In an officers v sergeants game, he played at outside left, me at right half, was I glad to hear the final whistle.' In July Generals Brian Horrocks and Erskine gave talks on the lessons to be learned from Operation 'Husky' in Sicily. The 'X' Corps were now put on alert in Operations 'Manna', 'Woolwich' and 'Bustard', codewords for possible enemy sea or airborne landings in Tripolitania.

During August belatedly the Red Fox's mask flash was issued, worn with pride, but not for very long. There has always been a 'feeling' between smart cavalry regiments and the down-to-earth practical 'tankies'. 3rd Battalion's Brunswick Green colour signifies the title of this poem, penned probably by Captain John Dunlop, certainly someone who knew 'Paddy' Hehir well, the RSM now Lt QM.

A WEARING OF THE GREEN

Oh, Paddy Hehir did you hear the griff that's in the air,
That the Yo Yo boys have won the war and the Third Tanks were not there,
Oh, the Staffs were first in Mersa and the Notts they took Matruh,
When both led to Bhengazi oh, then where the hell were you?
Miles and miles ahead of them a 'probin' Jerry's screen,
A Tank Corps crew far up the 'Blue', a wearing of the Green.

You remember in September when we battered Jerry's flanks,
The Notts ran out of petrol and the Staffs ran out of tanks,
For the Grants they shot the Cruisers up and Jerry shot the Grants,
But the best of what was left did with 'Crisp' column get its chance,
As they swarmed around Himamel learned to see and not be seen,
A Tank Corps crew far up the 'Blue', a wearing of the Green.

When Rommel came to Alamein and Monty rolled him back,
Two famous Gee-Gee regiments were first in the attack,
Oh, the press was full of praises and the flicks were full of shots,
Of the story of the Staffords and the glory of the Notts,
But miles and miles ahead of them a 'probin' Jerry's screen,
A Tank Corps crew far up the 'Blue', a wearing of the Green.

Now when we came to Tripoli and toured around the town,
They went and told the story of the Eighth Brigade's renown,
Oh, they named the Greys, they named the Notts, the Staffords they
    did name,
And how they formed the spearhead all the way from Alamein,
But they never named the boys who were first upon the scene
A Tank Corps crew far up the 'Blue', a wearing of the Green.

Oh, the Eighth Hussars they sailed back home for the Victory
    Parade,
And the Gloucesters and the CLY with their medals well displayed,
Oh, the Tenth Hussars were shining and the Lancers spruce and
    spare,
And the boys were all bull-shitting, but the Third Tanks they were
    where?
Miles and miles behind them digging a latrine,
A Tank Corps crew still up the 'Blue', a wearing of the Green.

Oh, now we wear a Fox's mask but once instead of that,
We did display so bright and gay a crimson desert rat,
And when the show is over and friends ask about the war,
Our proudest claim we have to fame and the proudest badge we
    bore,
Is the little tank upon our sleeve and the flashes that are to be seen,
On any Third Tank crew from the desert 'Blue', a wearing of the
    Green.

On 12 July 7th Armoured Division carried out Operation 'Tortoise', and battalion lectures were given on 'Russia', the 'British Parliament', and 'First American expeditionary force to Tripolitania'. And rumours of a major move were floating as on 14 September a large 'sea party' left for 201 R&T Camp Tripoli to await embarkation moves back to the Delta. Lieutenants Jock Watt and Willy Macfarlane made a mad dash by jeep to the Del Mahari Hotel, Tripoli, then with the rest of the battalion back to the old Beni Yusef camp behind the Pyramids, to Cairo, the Opera Square, the Continental Hotel with its marble staircase and doormen in smart uniforms, and the Opera House Night Club, a balcony box for six above a wing of the stage, watching the belly dancers, listening to the wailing music. Outside in the streets the beggars cried '*Ana muskien, mafi flous*' (I am very poor, I have no money).

Major A.R. Leakey the newest-joined squadron commander was in charge of a 'tank party' of the few remaining tanks (presumably not wanted by 5th RTR!) on a very old merchant ship bound for Alexandria. Slowly, hugging the coastline they eventually arrived there. Both ship and her tank cargo were spurned by the dock officials, so it was on to Port Said. Spurned again they sailed to Suez and were refused permission to land. The skipper of the old tub was happy to sail south to South Africa but Major Leakey persuaded Egyptian State Railways to take the tanks to Cairo, meeting up with 3rd RTR. Anthony Eden visited the battalion on 13 October.

Sergeant Jim Caswell, recovering from wounds in Homs, was collected by Captain Johnny Watts and returned to light duties. But a month later he played rugby for Area 15 in the Cairo sector against the New Zealanders including some 'All Blacks'. On 1 November awards arrived with an MC to Major Bill Close, a bar to the MM for RQMS Stewart and an MM to SSM Quinn. A few days later Lieutenant-Colonel Silvertop took his squadron leaders into the desert to view enemy equipment captured at El Alamein.

On 3 November 3rd RTR boarded a luxury troopship SS *Tegelberg* in Alexandria harbour. Major A.R. Leakey was in charge of the rear party. He believed he was sailing back to England with 3rd RTR, but instead was posted to be 2 i/c 44th RTR then in the south of Italy. The convoy sailed on the 18th and Cambrai day on the 20th was celebrated with difficulty. The troopship called in at Port Augusta, Sicily on 27 November, then the Grand Harbour at Malta, passing Algiers on the 30th.

Dances were held with eighty quite well-chaperoned nursing sisters. ORs slept in hammocks below deck, and eight junior officers shared a cabin. The ship was supposed to be 'dry', but it wasn't.

During the desert campaign from 23 October 1942 to 28 April 1943 when 3rd RTR were part of 8th Armoured Brigade, there were 5 officers and 24 ORs killed, 14 officers and 81 ORs wounded. Awards totalled 9 MCs, 5 MMs and 8 Mentions in Despatches.

The Eighth Army had a great respect for the Afrika Korps. But they not only beat them on the ground but also pinched 'their' most popular song, broadcast every night on the German wireless station in Budapest: 'Lili Marlene'.

> Underneath the lantern
> By the barrack gate
> Darling, I remember
> The way you used to wait
> There where you whispered tenderly
> That you loved me
> Would always be
> My Lili of the lamplight
> My own Lili Marlene.

15

COUNTDOWN TO 'OVERLORD' – 'SO MANY OF MY OLD FRIENDS'

'It was quite pleasant to cruise through the "Med" without daily lifeboat drills. Our naval escort was increased at Gibraltar because U-boats were still operating in the Atlantic. We (Sergeant Jim Caswell, 'B' Sqn) reached Gourock near Glasgow on Christmas Eve 1943 to be rushed by train to Newmarket where home leave passes, ration cards, railway warrants were quickly processed. After being away for over three years I noticed women were now working on the railways. At Carlisle we stopped for a few minutes. I offered 2*d* for the "Times" newspaper but was informed they were 6*d* which I'd not got, so I had one for nothing. In the Sergeants' Mess in Newmarket it was porridge, bacon and mashed potatoes. The "Blighty" Sergeants were all refusing the mash. We had had only Egyptian sweet potatoes which were horrible. We relished the English mash and asked for more.' Bill Close had been parted from his wife for three years and she had joined the ATS. During his leave his promotion to Major and command of 'A' Sqn was confirmed. 'Our commanding officer was David Silvertop from the 14/20th Hussars. Us tankies had somewhat mixed feelings about a cavalry officer ('Donkey Wallopers') commanding a regular tank battalion. There had always been a friendly rivalry between us though we had no illusions about their keenness and ability.'

'Pip' Roberts was now the youngest Major-General in the British Army and in early 1944 now commanded an armoured division originally formed and trained by General Percy Hobart. The 11th Armoured Division, with a Hobart family emblem – a charging black bull on a bright yellow background – had never fired a shot in anger. They had exercise after exercise and were destined for North Africa at one stage. 'Pip' Roberts ensured that '*his*' old tank regiment, 3rd RTR, joined the 'virgins' of 11th Armoured. The 29th Armoured Brigade of 265 tanks which included 3rd RTR, 23rd Hussars and 2nd Fife and

Forfarshire Yeomanry was commanded by Brigadier 'Roscoe' Harvey DSO, MC – again well known to the battalion from their desert campaign. They were equipped with Mk V Sherman tanks, some diesel, many petrol (unfortunately), which were standard equipment. The recce regiment, 2nd Northants Yeomanry were equipped with British-made Cromwell Mk VIIs with a 75-mm gun, two Besa MGs, a top speed of 32 mph, and 28 tons of weight compared to the Sherman's 32 tons.

'We moved to Bridlington on the east coast and joined the 11th Armoured Division', wrote Lieutenant George Morris, 'C' Sqn, 'whose symbol was a bashing black bull complete with a red pizzle on a yellow ground. New tanks arrived, all Shermans including five new models armed with a 17-pounder, 77-mm gun, a great improvement over the 75-mm, for anti-tank use. This troop of "Firefly" tanks was mine. A revolutionary feature was the solid anti-tank shells, known as Sabots, being a small steel projectile encased in a wooden shell, the latter being discarded when the shell left the gun muzzle, the steel cone travelling on at a speed of around 4,000 feet per second, bringing the penetrative capacity up to the region of the Panzer 88 mm. We shot these guns in from a nearby cliff out to sea by arrangement with the Royal Navy.' There was much debate by armoured regiment COs whether to concentrate the limited number of Fireflies or to spread them in penny packets across the squadrons. The Firefly could knock out any enemy tank other than the formidable Tiger head-on. In practice and in action one Firefly was allocated per troop of tanks.

Major Bill Close saw a captured Tiger at the end of the campaign in North Africa. 'Even the side armour was thicker than the toughest part of the Sherman – the 76-mm turret front. The nose of the Tiger was twice as strong as our 50-mm. I looked at the long 88-mm (gun) sticking from the massive turret and swallowed hard. It was quite capable of knocking out any Allied tank at about 2,000 yards, long before we could get near enough to do any damage.'

Within 11th Armoured Division was the 159th Infantry Brigade from the Welsh borders, 1st Herefords, 3rd Monmouths, and 4th King's Shropshire Light Infantry. They were lorried and each had a Vickers machine-gun company from the Royal Northumberland Fusiliers. The 8th Battalion, Rifle Brigade with Bren-gun carriers and armoured half tracks was the motorized infantry support for 29th Armoured Brigade, each company working closely with a specific armoured regiment. The divisional artillery support was formidable. The 13th (Honourable Artillery Company) RHA with their 25-pdrs mounted on Ram tank chassis called 'Sextons', and the Ayrshire Yeomanry with towed 25-pdrs, supported the infantry battalions. Both artillery regiments could synchronize quickly and efficiently their combined forty-eight guns on a divisional target. The 75th A/Tk Regiment had two batteries of the M-10 tank destroyer, an American 76-mm gun mounted on a Sherman chassis. The 58th Light Anti-Aircraft Artillery Regiment had one battery of self-propelled and two batteries of towed Bofors AA guns. Divisional sappers, signals, RASC, RAMC, RAOC, and REME were closely integrated within the division. It was an awesome fighting unit, far better organized and equipped than an armoured division in the desert. But the men were green and untried. So January 1944 was spent near Chippenham. A ceremonial parade was held for General Anderson at Moulton Paddock. Courses were run on the Sherman Mk V. There was wireless practice, and besides leave, amenities offered included a mobile cinema, which showed *The More the Merrier*, and educational films such as *World of Plenty*, and *Dakota*. One lecture given was on the 'Problem of Japan'. A mobile library manned by the WVS, and ENSA shows added to the strange background of preparing again for war. On 6 February training started on the AFV ranges at Kirkudbright in south-west Scotland.

The main body of 3rd RTR moved to Bridlington on the Yorkshire coast in early February and were visited by Monty on the 8th. In the grammar school grounds he gave them a rousing talk and was pleased to see 'so many of my old friends of the 3rd RTR'. Indeed, there were many desert warriors: Majors Bill Close, George Upcott-Gill (2 i/c), Guy Barker ('C' Sqn), Johnny Johnson ('D' Sqn echelons), John Watts, Captains Bill Morris, John Dunlop, Jack Balharrie (Adjutant), Paddy Hehir (Lt QM), Jock Watt, Stubbs and many more. In the sergeants' mess were just as many wearing the Africa Star ribbon: Jim Caswell, Geordie Reay, 'Buck' Kite, Fred Dale, SSM Quinn, RQMS Stewart, Bill Jordan and many others. An important non-military veteran with sand in his shoes was the RMO, Doc MacMillan MC. Brigadier 'Roscoe' Harvey visited on 6 February, Major-General 'Pip' Roberts on the 11th and Exercise 'Eagle' started on the 13th, and again on the 22nd and 24th. Four young second-lieutenants joined from OCTU: Lindquist, Philip Pells, Stuart Montgomery and Robin Lemon. The latter wrote: 'I was 19½ years old when I joined 3rd RTR as Second Lieutenant in Bridlington having trained on Shermans at Sandhurst. With Philip Pells we were sent straight out on to the moors in bitterly cold weather where the regiment was on exercise. Sergeant Salmon an old sweat was most helpful in putting me in the picture.'

Lieutenant Jock Watt found Bridlington to be a lovely peaceful seaside town, with golden sand, a long promenade, the Yacht Club and Spa Ballroom. The tanks were parked under trees in the residential part of the town and crews were billeted in houses. One squadron billeted their officers in a large house near the promenade; one half was occupied by WAAFS. There were of course a number of regimental dances.

The *London Gazette* on 23 February published ten Mentions in Despatches for 3rd RTR Major Alec Doig, Captain Watts, Sergeant Lister, Sergeant Fred Dale, Sergeant Ellis, Sergeant Craik, Corporal Williams, Troopers Wilde, Cook and Tuffs.

Lieutenant George Morris, 'C' Sqn was ordered to demonstrate a Sherman tank on Fylingdale Moor's Gunnery Range to the Corps Commander, General O'Connor, who had been a POW in Italy for nearly two years. 'Without a word he climbed into the turret and said "shoot". So we fired armour piercing projectiles at canvas targets representing tanks at some 1,000 yards. Easy when stationary but not very effective on the move.' Morris then demonstrated firing HE shells at the General's request at the range-limited corrugated iron boards about 3,000 yards away, finally on a flock of sheep. 'The General left without a word seemingly unimpressed with the HE performance.' Nevertheless on 2 March Lieutenant-General Sir Richard O'Connor addressed all officers of the division in the Spa theatre on his Exercise 'Eagle' conclusions.

Waterproofing of tanks and lorries started in May which indicated a 'wet' loading somewhere, presumably across the Channel. 'Beverley IV' (corps wireless) was another exercise and wading practice took place at Hull. Even more exercises followed: 'Frederick Uncle IV' (divisional move), 'Honey' (Recce Troop), 'Tatler' and 'York'. The latter was to prepare a secure welcome for the visit of King George VI, Queen Elizabeth and Princess Elizabeth. Sergeant Jim Caswell recalled: 'We felt the atrocious winter weather after three years of desert sunshine.' At the end of January he had married a girl in the Auxiliary Fire Service and then 'went on a "waterproofing" course in Scotland, to seal tank and guns so we could land on the beaches in up to five or six feet of water.' Caswell was made responsible 'for waterproofing "B" Sqn's twenty-four tanks with Bostick sealing material. In about six weeks they were tested under water. They all passed.'

Major Bill Close, 'A' Sqn had three new troop officers, all ex-infantry: Johnny Langdon, 'Basher' Bates and Bill Yates. 'Johnny Langdon became my most trusted and courageous troop commander, remaining with me until the end of the war, gaining an MC in the process.' Bill continued: 'Our training on the Yorkshire moors was of great value, particularly to the desert veterans who found operating in entirely different country an enlightening experience. It also gave us the opportunity to test out our new officers and tank crews.'

The battalion moved south to Aldershot early in April and shared barracks with the 23rd Hussars, a regiment which had been revived in 1940. In Cobham they saw a demonstration of captured German tanks and AFVs. The panzer divisions were equipped with improved Mk IVs with a 75-mm gun which could penetrate 84 mm of armour at 1,000 yards, and had 80 mm of frontal protection. But Panthers (Mk Vs) and Tigers (Mk VIs) were another matter altogether. The former, a 45-ton beast, could travel at 34 mph, had 1,200 mm of frontal armour and its special 75-mm gun could penetrate 100 mm of armour at 2,000 yards. These awesome statistics were of no comfort at all to the crews of Shermans and Cromwells.

Exercises continued, first 'Mush' then planning for 'Fabius VI', 'Hardwork', 'Martha', 'Bubbles' and 'Red'. Secret operations included cooperation exercises with airborne troops and separately with the 15th Scottish Division. Films on security, lectures on air photograph interpretation took place in May. 'Red' was the codename for an inspection and talk by General Eisenhower to the officers of 'VIII' Corps. On 23 May the first Operation 'Overlord' conference was held for 'VIII' Corps COs, who in turn lectured their own units on the 30th.

Lieutenant Jock Watt, Sergeants Reay and Kite were among a party of twenty from 3rd RTR who went to Buckingham Palace to receive their awards from HM the King. 'As there weren't any VCs there that day, but there was another DCM, I (Sergeant Reay) was the second one to go up and receive my medal. The King said to me "Good show. Keep it up." '

The British Liberation Army (as the force destined for Europe was now called) was well kitted out for war: French phrase books and 200 francs in new 'liberation' notes; 24-hour packs which contained dehydrated meat, dehydrated porridge, four bars of chocolate and chewing gum, plus a hexamite cooker heated by little circular tablets which when ignited by a match gave a very hot flame; little tins of water-purifying tablets; and for some a smart pair of water wings. The lifebelts were called 'Shirley Temples' and the more buoyant 'Mae Wests' were issued to all ranks.

Embarkation leave took place in the same month. It was clear to everyone that an immense invasion plan of, presumably, France was imminent. On 5 June a slightly sinister gas chamber test took place for all ranks, but to recover, 300 ORs were shown propaganda films such as *Battle of Britain*, and *Victory in Tunisia*. On 'Overlord' D+1, with successful landings established on the Normandy beaches, Major-General 'Pip' Roberts briefed divisional officers on 'General situation in France', while the battalion 2 i/c Major Upcott-Gill received a Trace map which gave, after the disembarkation action, the various routes to the divisional concentration area. On 9 June the 3rd RTR move was postponed by 24 hours and the next day the battalion moved into camps near Wapping: camps A-2 and A-13, with RHQ in A-11. Major Peter Burr led the main party into the marshalling area and then Stage 2 of the waterproofing of AFVs was carried out. Major Bill Close noted: 'Our waiting in the concentration area around Southampton was incredibly boring, but finally on 12 June we joined our tanks on the tank landing craft, already loaded some days before.' Sergeant Jim Caswell recalled: 'When all the regiment returned from leave we moved into the New Forest area where we were well concealed under the trees. We were never intended or trained for assaulting the beaches – our role was to break out from the bridgehead.'

Under Lieutenant-Colonel David Silvertop the squadrons were commanded by Major Bill Close, 'A' Sqn, Major John Watts, 'B' Sqn, Major Peter Burr, 'C' Sqn, and Major Johnny Johnson, HQ Sqn. Their respective 2 i/cs were Captains Bernard Hamill, 'A' Sqn, Freddy Dingwall, 'B' Sqn, and Johnny Dunlop, 'C' Sqn. Captain Stuart Farningham was OC the Recce Troop; Major George Upcott-Gill was the battalion 2 i/c; Captain Jock Balharrie, the Adjutant; Captain Ted Anderson, Technical Adjutant. Lieutenant Paddy Hehir was the Battalion Quartermaster and Captain MacMillan RAMC the regimental MO.

On 15 June RHQ embarked on Landing Craft Tank (LCT) *Stokes Bay* with four Sherman Mk Vs and a Sherman bulldozer.

Lieutenant George Morris recollected: 'We embarked from the Portsmouth Hards. There she was, our Tank Landing Ship, a substantial craft on which were to embark 18 Shermans including my five Fireflies. Hitherto we had only practised on a TLC capable of carrying three tanks.' So almost a year after the final victories in North Africa, 3rd Tanks set off to war again, in very different surroundings – no sand or palm trees this time, but peaceful green 'bocage' country, harbouring 'monsters'.

16

OPERATION 'EPSOM' – ENLARGING THE BRIDGEHEAD

Most of 3rd RTR disembarked on 'Juno' beach on 16 June 1944, near Courseulles-sur-Mer, in about 4 feet of water. The waterproofing had been worthwhile. The main convoy had sailed out of the Thames, round North Foreland, through the Straits of Dover and down the Channel. Lieutenant George Morris sailed on a US Navy ship fresh from the Pacific theatre and their Chief Officer said that chains to secure the eighteen Shermans to the decks were not necessary. 'We sailed into a rough sea, the tanks slid about in the hold causing damage to the hull. The hold was hell let loose. With the few men not stricken with seasickness we set about securing our monsters, in the process rendering the waterproofing useless.' In the night their LCT was rammed by another ship. On arrival near Arromanches, Morris refused to land his tanks in 7 feet of water, with faulty or ruined waterproofing. So the US Navy eventually beached their ship on the shore for a dry landing. Major Bill Close's craft was commanded by a bluff old Scottish skipper who shared a bottle of malt whisky and still managed to get his craft and cargo close to shore for a not too 'wet' landing.

'Pip' Roberts visited the battalion on 17 June, and church services were held the next day. On the 18th the CO, Lieutenant-Colonel David Silvertop, attended a conference at 29th Armoured Brigade HQ with Majors Burr, Close, Johnson and Captains Dingwall and Balhousie (the Adjutant). The next day plans for close cooperation were made with the CO of 4th KSLI (King's Own Shropshire Light Infantry) and with the OC of 'G' (motor) Company, 8th Rifle Brigade (RB). These pairings were to last for most of the next year of campaigning. On the 20th all the brigade and regimental VIPs inspected the British tanks knocked out since D-Day, and 3rd RTR's first European casualty (since Calais) occurred, when Trooper G. Hawkins was killed near

Cheux. Two days later the battalion had a sports meeting, won by their new friends, 'G' Company, 8th RB. Most of the division were concentrated round the villages of Cully and Lantheuil. Severe unseasonal gales on 19–22 June had partly destroyed the 'Mulberry' artificial harbour, wrecked hundreds of ships and delayed Monty's plans by three days. On 24/5 June conferences took place for Operation 'Epsom'.

'Throughout the war, the tactics used within an armoured division and its organisation were continually changing. It was not until our third battle in Normandy that we got it right,' wrote the GOC, Major-General 'Pip' Roberts, 'and that was an organisation of complete flexibility. At the shortest notice the organisation could be altered from an armoured brigade and an infantry brigade, to two mixed brigades, each of two armoured regiments and two infantry battalions and artillery as required. All units were entirely interchangeable. It was not until 21 June that we heard about our first operation. . . . 'VIII' Corps was to consist of 11th Armoured Division, 15th Scottish Division, 43rd Division (from 'XII' Corps), 4th Armoured Brigade, 31st Tank Brigade (with Churchill tanks) and 8th AGRA (Army Group RA, with a heavy, a medium and a heavy AA regiment). The operation was to take place about six miles west of Caen. Its objectives were (a) to force a crossing over the River Odon, (b) then over the River Orne: 'XXX' Corps with 49th Division would be on our right, and 'I' Corps with 3rd Canadian Division on our left.' In the event the weather was so bad the attacks by heavy and medium bombers in support were cancelled.

Some of the key codenames for Operation 'Epsom' were Caen = 'Park Lane'; Le Mesnil-Patry = 'Ritz'; St Mauvieu = 'Savoy'; Cheux = 'Green Park'; Le Haut du Bosq = 'Claridges'; Mouen = 'Hyde Park'; Gavrus = 'Piccadilly'; Esquay = 'Continental' and Maltot = 'Scotts'. The staff officers at 21st Army Group naturally had expensive stamping grounds!

'VIII' Corps were concentrated north of the Caen–Bayeux road and 15th Scottish were to lead with two brigades directed on St Mauvieu and Cheux, heading south behind a heavy barrage. Once these two villages were taken, 11th Armoured would pass through, exploit to, and if possible, over the River Odon – altogether a distance of 3 to 4 miles.

Sergeant Jim Caswell, 'B' Sqn commented: 'There was complete devastation of Cheux as 3rd RTR made its way in the dark towards the river; small infantry battles were cracking away in the ruins of the village. The Odon was not very wide and it was the steep wooded valley which caused the most difficulty. The weather was wretched (on the morning of 26 June), almost continuous rain for two days with aircraft being grounded in England. However, we received excellent artillery support as we crossed the river over a small bridge which remained intact. We climbed the south bank of the valley, and it now being light were pleased in the improved weather to find open fields ahead of us, more like tank country.' Trooper Barnes, Caswell's tank driver lived in a cottage alongside the famous 'Epsom' racetrack and promised Caswell a free pass after the war.

South of Le Mesnil-Patry 'A' Sqn were in action at 1615 hrs on the 26th, and engaged three or four Panzer Mk IVs. The Scottish brigades had more or less captured St Mauvieu and Cheux early that morning but it was not until 1300 hrs that 29th Armoured Brigade advanced with a squadron of 2nd Northamptonshire Yeomanry Cromwells on the right flank. The engineer battalion of 12th SS Panzer Division was holding the sector in front of 11th Armoured and south of Cheux (Chooks of course in Army 'English'), and was resisting strongly with tanks, A/Tk guns and infantry. One of the first tank casualties was the Divisional Commander's Sherman which went up on a mine in an *unmarked* minefield laid by the Canadians. General Roberts sent Northamptonshire Yeomanry on their dash for the Odon bridges; 23rd Hussars were on the left flank, the 2nd Fife and Forfar Yeomanry (2nd FFY) on the right and 3rd RTR in reserve. Tiger tanks on the Rauray spur, Hills 112 and 113, just to the south-west dominated the western flank advance. The Northamptonshire Yeomanry lost many tanks with one squadron knocked out, and the Fifes quickly lost nine. By the end of the day the Odon had not been reached, in a badly planned battle. 'Co-operation between 15th Scottish and 11th Armoured was not very close; they rather went their separate ways,' wrote the General.

The end of the first day of Operation 'Epsom' had produced an advance of a few miles in the 'Scottish corridor' where the cream of Scotland: the Gordons, Argyle and Sutherlands, Seaforths and Camerons had taken a terrible beating. The 'bocage' country came as a shock to the armoured regiments – the thick hedges growing on steep banks guarding small fields made excellent tank obstacles; in the sunken lanes lurked Panzer Grenadiers, A/Tk guns and camouflaged panzers. It was a disappointing start. It was also a dangerous and frightening start for the great majority of 11th Armoured and 15th Scottish formations which were in battle for the first time.

The next day the advance continued steadily through Mouen, Colleville and Grainville. At 1230 hrs 'C' Sqn was engaged against a screen of three to six A/Tk guns and six to nine tanks, losing a number of Shermans. Troopers T. Greavy and G. Sproat were killed. Three panzers and two 75-mm SP guns were knocked out. The leading armour reached the River Odon at 1730 hrs. An hour later two squadrons of 23rd Hussars were across, followed by 1st Herefords and 4th KSLI in the Baron area. The GOC wrote: 'I was delighted and relieved to see the tanks of 23rd 'H' winding their way up that hill, 159th Brigade were hurrying forward too. They had to enlarge the bridgehead in the dark and were subjected to both mortar and infantry fire. The Monmouths held and protected the bridge on the north side.' The Germans apparently had no intention of destroying the bridge as it would be required for their (successful) counter-attacks! On 28 June 'C' Sqn was heavily engaged in the Colleville area and lost three Stuarts. Sergeant P. Britt, Corporal E. Folkes and Troopers C. Burton, T. Crookes, G. Kersley, H. Lord (thirty-eight), H. Lord (forty-seven), P. Peters and W. Vane were all killed in action.

A platoon of Monmouths and a patrol of 'G' Company, 8th RB were killed or captured. On the flank of Hill 112, destined to become the most notorious battlefield in Normandy, the bridgehead, 1,000 yards long, extended from Gavrus on the right to the woods north-west of Baron on the left. A mile to the south-west was Hill 113 which overlooked the small town of Evrecy. 23rd Hussars and a company of 8th RB had fought their way up to the crest of Hill 112, although six Tiger tanks in the woods on the southern slopes caused casualties throughout the day. 'In the afternoon we [Major Bill Close, OC 'A' Sqn] received orders from Colonel Silvertop to relieve 23rd Hussars on the hill. A rather daunting proposition as we moved through some of the burnt out tanks of the Hussars.' Lieutenant Johnny Langdon, 12th Troop, with Geordie Reay as his troop sergeant led, with the faithful 'G' Company, 8th RB, commanded by Major Noel Bell, moving closely behind. In the village of Baron intense fire from enemy tanks knocked out a Sherman which burst into flames. 'We remained in these rather negative positions for the remainder of the day. We were able to knock out several anti-tank guns but could make no impression on the dug-in Tiger tanks. We remained in position on this hill for 36 hours. That first night was most unpleasant. We more or less stood to in our tanks as we were practically surrounded.' By nightfall 3rd RTR had relieved 23rd Hussars on the summit with 8th RB dug-in on the crest with the Fifes slightly to the north of the hill. Sergeant Jim Caswell recalled: '3rd RTR was now in the lead and 'B' Sqn fought its way to the top of Hill 112. My tank had a wonderful position from which we could see Carpiquet airfield, the whole of Caen and to the east the river Orne and the Bourguébus ridge ten miles to the south.'

Sergeant Geordie Reay in 'Jig One Able' Sherman, with the rest of 3rd RTR were lined up with 8 RB behind the crest of Hill 112 on the morning of 29 June. Just after a basic but welcome breakfast a deluge of *Nebelwerfer* mortar bombs (known as 'Moaning Minnies' for their horrible wailing noise in the air) descended. 'Jerry knew the range to a T and the bombs were stroking the top of the hill as they went over. HQ got the worst of it (noted Sergeant Kite) and we lost four NCOs who'd been caught outside their tanks.' Colonel Silvertop gave orders for 'A' Sqn to move to the left flank of the crest to take and occupy Esquay village. Mortar bombs landed on Major Close's tank causing a fire. Sergeant Reay advanced his tank to the top of the hill; on one side was Esquay, a clump of trees and a building. In some bushes he saw two SP guns dug in. 'I had a nice hull-down position and cover . . . then people started baling out of the troop corporal's tank on my left but not the corporal, as he and the driver had copped it. A high velocity shell had gone through the tank, though it didn't burn . . . then a tank burst into flame further on my left. It was Geordie's. I heard him say, "We've been hit. The tank is on fire" '. Reay and his gunner, Trooper Etock, and co-driver, Danny Wilson, escaped but all were very badly burned. Lieutenant Bill Yates, 'A' Sqn troop, lost two tanks and was unable to get forward despite their CO's impatience. Lieutenant Johnny Langdon pushed forward, found some cover and started to engage the Tigers on his front. At 1010 hrs RAF Typhoons were called up on 'Lime juice' (a wireless SOS to the RAF) and engaged a dozen Tigers and Panthers and six SP guns of 12th SS Panzer during the day.

Lieutenant George Morris spotted four Ferdinand tracked 88-mm SP guns and engaged them with his Fireflies. 'Near the crest of the hill all hell broke loose, most confused fighting. We had radio contact with a Typhoon Squadron who were armed with formidable 60 pound rockets. We carried canisters of yellow

smoke thrown in the direction of the targets.' During the night
Morris spotted a glowing red light. It came from a radio set in a
half-track vehicle manned by three dead soldiers.

Sgt Caswell, 'B' Sqn recollected: 'From my part of Hill 112 my
tank had plenty of good shooting at dug-in German infantry
about 1,000 metres range. So much so that we ran out of
ammunition and had to go back to the Odon to replenish. Back
in position I could not believe Colonel Silvertop's order to
withdraw. The CO told "B" Sqn leader (John Watts) to withdraw
but there was no response, not from the 2 i/c (Freddy Dingwall).
Eventually I plucked up courage and for one hour or so I was a
Sqn Commander.' During 29 June Troopers A. Bragg, H. Foxon
and R.D. Hillier were killed in action. During Operation 'Epsom'
3rd RTR lost nine Shermans, a Stuart and an armoured car,
mainly from 'A' and 'C' Sqns. Ironically 8th RB with 3rd RTR had
cleared the woods on the southern slopes when the orders came
for 29th Armoured Brigade to withdraw. The codebreakers at
Bletchley had intercepted messages indicating that the newly
arrived 9th (Hohen Staufen) and 10th (Hitler Jugend) SS Panzer
Divisions were about to launch a massive counter-attack from
the Rauray area which would cut off most of the 11th Armoured
Division in control of Hill 112. Major-General 'Pip' Roberts, the
GOC on Hill 112 wrote: 'I had to tell Roscoe Harvey of the
general picture. For the time being we would go on the
defensive. The bridgehead over the River Odon must continue to
be held by 159th Infantry Brigade.' The withdrawal of the armour
was done between 2300 hrs and 0400 hrs. Operation 'Epsom'
was over. During the month of June 3rd RTR suffered fifteen ORs
killed in action and thirty wounded (including Captain
Farningham). The RMO Doc MacMillan, who had tended the
wounded in the desert, now did his best for the badly wounded
Sergeant Reay. 'They can't kill men like you, Sergeant Reay,' he
said. 'Well,' croaked Reay, 'they're having a bloody good try.'

17

COUNTDOWN TO OPERATION 'GOODWOOD'

The three armoured regiments withdrew to Norrey-en-Bessin, 6 miles north of the River Odon bridge, while the infantry battalions tenaciously held their bridgehead until 6 July. Operations 'Martlet' and 'Albacore' had seen a tough defensive battle by 49th 'Polar Bears' Division at Fontenay, Rauray and Brettevillette against the Hohen Staufen Division, the battle group Weidinger and the 12th Hitler Jugend Division. This was the attack predicted by Ultra which would have left 11th Armoured stranded in an untenable bridgehead over the Odon.

On 1 July Brigadier Roscoe Harvey and then the GOC visited 3rd RTR before they spent a few days assisting 32nd Guards Brigade in an attack on Carpiquet. Lieutenant A. Carter and Trooper K. Benson were killed. On the 5th 'B' Sqn knocked out a Mk IV. The RAF shot down thirteen ME 109s who appeared in a rare daylight sortie.

Sergeant Caswell, 'B' Sqn noted: 'the RAF are happier. They have established a landing ground near to our resting and tank servicing area. They were even giving us flights behind enemy lines. Whatever happened to the Luftwaffe?' Trooper L. Slater, HQ Sqn recalled: 'First few weeks in Normandy I spent in an AA Crusader tank fixed with a mounted Oerliken gun. We quickly became redundant with few enemy planes about. We were used for escorting and recce duties. Just before "Goodwood" we were taking two Shermans and a "Gin Palace" as reinforcements to go up to the sharp end. We got stuck in a narrow sunken lane. Something had gone wrong. I jumped out to relieve myself in the woods which surrounded us. Then I got the shock of my life. A group of Jerry infantry were setting up a gun in the woods 30 yards away. I shouted out to Sergeant Jock McCord MM and jumped back into the tank. Jock swung the AA gun round and fired half a drum of .5 mixed rounds into them. The Crusader and Shermans continued round a bend in the road. One of the Shermans was "brewed up" and the other (with Captain Joe Clews) sprayed the woods. All of a sudden it was quiet and the Jerries had gone. The "19" set informed us we had arrived in the middle of a counter-attack.' Slater later watched the RAF bombing Caen and saw four parachutes fall as a crew baled out: 'Wished we were nearer to help them.'

In the two weeks spent recuperating from Operation 'Epsom' and preparing for the next great battle, one unpleasant chore had to be done. Herds of cattle had been unwittingly slaughtered by crossfire during June. The hot summer days meant that for health reasons urgent burial by bulldozing large graves was essential in the Renville village area. Mobile baths, cinemas, NAAFI canteens, ENSA shows and a divisional rest camp by the seaside kept morale fairly high. Lieutenant Robin Lemon:

> Up to the middle of July I had been taking ammunition POL (petrol, oil, lubricant) and rations in 'A1' Echelon up to the tanks which involved several hairy incidents but certainly not enough to know what real battle was like. On arrival in Normandy the Recce Troop consisted of 13 Stuart (Honey) tanks commanded by a Captain (Farningham) and a Subaltern (Jack Thomson) 2 i/c. With their high turrets mounting a rather ineffective 35-mm gun, they made conspicuous targets. Without turrets they provided a low silhouette, were fast with a good cross country performance. Soon the turrets were taken off and the gaps left half covered by the metal engine plates taken from knocked out Shermans and cut into half moon shapes. Browning machine guns were then mounted on these plates and manned by the Stuart tank commanders.'

General Roberts was not a happy man. After 'Epsom' he lost control of 159th Infantry Brigade who temporarily came under orders of 15th Scottish and then 53rd Welsh Division. The two field gun regiments, 13th RHA and Ayrshire Yeomanry were put under command of the 'VII' Corps Commanding Officer Royal Artillery. 'I am left with Division HQ and the armoured brigade', he confided to Major-General Bobbie Erskine, GOC 7th Armoured – who was in exactly the same state! He was to be even more unhappy when the plans for Operation 'Goodwood' were made known. Lieutenant-Colonel David Silvertop had an 'O' group on 10 July and detailed planning started. Since two night marches were involved all tank crews were told to get as much rest as possible.

On the east side of the River Orne, north of Caen, a small bridgehead of 3 miles by 5 miles had been established by the British Second Army. Montgomery's intention was for three armoured divisions led by 11th Armoured Division (in turn led by 3rd RTR) to break out of this bridgehead. Initially they would establish themselves on the Bourguébus ridge which ran east–west 3 miles south of Caen. Some very senior officers thought and said that 'Goodwood' would, if successful, mean the capture of Falaise some 20 miles to the south. 11th Armoured Division were given the objectives (on the right of 'VIII' Corps' attack) of the villages of Bras, Hubert-Folie and Fontenay. But General Dempsey's orders to General O'Connor, and then to General 'Pip' Roberts, was that the 159th Infantry Brigade had to clear the villages of Cuverville and Démouville immediately in front of the start line. Roberts wrote, 'I thought this was all too much. Why could not the 51st Highland Division infantry now holding the front line, get out of their trenches and attack Cuverville and Démouville?' Despite an urgent plea to the Corps Commander that if his division had to follow this plan, then integrated tank/infantry battle groups in which 11th Armoured Division had planned for so long, could not function. General Dick O'Connor refused outright. Moreover, Roberts was told that if he did not like the plan inflicted on him, then another armoured division would lead instead. He gained one concession. Cagny was a heavily fortified village on the left flank and would need to be taken by 11th Armoured before they could swing right (west) to their main objectives. Roberts was allowed to mask Cagny; that is, keep it subdued from a distance without an all-out attack (which in the event caused Guards Armoured Division a bloody nose).

Montgomery had organized a massive air bombardment on most of the strongpoints of the prepared defences. But Second Army Intelligence thought that they only extended to 4 miles from the start line. Actually the defences were *10* miles deep in five carefully planned 'lines'. In the first line were two infantry divisions; the second had the armoured divisions of 21st Panzer, 503rd Heavy Battalion of Tiger tanks and part of 1st SS Panzer Division. The third layer consisted of a dozen fortified villages and hamlets, with infantry and A/Tk guns. On the crest of the Bourguébus ridge was the fourth line with no less than 78 88-mms, plus most of the 194 field guns and 272 Nebelwerfers that Rommel had available in the Caen sector. There were even more defence lines of villages on the plateau with 1st SS Infantry Division, and the ultimate reserve was the battlegroup of 12th SS with forty tanks and a Panther tank battalion of 1st SS. There is little doubt that Rommel's many defence lines had not been correctly identified. Even if the RAF bombing and artillery barrages destroyed the first two or three lines, it can be seen that Operation 'Goodwood' was doomed from the beginning. 11th Armoured Division, moving on a very narrow front, were about to put their heads and tanks into a mantrap!

General 'Pip' Roberts did his best. He ensured that 'I' Corps made enough gaps in the various minefields, that they were widened and well signed. He tried to support his own 159th Infantry Brigade, attacking the two villages of Cuverville and Démouville, a mile and a half ahead, by allocating the divisional reconnaissance regiment, 2nd Northamptonshire Yeomanry with Cromwell tanks to support them. He made sure that Guards Armoured Division would tackle the defences of Cagny. Two units of General Percy Hobart's 'Funnies' (79th Armoured Division) were allocated to him, 26 Assault Sqn REs with Churchill tanks with spigot bombards for cracking open strongpoints, and 'A' Sqn flail tanks of 22nd Dragoons, whose Sherman 75-mms would turn out to be helpful. The 3rd RTR group now included 'H' Battery, 13th RHA with Sexton 25-pdr SP guns and 'G' Company, 8th Rifle Brigade.

Ironically the day before Operation 'Goodwood', Field Marshal Rommel, the architect of the Caen plain defences, was seriously injured by RAF fighter-bombers and was carried unconscious to the village of Ste Foy-de-Montgomerie.

Lieutenant Robin Lemon:

We lay hidden all day on the 17th, and that night the regiment crossed the river Orne into the concentration area in the bridgehead. Traffic control must have been a nightmare. There was dust and more dust, as our tanks rumbled through the night. Dawn broke bright and clear, as the light grew stronger, the shapes of the 6th Airborne gliders that had landed on D-Day appeared all round us. When it was much lighter bombers in their hundreds began to stream overhead to wreak devastation on the ground over which we were to advance.

What softening up! It did our morale good. The Recce troop was positioned behind the two leading squadrons on call for any task that may be required.

Major Bill Close, OC 'A' Sqn recalled: 'At my CO's 'O' Group, I learned that 3rd RTR were to lead the attack with my "A" Squadron on the right, "B" Sqn on the left and "C" Sqn in reserve.' The final 'O' group at 1600 hrs on the 17th, aerial photographs were handed round. 'The Fife and Forfar were to be right behind us and 23rd Hussars and the rest of the brigade bringing up the rear. Our job was to press on ignoring any opposition from the villages which should have been flattened by then, and having crossed a couple of railway lines on the way, establish ourselves behind Bourguébus. Any Panzers which got in the way, were to be destroyed.' Close went back to brief his troop leaders. No one was really happy at the idea of bypassing the villages. 'We had been told the zone of fixed defences was only *three* miles deep.' Then having instructed his tank crews to prepare their tanks for battle and get a brew of tea, he and Major Noel Bell, OC 'G' Company, 8th RB, walked down to inspect the minefield entrances with taped lanes, guarded by immaculate Provost NCOs – white belts and gaiters and of course red caps.

18

'GOODWOOD' DAY ONE – 'DARK SHAPES ROLLED ON THE GROUND'

The 3rd RTR War Diary in the usual laconic way noted: 'H-Hour 0745, tanks falling behind line of barrage due to speed of barrage, nature of country. 0800 Le Mesnil Frementel reported clear. 0805 reached Matilda difficult crossing railway line, unexpected depth of cutting, temporary loss of barrage.' The regimental column had formed up with 'A' and 'B' Sqns, then the second wave of RHQ, Recce Troop, carrier platoon; a troop of flails, half troop of RE AVRE Churchills, and then the third wave, Reserve Squadron 'C', plus 8th RB Motor Company, and a battery of 13th RHA Sexton SP 25-pdrs. Lieutenant George Morris, 'C' Sqn recollected: 'I studied the overlay map of the fire plan directed on a front of only a few miles wide and deep. One heavy regiment of 9.2-in guns, two medium 4.5-in and 24 regiments of 25 pounders plus a 2,000 bomber raid. We were to follow behind a creeping barrage. We were among the inferno of shells. My Squadron Leader (Major Peter Burr) had his head blown off, blood cascading into the tank. My tank was knocked out by an A/Tk gun. In spite of the enormous fire put down the German resistance was still intact, the fire coming from a number of Mk V Panther tanks well dug in, practically indestructible.' The War Diary continued: '0830 Grentheville bypassed on west side: 0930 crossed railway line 074624. 1000 reached 070623 engaged enemy tanks and A/Tk guns area Hubert-Folie 072618.'

3rd RTR had been sitting in their tanks since 0545 hrs watching the RAF armada of planes saturating the area in front and, at H-Hour (0745 hrs), watching and listening to the 600-gun barrage firing ahead on a 2,000-yard frontage. In 'A' Sqn young Lieutenant Philip Pells, 3rd Troop Commander, had been caught outside his tank and killed by a stray shell from the barrage. Major Close told his troop sergeant Freddie Dale to take over

Pell's troop; 3rd RTR adopted a square formation with the two leading squadrons lining up side by side and half squadrons of the third ('C' Sqn) forming the sides of the box, with the RHQ command tanks and vehicles in the centre, and 13th RHA SPs closing the rear.

After Major Peter Burr's tragic death, Captain Jock Balharrie took command of 'B' Sqn. Burr had been with 3rd RTR in the desert as Adjutant to 'Pip' Roberts when their Grant tank was knocked out at Gazala. For a time there was confusion at Burr's loss. Another serious blow to the GOC was the destruction of the RAF Link Forward Observation Officer (FOO) whose tank was knocked out early in the battle and not replaced. There was no facility to call down by radio 'Lime Juice' on selected targets. Yellow-coloured shells might produce air support – just might!

'There was little opposition to begin with. A number of Germans shaken by the preliminary bombing and shelling came out of their foxholes and gave themselves up. Others seemed to be staggering around in a daze.' Lieutenant Robin Lemon with the Recce Troop shot a German with a grenade in his hand. He noted that an RE AVRE with a 'dustbin' did an excellent job in blowing holes in the embankment. 'Stiffer opposition was met as Le-Mesnil-Frementel was approached. One of the Honey tanks was knocked out on the left flank. I saw several Shermans being engaged and brewed up.' Lieutenant Osbaldeston, a Troop Commander 'C' Sqn, was killed at an RHQ ORs group.

The railway cutting on the Caen–Troarn line, despite the AVRE bombards, caused considerable delay. Sergeant Jim Caswell, 'B' Sqn commented: 'We had advanced about 1,000 yards but found the railway embankment steeper than expected. This slowed us down considerably in our advance and gave the enemy time to recover. We also lost our artillery barrage. To make matters worse we heard over the radio the Guards Armoured were late in arriving.' Major Bill Close, 'A' Sqn, sent a radio message back asking for the artillery barrage pause to be extended as tanks were slowly deploying through the railway tunnels. 'Two tanks had shed tracks crossing the permanent way. It was clear that wheeled vehicles would have trouble when they arrived at the railway so I called up the sapper AVRES to blow gaps in the embankment and bulldoze a road through it.' Close reorganized 'A' Sqn during the pause. The 17-pdr Fireflies – four of them – were echeloned behind the standard Mk V Shermans in line abreast, 40 yards apart. The leading tanks met the railway line at 0920 hrs and the leaders were across a quarter of an hour later.

The CO, Lieutenant-Colonel Silvertop, ordered Lieutenant Lemon to climb the embankment on foot, observe the other side and report back to him. 'I could see all the ground from Soliers up to Bourguébus. The battle was raging there and I saw several German tanks. Two separate battles were going on with enemy tanks literally on a level with ours but only separated by the high railway embankment.' Major Close could see Lieutenant David Stileman's Rifle Brigade carriers rounding up prisoners and escorting them to the rear. He ordered Lieutenant Johnny Langdon, his 1st Troop Commander, 'Sugar One, move out to your right. Anti-tank guns firing from the orchard area, use your machine-guns to keep their heads down.'

The GOC, 'Pip' Roberts commented: 'Having got over the embankment, TAC HQ followed the armoured brigade's route. There was some firing on our left. We caught up with (Brigadier) Roscoe Harvey in a wooded area facing up to a little hamlet called Le Mesnil-F02rementel, about 1,000 yards west of Cagny. The area where Roscoe was being heavily mortared, the flail tanks were firing at the hamlet and on the left, some 300 yards nearer Cagny, a whole squadron of the Fife and Forfar Yeomanry, all knocked out and some burning. (Colonel Hans von Luck had ordered four 88-mm guns of a Luftwaffe AA regiment – at pistol point – to fire in an anti-tank role on the unfortunate Shermans of the Fife and Forfars). It was rather a daunting picture. I had to go up, mortars or no mortars and find out the form.' Roberts went forward and saw that 3rd RTR, moving in a south-west direction, had put a squadron across the railway embankment; the Fifes were moving south bypassing Le Mesnil-Frementel being cleared by flail tanks; and 8th RB, and 23rd Hussars were well back on the left keeping the route open for the Guards Division – when they arrived. But when 3rd RTR and 2nd FFY pushed across the railway line they were soon checked not only by resistance from the villages ahead – Fours and Soliers – but also by Panthers and SP guns arriving on Bourguébus ridge.

'The reports coming over the air were fast and furious and I saw more of our tanks being brewed up. Lieutenant Stubbs "C" Sqn, notoriously bold and dramatic encountered an enemy tank. Both traversed on each other. There were tense moments before Stubby reported he had won,' noted Robin Lemon. Lieutenant Gibson Stubbs had won an MM at Sidi Rezegh in June 1942 and was now to win an MC by knocking out a Panther and Mk IV tank around Hubert-Folie and Bras.

On the right flank 159th Infantry Brigade reached Cuverville and cleared it by 1015 hrs and Demouville by 1430, aided by Cromwell tanks of 2nd Northamptonshire Yeomanry. The CO told Major Close, 'in no uncertain terms to get "A" Sqn moving on towards Grentheville, some 1,500 yards on my front. I could see "B" Sqn on my left had two tanks hit which were blazing furiously. Hatches flew open. Dark shapes rolled on the ground. The corn caught fire.' Sergeant Jim Caswell, 'B' Sqn recalled: 'The right flank of my squadron was threatened by three camouflaged Tigers concealed in a wood to our left on Bourguébus ridge. Most of our 20 tanks were hit in a matter of minutes. I spotted an 88-mm gun pointing at me. I saw the terrible flash of its muzzle and heard the shell whistle by. I ordered my driver to reverse which he did – promptly. A few yards gone when another shell hit us. There were 3 of us in the turret. The navigator was killed outright and my wireless operator was seriously wounded.' Trooper Bill Slater was killed and Stan Duckworth seriously wounded in both legs. The front gunner Trooper Russell had been singing 'Come come Vienna mine' just before the shells hit. Trooper Barnes, the driver did his best to get the tank to safety. Sergeant Jim Caswell, wounded in his left knee, got out of the tank, administered morphine to Duckworth and *carried* him for an hour to an Advanced Field Dressing Station. Caswell then spent three months in hospital and on convalescence leave. 'The RAP was hard pressed. My (Lieutenant Robin Lemon's) next task was to collect the wounded and take them back to the MO (Captain MacMillan MC). With our turretless Honeys we motored through the high corn and picked up as many wounded as we could. I picked up two of Johnny Langdon's wounded crew members. One was very badly wounded and he died later.'

General 'Pip' Roberts noted that at 1100 hrs 'the whole of 3rd RTR were west of the embankment and had received casualties from right and left. The 23rd Hussars were facing up to Grentheville, east of the embankment, with one squadron further east facing the village of Fours, from where 2nd F&F Yeomanry had lost many tanks from one Panther and some A/Tk guns.' By midday fierce battles – rather one-sided ones – were being fought north of Cagny and towards Frénouville. The traffic congestion through the minefields behind meant that Guards Armoured and

7th Armoured were, like Blücher at Waterloo, rather late in arriving on the battlefield. The 3rd RTR War Diary notes: '1400 position 070623 covered by tanks and anti-tank guns, withdrawn to 072628.' At 1445 hrs the expected enemy counter-attack came in launched from the Four–Frénouville area by Panther tanks. Although six were knocked out the Fife and Forfars were again badly mauled with thirty-eight killed in action during Operation 'Goodwood'. Continued pressure on the left flank forced a withdrawal to the area of Grentheville cleared by 8th RB.

As 'A' Sqn approached Grentheville Major Close could see crews of anti-tank guns swinging their weapons into action. 'Nebelwerfer bombs howled overhead. There were some twenty or thirty gun positions out in the cornfields in front of the village. Woompf . . . a Sherman right next to me burst into flames and two more were ablaze within minutes. "B" Squadron on my left were also receiving an alarming number of casualties.'

When 'A' and 'B' Sqns – what was left of them – were within 500 yards of Bras and Hubert-Folie all hell was let loose. Intense fire from every direction fell on all three squadrons. The corn was blazing and crews were dying as they rolled in agony on the ground. The Rifle Brigade carriers and half-tracks came up to the wrecked tanks and did their best to rescue their crews. Major Close's tank was hit and the crew baled out unhurt. Lieutenant Bill Yates was wounded and Sergeant Mason commanded his troop. Sergeant 'Buck' Kite was sent right to flank Bras and deal with Panthers lurking there. Ammunition and petrol were getting low. By any standards it was a desperate situation. Lieutenant-Colonel Silvertop now ordered the shattered regiment over to the west side of the Caen–Bourguébus railway. From Caen three railways crossed the path of the 'Goodwood' armoured advance. Although they were ideal ranging points for the enemy gunners on the lee-side, they offered some protection from shells.

Lieutenant Johnny Langdon and Sergeant 'Buck' Kite had both lost two tanks from each of their 'A' Sqn troops. 'Buck' Kite now earned another Military Medal by engaging the enemy A/Tk guns with his Firefly, its 17-pdr gun knocking out two quickly; the latter hit two enemy SP guns and burnt them out. Each of the leading squadrons had FOOs of 13th RHA with them. 'H' Battery took seventy-five POWs during the day, had one FOO killed and another wounded. More importantly they brought down fire on the villages ahead. Sergeant Buck Kite, 'A' Sqn recalled: 'Bras is at the top of a slope beside a small wood. We started copping it there and I fired back hitting a couple of SP guns and a tank before the Sherman on my left brewed up. The crew baled out and came over to my tank carrying the gunner, a Scots lad called Hume who played for the battalion football team.' Kite reversed his tank to the bottom of the hill and met Captain MacMillan the RMO who was in the thick of the battle in his half-track. Hume died in hospital. 'By the time I got back up the hill we were getting it really badly and my tank was hit two or three times but not penetrated.' When later in the day Brigadier 'Looney' Hinde, CO 7th Armoured Division's tank brigade, surveyed the battlefield, he told Major-General 'Pip' Roberts: 'There are too many bloody tanks here already. I'm not going to bring my tanks here.' Hinde, an experienced desert warrior, failed to realize that at least half the Black Bull Shermans he could see were knocked out, blackened and motionless; 3rd RTR at the end of the first day had only seventeen battleworthy tanks.

The General noted:

At 1720, 2nd Northants Yeomanry were west of the railway embankment facing W and NW linking up with 3rd RTR who were facing south towards Bras and Hubert-Folie. 23rd Hussars were in Grentheville and Four. 2nd Fife & Forfar were in reserve reorganising 1,500 yards north of Grentheville. At 1800hrs
7th Armoured Div started to arrive directed on La Hogue, south of Four. Up until 2200 hrs small but strong counter-attacks by Panthers and some Tiger tanks continued but were driven off with losses by the armoured regiments helped by the SP anti-tank batteries. Our tank casualties had been heavy. 23rd Hussars had lost 26, 3rd Royal Tanks 41, 2nd Fife & Forfar 43 and 2nd Northants Yeomanry 16.

The CO saw that 3rd RTR were losing tanks all the time on the attacks on Bras and Hubert-Folie, so for the rest of that long hot day the battalion stayed in 'negative' positions, unable to get forward. The War Diary recorded: '1700 further shelling by tanks and anti-tank guns withdrew to position 075637: 2100 fired on by four Tiger tanks from 083634: 2200 fired on by 3 Tiger/Panther tanks from Bourguébus ridge: 2215 6 Sherman tanks knocked out: 2230 withdrew to leaguer at 076638 – 12 tanks in leaguer.' RHQ down by the embankment was heavily bombarded. A German OP was dug-in nearby. 'Just before the light faded a terrific "stonk" came down on us and one shell landed on my tank,' Lieutenant Robin Lemon noted. 'No one was hurt but we had to bale out. As more shells exploded all around us we crouched between the tank and the railway embankment. My operator then took a photograph of me.' 'A' Sqn leaguered beside a quarry near the railway embankment. Lieutenant Maurice Thompson from the Recce Troop 'supplied' two troop officers to Major Close. Captain Bernard Hamill, his 2 i/c, had been badly wounded, but Lieutenant Johnny Langdon was only slightly wounded and shaken and rejoined 'A' Sqn. 'B' Sqn OC Jock Balharrie, though knocked out and wounded, rejoined the battalion.

At the end of an exhausting and frustrating day the death toll was grim: Major Peter Burr, Lieutenant D. Osbaldeston; Second Lieutenant R. Pells; Corporal J. Smethurst; Lance Corporal E. Crisp; Troopers G. Wilson, A. Turner, J. Swift, H. Spencely, M. Allbrooke, A. Barned, Lance Corporal J. Chipping, Trooper R. Clarke, S. Cusworth, R. Snape, W. Slater, A. Hartnell, J. Hooper, M. Hume, J. Lyons, and E. Mellor. In addition four officers and thirty-five ORs had been wounded.

19

'GOODWOOD' DAY TWO – 'ENGAGED ENEMY GUNS AT POINT-BLANK RANGE'

During the night the Luftwaffe bombed the salient and the bridges back over the Orne. *Brigadeführer* Theordor Wisch commanding the 1st SS Panzer Division (Leibstandarte), had launched a series of counter-attacks with his eighty Panther Mk IV special tanks around Frénouville and Roquancourt. At close range he saw forty British tanks go up in flames, although many of them were abandoned derelicts knocked out during the day. The counter-attacks continued into daylight on the second day of Operation 'Goodwood', while 3rd RTR stubbornly held the salient gained between Bras and Soliers. Wisch admitted to losing twelve Panthers and a light tank in his counter-attacks.

The 3rd RTR War Diary notes: '0430 broke leaguer and took point of observation in area 076638: 0800 move to 084658, period of reorganisation: Two squadrons formed "A" under Major Bill Close, "B" under Major J.A. Watts, "C" personnel and tanks divided between "A" and "B".'

The good news was that 159th Infantry Brigade had come up to join in the battle, and that several medium artillery regiments were now within range and on call for the next attacks. The arrival of eleven replacement Shermans brought up by the Tank Delivery Squadron (OC Captain Joe Clews) enabled 3rd RTR to make up three squadrons each of ten tanks. The LOB (left out of battle) personnel came up from echelon to make up numbers.

General O'Connor the Corps Commander held a conference at the GOC's TAC HQ at midday. His plan was that, '11th Armoured Division at 1600 hrs would capture Bras on its eminence, despite the 88-mm guns covering it, and thereafter its satellite village Hubert-Folie. An hour later 7th Armoured would undertake the major role by capturing Soliers and then taking Bourguébus. At the same time Guards Armoured Division were to attack Le Poirier and exploit towards Frénouville.' 'Pip' Roberts called an 'O' group for 1400 hrs on the embankment, 1,000 yards north of 29th Armoured Brigade TAC HQ. The plan was for the recce regiment 2nd Northamptonshire Yeomanry to support 8th Rifle Brigade into Bras, and 3rd Monmouthshires (from 159th Brigade) would complete the clearance. The 8th RB would advance from Bras to Hubert-Folie with 3rd RTR, with 4th KSLI following up, to occupy and hold the two villages. While the reorganization took place and plans were being made, enemy shelling around 3rd RTR area during the morning was intense.

Major-General 'Pip' Roberts recalled: 'On the previous day 3rd RTR had lost two or three tanks from 88-mm guns firing from the little village of Ifs some 2,000 yards west of Bras.' Roberts personally warned the CO of 2nd Northern Yeomanry (2nd NY) not to get *too far* north of Bras or he would run into trouble. Despite this advice 'his regiment went too far west and immediately lost five tanks. They therefore withdrew in some disorder. The CO (Lieutenant-Colonel Silvertop) seeing what had happened requested Roscoe (Harvey, the Brigadier) that 3rd RTR should take on the supporting role for Bras. This was agreed. 2nd NY were told to reorganise themselves and prepare to support 8th RB in their attack on Hubert-Folie from Bras. The Bras operation went well. It was held by 3rd Bn No. 2 SS Panzer Grenadier regiment and such was the dash of 3rd Royal Tanks and the effective mopping up of 8th RB that almost the whole garrison was either killed or taken prisoner. 3rd Monmouths following up, took over from 8th RB.'

Generals have to present an optimistic viewpoint of all the battles they fight. Undoubtedly General 'Pip' Roberts was one of the finest divisional commanders of the Second World War. But on the ground events were not quite as positive. The Battalion War Diary noted: '1445 Brigade ordered to take Hubert-Folie, 2nd NY to attack Bras at 1600, immediately after 3rd RTR to attack Hubert-Folie under full artillery support; 1600 2nd NY move towards Bras, not able to enter village. CO suggests, Bde agreed, 3rd RTR to take Bras: 1625 Bn move towards Bras: 1640 Bn on edge Bras, progress slow due to rubble (heavy bombing result), snipers, bazooka teams: 1615 8th RB arrive to mop up in Bras, Bn tanks withdraw north from Bras; 1800 CO asks Bde if possible to withdraw to reorganise for 24 hours back to 'A' Echelon: 2100: leaguered 105670 at 2300.'

'We were very short of officers, both the other Sqn leaders (Burr and Watts) had become casualties and all but one of my troops were commanded by Sergeants,' Major Bill Close commented. 'The artillery was as good as its word and an excellent smokescreen enabled us to move up the slope rapidly and properly, troop by troop, giving each other supporting fire. When we made the final assault I had five tanks left in "A" Sqn, "B" Sqn (Captain Dingwall) had about the same number and "C" (Captain Dunlop) four. The enemy had machine-gun emplacements in the houses, infantry in the cellars and there were anti-tank guns in the gardens and behind walls. But we were able to get right up to the edge of the village and engage the enemy guns at point blank range. We fired AP shot through buildings and even knocked down walls and parts of houses by ramming them. With two of my remaining tanks I took up a position on the western end of the village and held off German tanks which tried to come in from that side. We had a very good shoot.' Lieutenant Gibson Stubbs, 'C' Sqn led his troop into Bras with dash and quickly pushed through it, although it was garrisoned by 300 infantry of 3rd Battalion, 1st SS Panzer Grenadier Regiment. He destroyed a Mk IV and when his 75-mm tank gun was damaged, he dismounted his crew and engaged the enemy with small arms.

Allan Cameron Wilson, 'C' Sqn recalled: 'We counter-attacked near to Soliers with rather scratch crews, Stubby (Lieutenant Stubbs) led we three tanks (supposed to be in reserve) straight at Hubert-Folie (Bras in fact) and we captured it. I took an SS Major and 14 men prisoner with my empty pistol. Then the Rifle Brigade took them off to the cages.' Lieutenant George Morris, 'C' Sqn, after losing his tank on the first day remarked: 'I was sent back to our transport lines to organise a left-out-of-battle reserve of officers and men. A thankless job and quite demoralising, the only way to be involved in war is in the firing line.'

Two of Sergeant 'Buck' Kite's troop of tanks were hit by heavy anti-tank gun fire on the way up the slope. Major Close could see several other tanks of 'B' and 'C' Sqns also hit and blazing furiously. Lieutenant Johnny Langdon led his troop between the two villages, knocking out two Panthers in the process but once again losing two of his tanks, including his own. 13th RHA FOOs supporting 3rd RTR put down stonks on both villages for most of the afternoon. When Major Close's own tank was hit by an 88-mm shell, killing his driver and co-driver, he sent the two survivors back to the railway embankment and took over Sergeant Freddie Dale's tank. When 'B' and 'C' Sqns entered Bras they were reduced to two or three tanks each. German anti-tank guns in Ifs continued to hammer tanks of 29th Armoured Brigade throughout the day. Close admitted: 'We were completely unable to advance (beyond Bras). The whole brigade was pinned down.' RAF fighter-bombers made sorties on the many fortified villages in Rommel's third, fourth and fifth defensive lines. But eventually Hubert-Folie was taken by 2nd Fife and Forfars. Both key villages were then occupied by 3rd Monmouths and 4th KSLI. But the key German defences on Bourguébus ridge remained intact.

The Guards Division captured Le Poirier and 7th Armoured took Four. At 1900 hrs Lieutenant-Colonel Silvertop rallied the remaining 3rd RTR tanks on the western edge of Bras. As he was holding his 'O' group by a Dutch barn a shell landed in the middle, killing Lieutenant Maurice Thompson, Recce Troop OC, and two other RTR crew members.

During the second and final day of Operation 'Goodwood' 3rd RTR lost sixteen tanks. 'A' Sqn started with nineteen Shermans and lost seventeen of them, over half completely destroyed. All Bill Close's officers were casualties and only one troop sergeant, 'Buck' Kite, was with him by the end of the battle. In two days 4 officers had been killed and 21 ORs, 11 officers wounded and 67 ORs. On 19 July the battalion losses killed in action included Lieutenant J. Thompson, Sergeant J. Dickson, Sergeant T. Yeomans, Lance Corporal S. Harris and Troopers S. Hart, W. Jordan, S. Petch and R. Russell.

'Goodwood was a shambles, but only because the method of advance was forced on us without infantry support to clear up the villages. Certainly the fact that 159th Infantry Brigade were divorced from 29th Brigade for practically the whole of the first day had a great effect on the conduct of the battle,' wrote Major Close. Colonel von Luck, the experienced German battlegroup commander who played a key role in 'Goodwood' (for his side), suggested that German troops trained on the Russian front would have done things differently: 'Our attack would have been made very early in the morning with one infantry division in front assisted by armoured assault guns to break through the first resistance followed at *once*, by armoured divisions to break through.' General 'Pip' Roberts wrote in his autobiography: 'The real set back was the enemy gun position along the Bourguébus ridge. In all there were 78 88-mms, 12 heavy flak guns, 194 field guns and 272 eight barrelled Nebelwerfers. These were scarcely touched by the bombing and were out of range of the majority of the Corps artillery which was on the west side of the River Orne.'

Not only were the Bourguébus defences not taken out by the massive RAF preliminary bombardment, but the lack of target direction to the RAF Typhoons (since their FOO link had been knocked out) meant that during the two-day battle the enemy tore 11th Armoured Division tanks to pieces. Nearly 200 had been knocked out during Operation 'Goodwood'.

Major Upcott-Gill, 2 i/c, Major John Watts, Captain Hamill, Lieutenant 'Basher' Bates, Lieutenant Hudswell, Lieutenant Wilfred Brooks, Lieutenant Stuart Montgomery, and Lieutenant Harry Bennett were all wounded (Lieutenant Johnny Langdon and Captain Balharrie were wounded and carried on!).

That evening a violent thunderstorm burst over the battlefield; 'II' Canadian Corps took over the 30 square miles so painfully gained by 20 July. Two days later 11th Armoured moved back across the River Orne, concentrated north of the Caen–Bayeux road and awaited reinforcements of men and replacement tanks.

20

OPERATION 'BLUECOAT' – 'SOME BEAUTIFUL STONKING'

On Thursday 20 July it was clear that the three armoured regiments of the division were in a critical state. The Commanding Officers of each had been told that either they would reorganize their regiments and get immediate reinforcements to be ready to go back into battle *in full strength* within five days or else the whole 29th Armoured Brigade would be taken out of the line and be completely re-equipped, which would take about six weeks. Moreover, there would be no guarantee that they would fight again, either as individual regiments or as a brigade. General Miles Dempsey, the Army Commander told journalist Chester Wilmot that replacement of Sherman tanks was no problem. There were about 500 piled up in the bridgehead. But replacement of trained crews and commanders was a problem. Major Upcott-Gill's place as 2 i/c was taken by Major N.H. Bourne DSO. The squadron OCs were Major Bill Close, 'A' Sqn, Jock Balharrie, 'B' Sqn, Johnny Dunlop, 'C' Sqn. Captain Neil Kent became 2 i/c 'A' Sqn; Captain Bill Morris 2 i/c 'C' Sqn.

General Richard O'Connor had seen the light of day after the damage done by faulty tactics during Operation 'Goodwood'. He talked to General Roberts: 'told me we were going to operate on the right flanks of Second Army, right in the middle of the "bocage" country. He said "You must be prepared for the very closest of tank/infantry co-operation on a troop/platoon basis". (Quite simple for the three armoured regiments and three infantry battalions as they had done it on a squadron/company basis.) It was my intention to have two brigades each containing two armoured regiments and two infantry battalions. Who commanded each group must be decided by the brigade commander and would depend on the type of operation. It must be entirely flexible and *any* armoured regiment must be prepared to work with *any* infantry Bn.'

For the last ten days of July 1944 the division, except the guns of 13th RHA and Ayrshire Yeomanry, were out of action. The 3rd RTR War Diary notes: '21st 'C' Sqn reformed under Captain J.D. Dunlop, heavy shelling, heavy rain. 22nd Bn to ruined Cussy, very muddy, ARVs and Stuarts had to tow out wheeled vehicles. 23rd 1130 memorial service held (for those killed in 'Goodwood'. Captain T.L. Kinton becomes Adjutant; Major Balharrie O.C. 'B' Sqn; 24th visits by CRA and CREME: 25th parties sent to baths, cinema and Corps rest camp (at St Aubin-sur-Mer): 26th, Major N.H. Bourne DSO new 2 i/c, new draft arrived (reinforcements); 27th Film show in Authie 'Stars in Battledress': 29th leave Cussy.'

In July, mainly during 'Goodwood', 3rd RTR claimed enemy losses of 2 Mk IVs, 6 Mk Vs, and 8 assorted 75- and 88-mm A/Tk guns. Each armoured regiment disbanded its AA troop and reduced the size of the Recce Troop.

General Montgomery now mounted an ambitious attack to the south of Caumont in the direction of Vire and the commanding Mont Pinçon. It would be in conjunction with (a) a Canadian Army attack towards Falaise and (b) the American Third Army's offensive heading towards Avranches and Granville.

General O'Connor's 'VIII' Corps composed of 15th Scottish, Guards Armoured and 11th Armoured were to mount an attack, Operation 'Bluecoat', on 30 July on the right of the British line, to support the breakout from the bridgehead. 15th Scottish with 6th Guards Tank Brigade with Churchill tanks, led towards Point 309, some 2,000 yards east of St Martin-des-Besaces. The GOC, 'Pip' Roberts, wrote: 'We, 11th Armoured were to fight forward protecting the right flank of 15th Scottish and in touch with the Americans on our right flank.' Roberts had decided on his 'mix': 29th Armoured Brigade with 23rd Hussars, 3rd RTR, 8th RB and 3rd Monmouths; 159th Brigade (under Brigadier Jack Churcher) comprising 2nd Fife and Forfars, 2nd Northamptonshire Yeomanry, 4th KSLI and 1st Hereford. On 29 July the division moved across the Second Army bridgehead via Bayeux and eventually concentrated between Balleroy and Caumont. The 2nd Household Cavalry, an armoured car regiment, were allocated to 11th Armoured as the attack began at 0700 hrs on the 30th.

Major Close had reorganized 'A' Sqn. Captain Neil Kent who was left out of battle during 'Goodwood' rejoined and took over 2nd Troop. Lieutenant Johnny Langdon also returned to take over 1st Troop and Sergeants 'Buck' Kite and Freddie Dale retained command of 3rd and 4th Troops.

15th Scottish seized Hill 309 overlooking St Martin-des-Besaces (Beggars) and 3rd RTR and 8th RB advanced on St Martin after bypassing Dampierre and Sept-Vents. A patrol of the Household Cavalry found an unguarded bridge over the little River Soulevre on the boundary between the German 326th Infantry Division and its neighbours, 3rd Parachute Battalion. The direction of the divisional advance changed and the objective of Le Beny Bocage made easier. 'C' Sqn RTR entered the small town at 1030 hrs on 1 August with 'A' Sqn, 'C' Sqn moving up onto the high ground at Point 243 and Point 266, and 'B' Sqn with two companies of 4th KSLI exploiting towards Le Tourneur. Meanwhile, 8th RB and 3rd RTR tanks neared Charles de Percy moving south-east and thus cutting the main Caen–Vire road. On 2 August 3rd RTR followed 4th KSLI in their troop carrying vehicles from Cathéoles, passing Aigneaux towards Point 218, just short of Presles. In the evening they attacked the little hamlet of Le Grand Bonfait. 3rd RTR were now the left flank guard on the Vire–Estry road.

Day by day 3rd RTR pushed on, usually with 4th KSLI infantry on the back of their tanks, through 'bocage' country, narrow roads, hedgerows, copses, a forest or two and small hamlets towards the dramatic finale of Operation 'Bluecoat'.

General Montgomery now fired Lieutenant-General Bucknall, GOC 'XXX' Corps, also Major-General Erskine, GOC 7th Armoured and Major-General Bullen Smith, GOC 51st Highland Divisions. The German General von Kluge realized that he must stop the British 'Bluecoat' attack or his whole front would collapse, so he committed 21st Panzer, 9th SS Panzer and 10th SS Panzer, plus a Tiger tank battalion to close the gap that 11th Armoured had opened up between his two armies.

Vire could have been captured and 11th Armoured Division patrols sent in, but as it was an agreed American objective they were pulled out! General 'Pip' Roberts now had two alternatives, 'enormous chaos can be inflicted on the enemy by the armoured division thrashing around in his rear areas, but (in continuing the advance *past* Vire) I decided to hold the two very dominating ridges, one four miles from Beny-Bocage and the other, one and a half miles further on, and higher than the first. The east–west Vire–Vassy road ran in the valley beyond the second ridge and was our objective.'

For three or four days almost non-stop battles were fought around the villages of Burcy, Presles and Chênedollé and in the hamlets of Pavée, Bas-Perrier, Le Moulin and Le Grand Bonfait. The latter was to be the battleground where 3rd RTR and 4th KSLI fended off desperate counter-attacks from the German-held village of Estry 2 miles due east. Moreover, panzers, mainly from 9th SS Panzer Division, moved to cut off 11th Armoured formations in the Presles–Burcy sector and reopen two vital roads for their supply columns (Vire–Estry and Vire–Vassy). 13th RHA and the Ayrshire Yeomanry 25-pdrs were in Le Desert area 2 miles north-west of Le Grand Bonfait. They were in action for three days and nights helping to subdue the ferocious German counter-attacks.

'We did a really rough night march with the Shropshires. It was pitch black and the CO congratulated us on finding the way. We formed one of the four troops of Bill Close's "A" Sqn. Two troops, mine and Captain Kent's took up position in an orchard beside a farm (in the small hamlet of Le Grand Bonfait). We did our best to space our tanks out. My Sherman was right under a tree.' The other three troops were scattered over a 400-yard frontage. 'I (Sergeant 'Buck' Kite) had a Firefly and there were 75-mm Shermans with me.' 13th RHA had two FOOs almost permanently with 3rd RTR, and 4th KSLI were dug into a huge field of high corn in front of the orchard. The battalion stood-to at dawn, had breakfast, netted the tank wireless and Captain Neil Kent went off to talk to Major Close. 'At 0930 we were all out of our tanks when shot and shell came whistling all around us, arriving from nowhere.' Kite climbed on to the back of his tank and saw two panzer Mk IVs creeping down the hedge 200 yards away. Sergeant Freddie Dale's troop lost a Sherman immediately but their Firefly destroyed one Panther and forced the other to retire. Although the 4th KSLI infantry were confident they could defend themselves with their PIATs, Close asked Lieutenant-Colonel Silvertop for support. A squadron of the Guards Armoured would – perhaps – arrive to support 3rd RTR on their flank. Corporal Peter Elstob of 'A' Sqn reported over the air that Sergeant Kite had been badly wounded, his tank knocked out and another troop tank completely destroyed. Little Trooper Herbie Barlow and Trooper Shaw rescued Kite and carried him to the KSLI RAP where Kite was again wounded. He had been recommended for the DCM for Operation 'Goodwood', and received the MM. In 'Bluecoat' exactly the same thing happened, DCM, no – bar to MM, yes.

Captain Neil Kent, 'A' Sqn recalled: 'The attempt to get the Guards squadron to shoot into the flanks of those Panthers was only partially successful. The CO sent Lieutenant Johnny Langdon's troop up to give further help. The Divisional gunners organised a helluva big Defensive Fire Plan. Any further movement down came some beautiful stonking. At last light we were bristling with all forms of A/tank defence.'

Intermittent fighting went on during the 4 and 5 August (although the rest of the division were under immense pressure on the 23rd Hussar and 2nd Fife and Forfar fronts). On the 6th a minor counter-attack was repulsed and Captain Farningham MM rejoined as 2 i/c 'C' Sqn. On the next day 'A' Sqn were lent to 2nd Warwickshires of 3rd British Division to relieve the 23rd Hussars. Major Len Hagget told Major Close that after 24 hours of constant attacks from Panthers *in his rear*, he had lost half his squadron. Led by Lieutenant Johnny Langdon 'A' Sqn sped through an enemy-occupied village (Presles) up the Bas Perrier ridge towards the Hussar tanks, some still burning. The only casualty in the next 24 hours was Major Close's own tank which received an enormous blow on the tank turret. All the crew were having breakfast so there were no casualties. But at 1000 hrs back at Le Grand Bonfait mortar bombs fell near Battalion HQ, wounding the Adjutant, Captain T. Kinton and three ORs. A Tiger attack on 8 August was fended off by armour, anti-tank guns and divisional artillery. Even General 'Pip' Roberts admitted, 'there is no doubt that we remained in a highly precarious situation for several days'. 10th SS Panzer Division were sent south-west from Mont Pinçon to launch a full-scale attack which fell mainly on the two defensive 'boxes' at Le Bas Perrier and Pavé. They hammered away and were hammered back and on the night of 8 August 10th SS Panzer and 363rd Infantry Divisions slipped away; 11th Armoured Division fought a splendid defensive victory and held their ground. Operation 'Bluecoat' was the first decisive Second Army victory: a 20-mile advance through difficult 'bocage' and a great test of endurance at the end.

Around Le Grand Bonfait, 3rd RTR had killed in action: Lieutenant C. Groom, Lieutenant D. Mathers, Lance Corporal A. MacDonald, Lance Corporal A. MacMillan, Troopers R. Baker, R. Hamilton, G. Smith, and W. Walker.

21

BREAKOUT ACROSS NORMANDY – 'CHARGE! GO LIKE HELL'

3rd RTR were relieved by a Guards Armoured formation and 3rd British Division took over the infantry positions and made contact with the US forces east of Vire. On 11 August 1944 the Inns of Court armoured cars replaced 2nd Household Cavalry as the recce regiment. The next day the division was switched from 'VIII' Corps to 'XXX' Corps, now commanded by Lieutenant-General Brian Horrocks who had recovered from his severe wounds in North Africa. He visited the division on the 13th and explained his plan – a cautious advance eastwards through 'bocage' country easily defended by blown bridges, minefields, booby traps, snipers, an A/Tk gun, and a platoon of infantry backed by a couple of Nebelwerfers.

On 15 August General 'Pip' Roberts visited the battalion with Brigadier Jack Churcher, the tall Herefordshire infantryman now commanding 159th Brigade; 3rd RTR, 2nd Northamptonshire Yeomanry, 4th KSLI and 1st Herefords were now part of 159th Brigade. Their line of advance would be Estry–Vassy–Flers–Briouze. Several changes were made: Captain J.A. Kempton joined 'B' Sqn, Lieutenant J.G.H. Moorhead 'A' Sqn, Lieutenant J. Ormrod went to RHQ but was wounded four days later and Lieutenant H.P. Brookshaw joined 'A' Sqn. Lieutenant C.T.W. Lindquist became OC RHQ troop.

3rd RTR leaguered south of Vassy and then on 16 August made an 8-mile advance, 'B' Sqn leading, and crossed the River Vere north of Flers. The next day 'C' Sqn went into Flers, now the Normandy town most associated with the Black Bull – handsome wall statue and murals celebrate the division's victories in Normandy. A 6-mile advance was made from La Fosse (Montilly) to St George de Groseilles.

The unfortunate Northamptonshire Yeomanry had had 88 officers and men killed in action and double that amount wounded in the 'Epsom', 'Goodwood' and 'Bluecoat' battles. They had fought gallantly in their Cromwells but were now replaced by 15/19th Hussars.

On the 18th 3rd RTR 'motored' 6 miles in two hours, fought a brisk action at Sainte Opportune, entered Briouze and 'Pip' Roberts made contact at 0930 hrs with the US forces commander. Just as well, because the American batteries had just shelled 'A' Sqn. The following day despite several tanks being blown up on mines, Ecouché, east of Mont Caroult was reached at 1330 hrs.

The two centre lines were coded 'Diamonds' for the left line of advance by 29th Brigade, and 'Clubs' for the right for 159th Brigade, including 3rd RTR. On the morning of the 19th, the advance continued on the axis Ecouché–Montgaroult–Sentilly. 3rd RTR were linked with 1st Herefords then with 4th KSLI. The 20th was a day of rest spent 4 miles east of Argentan. The advance continued but both brigade groups were held up by blown bridges, mines and booby traps, roadblocks and demolitions, and by efficient (and brave) rearguard actions. The divisional sappers were always busy repairing bridges or constructing new ones or clearing minefields. AVRES of Hobart's 'Funnies' bombarded roadblocks and brought up mobile Scissors bridges, west of Villebadin and at Omméel.

Lieutenant Johnny Langdon led his troop of tanks into a wild charge through the centre of Gacé, 11 miles east of Argentan. Both brigade groups were held up by enemy infantry, A/Tk guns and bazookas. 'From the 15th/19th Hussar HQ I could see the road led straight downhill into Gacé with high banks on either side, as far as a bridge over the river Touque then rose steeply into the main buildings (and square) of the town. At 1730 with Corporal Elstob immediately behind, I broke cover and started down the road.' An SP gun fired but missed them. Trooper Todd fired AP into an AFV by the bridge which blew up. 'I shouted down the intercom to Trooper Arthur to get moving and we hurtled down the slope.' Langdon's tank was hit twice by HE shells, but the enemy AFV had slewed across the road blocking it behind. So alone they tore up the hill into the main square and turned round to block the only town exit. A German staff car was knocked out and Langdon and Trooper Dunning took two unhurt prisoners. Over the air Langdon told Major Close that he was on the far side of town 'on my own and would like reinforcements as soon as possible'. Corporal Elstob and the rest of 'A' Sqn soon arrived and

4th KSLI cleared up, taking 190 POWs. Langdon was awarded the MC for his charge and capture of Gacé. On 22 August 3rd RTR pushed on to La Trinité-des-Laitiers, found clear, turned south and concentrated near St Gauburge. L'Aigle was taken and held by 3rd Monmouths. 11th Armoured then settled down for a few days of rest and rehabilitation. 'We had five days rest, parked our tanks in orchards around the town, enjoyed ourselves. Baths, washed our filthy clothes, self decontamination, cinema, shows and dances organised by the Mayor, with the local ladies well chaperoned,' recalled Major Close.

Aube-sur-Rile was the centre of the divisional concentration. A Radio Diffusion van gave gramophone recitals, ENSA appeared, mobile baths and laundry facilities were available and the GOC visited the battalion. On 26 August an advance party got under way led by Majors N.H. Bourne and F.I.C. Wetherell. Sam Wetherell had been GSO II in the Armoured Training Branch at the War Office. As there was no vacancy with 3rd RTR as Squadron Commander he arrived in Normandy as a reinforcement and served as a tank crewman. By the time the battalion reached Antwerp he was OC 'B' Sqn. On Sunday the 27th there were Roman Catholic and Church of England services, a cinema show for fifty ORs in a factory canteen and a cinema show in L'Aigle theatre for twenty-five ORs.

The notorious Argentan–Falaise 'pocket' had been closed. In twelve days the division had taken 3,000 POWs, out of the grand total of 40,000 claimed by British, American, Canadian, Polish and French formations. The five SS divisions (1st, 2nd, 9th, 10th and 12th) had been devastated. The converging formations had squeezed and finally crunched and the RAF Typhoons had wreaked havoc in their last corridor of escape. Nevertheless 20,000 German troops, 24 tanks and 60 guns were eventually ferried over the River Seine to continue their professional rearguard actions.

22

OPERATION 'SUPERCHARGE II' – THE 'GREAT SWAN'

The Eighth Army in North Africa had two successful operations codenamed 'Supercharge'. Possibly General Montgomery realized that it could again be a 'lucky' codename for what became known afterwards as the 'Great Swan'. Operation 'Bluecoat' had been successful and the breakout to close the 'corridor' and the advance up to the River Seine now convinced many VIPs that the war might be over by Christmas.

'There was no doubt', the General wrote, 'all the regiments which I visited (at L'Aigle) were in very good shape and keen to get on with the chase.' The 43rd Wessex Division in Operation 'Neptune' had spent five days forcing a bridgehead at Vernon. 'Pip' Roberts wrote: 'Clear from the success and speed of the crossing that the opposition was not strong so I decided we would operate with normal brigades with 29th Armoured brigade leading.' The pursuit would be mainly carried out by the Guards Division on the right flank, and 11th Armoured on the left. 'Our sights were now fixed on the River Somme and Amiens.'

3rd RTR moved north-east from L'Aigle, and at 1950 hrs on 28 August crossed the River Seine through the 43rd Wessex bridgehead and harboured at Tilly. Starting at 0700 hrs on the following day, leading the right column, the battalion set off on the 'Great Swan'. By 1330 hrs the battalion had reached Etrepagny, a distance of 16 miles. At Heidicourt, in very heavy rain, many POWs were captured from the German 49th Infantry Division. They entered Sancourt at 1700 hrs, a further 5-mile advance. But 6 miles north-east at Mainneville the enemy rearguard occupied an awkward reverse slope with infantry, SP and A/Tk guns. The battalion crossed the little River Levrière, made a flanking movement through Rouville and regained their original axis. 'B' Sqn came under fire and lost three tanks. 'C' Sqn also had three tanks knocked out just south of Mainneville. Sergeant C. Remane, Lance Corporal W. Oliver and Trooper R.

Lawson were killed in action. A determined and well-planned German rearguard would unfortunately always produce a 'bloody nose'. However, at least one Panther was destroyed in the action.

The advance resumed at 0700 hrs on the 30th as the battalion reached the River Epte at Talmontier. 8th RB were invited to clear the troublesome rearguard in Etrepagny. The Epte bridge was blown and in house-to-house fighting in Amécourt the 3rd RTR/8th RB partnership took 150 POWs. 3rd RTR tanks forded the little river and for a while observed enemy troops in thick woods beyond Talmontier until 4th KSLI could clear the area. 23rd Hussars took the lead and rushed north-east, bypassing Gournay through Marseille-en-Beauvais and east to Crévecoeur-le-Grand, a 30-mile advance! Here 3rd RTR caught up, and with 8th RB captured guns, half-tracks and 150 POWs. The town's gendarmerie gave cases of cognac away to the liberators, who now saw for the first time how the FFI Resistance (Forces Françaises de l'Intérieur) treated those people suspected of collaboration with the enemy – mostly young girls who fell for the blond young men of the SS and Wehrmacht. As darkness fell the battalion, with the faithful 8th RB entered Croissy-sur-Selle, 18 miles south of Amiens. Earlier in the day at 1600 hrs General Horrocks met the GOC at St Germer (4 miles south-east of Gournay). General M.C. Dempsey ordered General Horrocks to capture Antwerp and Brussels respectively with 11th Armoured and the Guards Divisions. The GOC in his autobiography wrote: 'Ike said to Monty "Amiens tonight." Monty said to "Bimbo" Dempsey "Amiens tonight." "Bimbo" said to "Jorrocks", "Amiens tonight" and "Jorrocks" said to "Pip" Roberts "Amiens tonight" and then the planning started.' It makes a good story anyway!

To capture a large town like Amiens, infantry were indispensable and supplies of petrol were essential to keep the armoured columns moving. The RASC echelons were 50 miles behind near the River Seine, but the divisional RASC pulled out all the stops with a column of petrol lorries coming and going, often through half-cleared sectors. General Roberts decided on two centre lines, the right route from Crevecour up the main road east to Breteuil, north to Amiens; and a winding country road via Conty and Taisnil north-east to Amiens. 3rd RTR and 8th RB would lead the right-hand column and 2nd Fife and Forfar with 3rd Monmouths the left-hand column. At last light both columns were almost level: the right near Catheux and the left around La Houssoye, about 20 miles from Amiens. The key objective was 'to bounce the Germans out of Amiens before they can blow the bridges' – not an easy task.

Up to now the advance of some 60 miles from the Seine had been in daylight over high rolling countryside, often with 3rd RTR advancing as a battalion in open battle formation. Now a night march was planned, with menacing clouds building up to hide the full moon, and in drenching rain moving nose to tail in armoured convoy through enemy-held country. The battalion Signals Officer Hugh Abercrombie and Lieutenant James Ramsden, 8th RB went ahead in a carrier into the village of Fontaine just ahead to check that it was clear before the night march could start. Major Bill Close and 'A' Sqn, with Major Noel Bells's 'G' Company, 8th RB in half-tracks and lorries, were the vanguard of 11th Armoured Division's famous night march. In pitch-black darkness in pouring rain Lieutenant Langdon's 1st Troop leading the Shermans started at 2230 hrs from the little village of Fontaine Bonnelieu. Major Bill Close commented: 'Water was streaming off the Shermans as I went down the column warning tank commanders that nothing was to stop us and if we bumped into anything on the way it was to be brushed aside.'

Only tail lights were permitted and the tanks moved closed-up at 5 mph. Huddled in their turrets maps were studied by shaded light, operators tinkered with radios, their headphones humming. Keeping the tank drivers awake was vital. The GOC remarked that 'By 1 a.m. drivers were very tired. There were occasional halts. German vehicles joined the column, once vehicles stopped for any length of time some drivers dropped off to sleep. I personally got out of my White scout car to wake up a driver at least five times during the journey and I'm sure many officers and NCOs did the same. The greatest pressure was on the leaders; to take the wrong turning, turn round in the dark with the column pressing up behind was anxious work.' 29th Armoured Brigade had a strength of 139 Shermans (of which 30 were Fireflies) and 20 Stuarts. During the 'Great Swan' to Antwerp 26 Shermans and 2 Stuarts dropped out for repairs.

The CO, Lieutenant-Colonel Silvertop, was on the wireless exhorting the battalion to 'Push on, push on.' Lieutenant Langdon's leading tank, 'Sugar Two' reported a column of horse-drawn artillery and limbers at a crossroads and was promptly ordered to 'motor through them', which he did. Lieutenant Johnny Langdon recalled: 'Soon all hell was let loose, machine-guns firing at random, horses stampeding mad with fright, tanks mixed up with enemy wagons, horses were dying in their traces, wagons upturned with horses lashing out to regain their footholds. It was a sad sight illuminated by star flares fired from Very Light pistols.' A Volkswagen and its occupants were crushed and then 'Sugar Two' fired three AP shells from a range of 20 feet into an enemy tank. 'It was quite the biggest and best explosion we had seen for some time.' Lieutenant Philip Brookshaw led the advance for the first two and a half hours and then it was Lieutenant Johnny Langdon's 1st Troop's turn to lead.

By 0400 hrs on 31 August 'A' Sqn was 3 miles south of Amiens and Majors Close and Bell decided a quick brew of tea was possible while they waited for the column to catch up. On the left flank 2nd Fife and Forfars were about 5 miles short. The GOC noted: 'At this point I gave orders to 29th Armoured Brigade that 3rd RTR with the Company of 8th RB push on with all speed to Amiens and aim specifically for the main bridge over the river Somme. 23rd Hussars were to occupy the high ground south of the city astride the main road. 2nd Fife and Forfar on the left, would occupy the other main feature west of the little river Celle. At 0500 the leading tanks entered the outskirts. By 0600 the centre of the city was reached.' At dawn 'A' Sqn engaged target after target. 'The countryside was littered with burning wrecks, alive with running figures . . . clattering over the uneven pavé past patches of wasteground, rows of dingy houses and dilapidated factories, I thought "What a place to die for." ' At 0530 hrs the ten Shermans left of 'A' Sqn rumbled over the first railway bridge. The FFI then told the point troops that the German garrison in Amiens numbered 4–5,000. 'G' Company, 8th RB had only 70 riflemen! Guided by the excited FFI members huddled on the backs of the Shermans they reached the main bridge over the Somme. 'Sugar Three' crossed it and the rest of the troop under Lieutenant Bill Yates followed but were promptly cut off as by remote control the German defenders blew the bridge up, which collapsed into the river. Yates reported over the wireless that he could see four 88-mm A/Tk guns limbered up with their half-tracks ready to move off. Yates then captured all four guns and their crews and later was awarded the MC for this action. Fortunately the FFI were guarding another unmined bridge 800 yards away which 'A' and 'C' squadrons crossed; 4th KSLI were now brought in swiftly to clear up and finally three bridges were captured intact – 23rd Hussars captured one and 2nd Fife and Forfars the other. By midday the whole of 3rd RTR were across the Somme and occupied a German artillery HQ with a field kitchen where an excellent meal had just been cooked. General Eberbach, GOC of the disintegrated German Seventh Army was captured by the Fife and Forfars while he was having breakfast. During the afternoon the bridgehead over the river was enlarged to 3 miles in diameter. By 1800 hrs a brigade of 50th Division had taken over Amiens. The division were responsible for the capture of 800 POWs and a large quantity of German equipment. The battalion tank strength was now forty-seven, as twelve had fallen by the way with mechanical failures. The night march to Amiens and its dawn capture by 3rd RTR and 8th RB (with a great deal of help from 23rd Hussars and 2nd Fife and Forfars!) was a notable triumph.

23

OPERATION 'SABOT' – THE CAPTURE OF THE VITAL BOOM BRIDGES

On 1 September 1944 the division covered another 50 miles via Doullens, and north-east to Aubigny-en-Artois; 23rd Hussars led on the right and 2nd Fife and Forfars on the left. Numerous flying-bomb sites were overrun which was very satisfactory as London and the south-east coast had been terrorized by the V-2s for several months.

At 0730 hrs on 2 September, in heavy rain, each of the three regiments had a centre line: 3rd RTR in the centre, 23rd Hussars on the right, 2nd Fife and Forfars on the left. It was 15 miles to Lens via Servins, then north to Bauvins and 6 miles north-east to Seclin. The division had no intention of trying to capture the city of Lille. 'B' Sqn led, found the bridges in Lens blown but managed to cross by 1130 hrs. Major Bill Close wrote: 'We had leaguered overnight on some flat ground about 7 miles from Seclin where there were supposed to be a lot of Germans. The halt puzzled us until it was explained that our next objective was Antwerp. 'A' Sqn formed the advance guard but within a mile of Seclin both Honeys went careering off the road in flames . . . 88-mms.' The German defenders remained hidden in woods west of the town. Lieutenant-Colonel Silvertop ordered 'A' Sqn to charge across open ground at speed to draw the enemy's fire while 'B' Sqn identified the opposition and dealt with them. Although AP shot whistled around them the only casualties were two tanks hit, including that of Captain Neil Kent, 'A' Sqn 2 i/c, though both were still 'runners'. 'B' Sqn entered the town, knocked out several A/Tk guns, including a battery of seven 88-mms and demolished a transport echelon fleeing the town. Lieutenant Gibson Stubbs found a crossing over the canal to the north-west which led to the enemy being outflanked. The key find was by Lieutenant Johnny Langdon whose troop had discovered a

Wehrmacht liquor store crammed with champagne, brandy and wines. Major Bill Close gave the appropriate orders and every tank carried 'hooch' hidden under the bedrolls behind the turrets. Yes, Seclin was a most satisfactory little battle – over before lunch. By 1530 hrs 'A' Sqn led the battalion across the Belgian frontier at Willems just east of Lille. The bridge at Pecq over the Escaut Canal was blown, but 2 miles north a wooden bridge was discovered at Warcoing by Lieutenant Bill Yates. Tested first by a lighter Honey then by heavier Shermans the rest went over carefully one by one in pouring rain. Then it was 16 miles east to Renaix (Ronse) and 6 miles north to Oudenarde. Now Major John Dunlop's 'C' Sqn were in the lead. The Belgians were even more enthusiastic in their 'liberation' welcome. A solitary 88-mm gun was destroyed and when 3rd RTR refuelled at Zotteghem at 1930 hrs a 'bazooka' Panzerbuchse team claimed a 'C' Sqn Sherman. The Germans were hosed in their hedges and ditches with violent Besa fire and that was that. The GOC was hounding his brigadiers who were in turn hounding their regimental commanders, who were, etc. So the night advance continued for another 20 miles to a leaguer reached at 0300 hrs on the 4th, east of Aalst (Alost). Service life is often unfair. Brigadier Roscoe Harvey had heard of 'A' Sqn's 'hooch' find at Seclin and reluctantly the Quartermaster, Lieutenant Paddy Hehir had the difficult job of 'reclaiming' the alcoholic loot. Curiously he found only the unpopular bottles of white wines. Reveille was at 0530 hrs.

General 'Pip' Roberts said: 'I did not want to try getting into Antwerp in the dark, the possibility of absolute chaos was much too great – but we had to start dead on first light on 4 September. The Inns of Court (reconnaissance regiment) reports helped the (GOC) agree on the right route. 23rd Hussars would enter Antwerp via Malines and 3rd Royal Tanks on the left route would enter via Boom.' The General's map was of the school atlas type which showed the great port as a little circle with a blue line, presumably a canal, going through the middle of it. The day before, the Guards Armoured had entered Brussels to a delirious welcome. The division's orders were to reach the harbour area and forestall demolitions. Major Johnny Dunlop's 'C' Sqn would lead, followed by 'A', and 'B' Sqn under Major Jock Balharrie, in support. After a few hours' rest at Termonde, 'C' Sqn and 'G' Company, 8th RB started at first light, east for 10 miles to Willebroek. The town of Boom on the River Rupel guarded the approach from the south to the great port and city of Antwerp. If a bridge or bridges at Boom could be seized before they were blown the division led by 3rd RTR could reach their main objectives – quickly.

Wrote Major John Dunlop: 'Even after our speedy advance into Belgium it seemed most unlikely that we should be unopposed, and, in that country with many water obstacles, the likelihood of being blocked seemed high. But we had plenty of the success that followed a quick side-step and the use of secondary routes.'

Trooper R.C. Payne, 'C' Sqn noted: 'We were the point troop approaching Boom when we arrived at a bridge on the main road which was mined. I think some of the Inns of Court were there too. After the usual hanging about the regiment turned round and with Belgian Resistance chaps on the back we crossed the river or canal by a mighty flimsy narrow wooden bridge. Actually some of us unlaced our boots as we went across. Colonel Silvertop was very insistent that the Inns of Court cars didn't overtake us on the way into Antwerp. As a co-driver in a Sherman, I came in for more than my fair share of cognac and kisses on the way into the town. Our driver Jim Cockraw from Liverpool very nearly lost his false teeth when he drank champagne from the bottle for the first time.' Later in the dock area a crew of a German 75-mm gun pointing in the wrong direction surrendered to the Payne/Cockraw tank crew.

Lieutenant Robert Vekemans, a Belgian engineer officer and a repatriated prisoner of war was a dedicated patriot. He had discreetly surveyed the two main well-guarded road bridges over the Rupel. If, however, he could stop the British troops short of a large railway viaduct, he could lead them across the Breendonk crossroads to cross the canal at Willebroek. The tanks would be concealed by buildings and they might reach the Pont Van Enschodt before being identified as hostile. The first of 'C' Sqn's Shermans ignored the man in a grey shabby mac (Vekemans) who tried to halt them, ignoring his signals. Lieutenant Gibson Stubbs in the second tank talked briefly to Vekemans and then to Major Dunlop, who asked permission from the CO on the radio to follow the flanking route suggested. Silvertop agreed and Vekemans confirmed that the minor road bridges would take a Sherman's weight, across 160 yards of river.

Led by Lieutenant Stubbs, two Shermans and a scout car with Vekemans in it went across the crossroads to Willebroek, crossed the canal to a cinder track and made for the Pont Van

Enschodt at top speed. Vekemans suggested the leading tanks turned their guns to face backwards and covered them with camouflage netting. Stubbs's troop crossed the bridge and the resourceful Vekemans halfway over cut the firing leads to the mines below the bridge and the rest of 'C' Sqn crossed. 'G' Company, 8th RB then guarded the bridge. 'C' Sqn tanks turned left through the narrow waterside streets of Boom to reach the town square. With the FFI who now appeared at about 1300 hrs, they charged up on to the main road to seize the great bridge from the rear taking the Germans by surprise. The bridge guard of about fifty tried to hold off the tanks as their engineers rushed to the bridge with primers, detonators and leads. Faced with most of 'C' Sqn tanks they surrendered. Vekemans at revolver point found the firing point and cut the leads. The other canal bridge to the south was exploded but divisional sappers put a Bailey bridge across that night. The CO arrived and met Vekemans and Pilaet, head of the Belgian Resistance in Antwerp. With 'B' Sqn as vanguard, the CO took the two key Belgians on his tank through cheering crowds down the main road for Antwerp 12 miles due north. The Rupel bridges were now to be guarded by the Resistance and 'G' Company, 8th RB resumed their usual role. Major Close took 'A' Sqn on the left by the river bank route through Niel, Hemiksem and Hoboken to enter the city of Antwerp along the bank of the River Scheldt. Close was guided by M. Gaston de Lausney, a member of the FFI, in a dirty raincoat armed with a Sten gun.

24

THE CAPTURE OF ANTWERP – 'THE RIGHT WAY TO FIGHT A WAR'

The defence of Antwerp district was in the hands of Major-General Graf Stolberg-zu-Stolberg with 15,000 troops under his command, widely scattered, modestly equipped and of poor quality. There were roadblocks at the important crossroads covered by mines, anti-tank and machine-guns, bazookas and mortars. Antwerp was a large sprawling city of 2½ million inhabitants and if well-defended would have needed several divisions for its capture. M. Pilaet and the Resistance leaders told Lieutenant-Colonel Silvertop, who in turn passed on to Brigade and Division, that Stolberg's HQ was in a network of concrete bunkers in the central park, garrisoned by up to 5,000 infantry. Neither Eisenhower, Montgomery or Dempsey realized that the important River Scheldt would be mined and defended and that it would take several months before the port of Antwerp would be usable. All the top brass were concentrating on the Rhine and breaching the Siegfried Line defences. Subsequently General Schwabe, commanding the German Fifth Army, was able to evacuate more than 65,000 men from eight battered divisions, then trapped in the coastal areas across the mouth of the Schelde from Berskens to Flushing.

The GOC had, with TAC HQ, arrived in Boom and was most disconcerted to find 3rd RTR echelon vehicles impeding progress. 'I was very angry and bawled out the officer in charge. The route was soon cleared.' The 23rd Hussars' route to Antwerp via Malines was held up by a flak site of 88-mms and other AA guns all dug-in and sandbagged. The approach to them was under a bridge in a steep embankment. This meant that it would be some time before they appeared in the suburbs of Antwerp from the south-west quarter. The whole of the battalion was able to cross the bridge in Boom, although small-arms fire came from some other pillboxes on the other side of the river. Major Jock Balharrie of 'B' Sqn was badly wounded crossing the bridge. When he reached the outskirts of Antwerp, Major Bill Close was ordered to branch off to the left of 'C' Sqn and make for the main railway station. Major Johnny Dunlop, 'C' Sqn, was to push hard into and secure the docks. Having no accurate maps it was difficult to realize that the huge deep-sea complex extended to 1,000 acres, with warehouses, cranes, bridges, 6 miles of wharves, quays, locks, railway rolling stock, barges, tugs and shipping!

The main bridge outside Antwerp was defended by anti-tank obstacles and covered by MG fire. 13th RHA put down a smokescreen; 3rd RTR and the company of 8th RB attacked and cleared the defences. It took two hours but by 1500 hrs 3rd RTR were deep in the heart of the city. The CO, with M. Pilaet, made for the Resistance HQ near the central park. Major John Dunlop led 'C' Sqn into the dock area. He could speak French, had visited Antwerp as a schoolboy, so knew the way to the docks. His Flemish was quite adequate. The Resistance had dealt with many of the anti-tank guns. Dunlop recalled: 'We never closed the lids of our turrets because we then became so blind and so deaf that we felt too vulnerable. We felt a LOT safer with them open. But that afternoon I remember seriously closing down. This sporadic firing from above (by German snipers) was confined to the outskirts of the town and later more intensively to some parts of the centre. Our biggest problem was with the crowds of excited civilians who thronged the streets and climbed on our tanks. We had no objection to kisses from charming girls, cigars or bottles of champagne. But we kept meeting bursts of small arms fire and an occasional grenade and there were civilian casualties.'

Corporal Cliff Wicks joined 3rd RTR in June 1942 and saw action from Alamein to Tunis. He was always in 4th Troop, 'C' Sqn, and with his tank commander Lieutenant Stubbs, 'entered the main tree-lined boulevard of Antwerp at 1100 hrs. The first tank in. Suddenly we were surrounded by hundreds of cheering civilians and had our first real contact with the Resistance, "White Brigade". One showed us the way to the docks where we sank a German ship just moving out. HE on the bridge and two AP below the water line soon put it out of action. The White Brigade showed us where there were pockets of Germans and took prisoners off our hands (put into the Antwerp Zoo) so we could continue to clear the dock area which we did in quick time. We then remained on guard in a square near the docks until 2000 hrs. We had only half a dozen rounds of 75 left and no petrol. We had to stay while the rest of the regiment moved back a bit.' Wicks knew Lieutenant Stubbs when he was a young corporal and sergeant in the desert and always called him 'Stubby'. Trooper Allan Cameron Wilson, 'C' Sqn recalled: 'Actually after a shoot up at ships and a train on the far side of the docks we were swamped by the civilians – flowers, fruit, drink, food.'

Lieutenant Gibson Stubbs now earned a bar to his MC. He had done sterling work at Seclin, and was the first tank across the Boom bridge earlier that day. He crossed a minefield on the outskirts of Antwerp and was the first tank to enter the harbour area. While he was busy knocking out German 75-mm guns and staff cars to prevent sabotage of the vital Kruisschans Lock, he spotted a 3,000-ton minelaying merchant vessel manned by 200 Germans. His first shell struck the bridge, the second the wheelhouse and the third and fourth made direct hits below the waterline. An RTR witness said 'A battleship could not have done a more destructive job.'

Major Bill Close, 'A' Sqn remarked: 'The city was in turmoil. German horse artillery columns were milling about and being shot up by the Shermans' MGs and PoWs were being rounded up. The Belgian population surged on to the streets and it became impossible to advance. Every tank was greeted by cheering crowds who clambered up on to the turrets. Crews were overwhelmed with flowers, bottles and kisses.' His Belgian guide, Gaston de Lausney, took Close and 'A' Sqn through several side streets to the railway station buildings, where they came under fire from small arms and at least one A/Tk gun. Most of the company of 1st Herefords had disappeared among the welcoming populace who now impeded 'A' Sqn's action. Close had his tank near a café opposite the station entrance and knocked out the A/Tk gun while a section of the Herefords rounded up forty Germans. A Firefly called locally 'a beeg cannon' smashed up a large private house which was a German HQ and the shaken and bewildered staff gave themselves up. Major Close thought about destroying the railway locomotives but decided they might be put to good use later on.

At 1600 hrs 4th KSLI were ordered up to establish themselves in the central park. The GOC commented: 'Clearly what we wanted as soon as possible was our infantry brigade forward and

I ordered Brigadier Jack Churcher with 4th KSLI, with 'B' Sqn 3rd RTR to be responsible for the reduction of the garrison' (in the central park). The 3rd Monmouths would move to the dock area and be responsible for the main sluice-gates under 29th Armoured Brigade. By 2000 hrs after a fierce battle they captured the park and enemy HQ with Major-General Graf Stolberg-zu-Stolberg and 6,000 prisoners.

The CO withdrew the main body of 3rd RTR to an open area off Boomse Steenweg, although 'C' Sqn and 'G' Company, 8th RB leaguered near the Resistance HQ at Bonapartedok. Two tanks were sent halfway along Kattendijkdok in the south-east corner of the docks and 'A' Sqn guarded the railway station area. All through the night Major Dunlop was kept awake by Germans coming in to surrender as the Resistance cleared the dock area south of the Albert Canal.

At 0900 hrs on 5 September General 'Pip' received an unpleasant shock. The main bridge over the Albert Canal had been blown up. It was north of the city and separated from Antwerp by the suburb of Merxem. RHQ and 'B' and 'C' Sqns were withdrawn to a large château while Major Bill Close kept a guard with 'A' Sqn on the railway station area.

But first a few more vignettes. Trooper Len Slater of HQ squadron recalled: 'Swanning round in Antwerp, an old lady asked me what part of London I came from. She had married a Belgian soldier after the First War. I gave her a chicken which we kept in a box for laying eggs.' Lieutenant Robin Lemon, Recce Troop remembered: 'People climbed on our tanks overwhelming us with garlands and kisses. Suddenly in the crowd I saw a very pretty girl pushing her way through and eventually coming up to me. I couldn't believe it was Milly Van Den Bemden. As teenagers we played tennis at parties in Wiltshire before the war. You can imagine the celebration we had on my 'Honey' tank. Later when we left Antwerp Milly was among the crowds lining the road watching the tanks go by waving goodbye with tears streaming down her face.' Major Johnny Dunlop ensconced himself with a RHA FOO on the top floor of a skyscraper block, bringing down artillery concentrations on enemy they could see across the River Scheldt. 'Meanwhile a trim little Antwerpoise office secretary was bringing in relays of café and cognac and playing us pre-war American blues on the office record player. Now that was the right way to fight a war.'

The next few days were spent in servicing the Shermans,

refitting, and receiving reinforcements after the 'Great Swan'. Major Bill Close developed malaria and he went back to Netley Hospital for a check-up. He then spent three weeks in the Military Hospital at Aldershot. He joined 152nd RAC, a rehabilitation unit stationed near Newmarket where he received the news that he had been awarded a bar to his MC for his efforts in the capture of Amiens.

Lieutenant-Colonel David Silvertop wrote home: 'Antwerp is behind us and very pleasant memories. I was first to the harbour and lived on champagne for three days' lunch and dinner parties and had to make speeches and I've even had a headline in the Antwerp paper. Now we're on the job again (11 September 1944) with 800 bottles of claret, 7,000 cigars, 8 dozen Cointreau and 8 dozen Cognac which should last us. It was a major feat of arms to capture Antwerp but we did it with such skill that I don't believe it will be realised. Everyone very pleased. The Corps Commander has given us a dozen cases of champagne!' A prominent street in the city has been named after Silvertop and a Black Bull tank stands proudly nearby. The 'Great Swan' was over, possibly a unique feat in the history of the British Army. Nearly 400 miles in eight days with determined German rearguard actions and the capture of two major cities – Amiens and Antwerp.

25

AUTUMN IN THE WATERLOGGED PEEL COUNTRY

Fierce fighting by 4th KSLI and 3rd Monmouths continued for several days around Merxem, the northern suburb of Antwerp, but the plan to push northwards across the Albert Canal was now abandoned. 'XXX' Corps needed help for the protection of their southern flank, so early on 8 September the armoured regiments moved to the Diest area via Malines and Aarschot. The enemy were active on the west bank of the River Scheldt. General Kurt Student's tough paratroops held the short stretch of heath country between the Albert Canal and the Meuse–Escaut Canal, an area sprinkled with small streams and swampy patches. Distinctly not AFV battlegrounds! Every village, hamlet and crossroads was held by determined enemy. All bridges over the canal in front of 11th Armoured Division were blown. 159th Infantry Brigade rejoined via Malines and Louvain as 53rd Welsh Division took over garrison duties in Antwerp; 3rd RTR was ordered on the 9th to clear north-west/north of Beeringen. The battalion and 15/19th Hussars were now under command of 159th Brigade regrouping on a mixed brigade group basis. On 11 September, 3rd RTR and 3rd Monmouths cleared around Laak and concentrated in Helchteren. The paratroops defended Hechtel with determination but the Welsh Guards pushed them out. 3rd RTR and the Monmouths moved in, cleared the woods to the east and guarded the important crossroads. In the afternoon of the 12th came news that Lieutenant-Colonelonel Silvertop had been awarded the DSO for the battalion's role in helping to capture Antwerp. The clearance of the area between the canals completed, the division concentrated around Hechtel, Peer and Petit Brogel for six days of rest and maintenance. Brigadier Roscoe Harvey visited the battalion on the 13th. The next day half the battalion had hot showers in a factory, and a mobile bath unit had 610 takers. About 150 ORs went to an ENSA show in Peer, and 75 to a mobile cinema. The 2nd Fife and Forfars beat the battalion at football quite comfortably 2–0.

On 16 September, together with 3rd British and 50th Tyne Tees Divisions, 11th Armoured came under the command of General O'Connor's VIII Corps. General Horrocks's 'XXX' Corps with Guards Armoured, 43rd Wessex and 8th Armoured Brigade would make a dash north to link up with three drop-landings (at the Grave, Nijmegen and Arnhem areas) by 82nd US Airborne, 101st US Airborne and 1st British Airborne Divisions. This was Operation 'Market Garden', possibly the boldest venture in General Montgomery's spectacular career. The 70-mile centre line – just the one – would bear immense convoys of men and tanks, and apart from the logistical problems, would be cut and cut again by the opposition. 'VIII' Corps would be responsible for right-flank protection and would also be responsible for clearing the 'Peel' country to the River Maas and down to Venlo. Besides the two depleted but vigorous panzer divisions 'resting' around the Arnhem area, battle groups named after their commanders – Grassmehl, Hubner, Haregg and Hermann – put up determined resistance ahead of 'VIII' and 'XXX' Corps.

One would like to think that the British Army could have recovered as quickly as the Germans did and in such unorthodox manner. Flak gunners, Luftwaffe ground crew, SS cadets, the invalid battalions (earless, limbless, bad stomachs, deaf), some steady Wehrmacht and a few tough ex-Russian front sweats were welded swiftly into battle groups with mines, booby traps, many cheap and deadly bazookas, and Spandau teams. And it was this motley crew that held up the British and Canadian Army for several months. Brand new Tigers were being thrust across the Rhine from Ruhr factories. *Nebelwerfers* were much in evidence, as were SP guns and a few 88-mm A/Tk guns. The defenders' numbers were also made up by the *Hiwis* or *Hilfswillige*, pressed or conscripted men, mainly Poles, Russians, Czechs and Alsace-Germans. Regrettably there were also highly enthusiastic Dutch and Belgian SS regiments who knew what their fate would be if they surrendered.

The Peel country had the reputation of being the most unfavourable battlefield terrain in Europe. A large tract of reclaimed marshland extended along the west bank of the River Maas for about 20 miles on either side of Venlo. Although each field was surrounded by a deep dyke to drain off water, in the autumn and rainy season, the whole became a quagmire. Slit trenches automatically half filled with water. Tanks got bogged if they strayed off the roads; these in turn rapidly broke up under the weight of 30-ton AFVs. The engineers and pioneers were always kept busy keeping roads and tracks passable. The opposition were always great minefield constructors and booby traps displayed Teutonic ingenuity. Every house, cottage or farm was a natural habitat for such devices. They were also well registered for defensive fire targets.

It was not until 20 September that the battalion was in action dealing with bazooka parties in the woods around Hamont and Budel; they then reached Soerendonk and patrolled towards Maarheeze, which was entered on the 21st. Geldrop and Mierloo were cleared next. From Geldrop on to Hout, just short of Helmond, and in the area around Gerwen enemy infantry were engaged. The next day opposition thickened and AP fire, LMGs, bazookas, snipers and mortars were encountered. 'C' Sqn had an action at a railway crossing and RHQ suffered *Nebelwerfer* fire. 23rd Hussars engaged seven Panthers and a Tiger near Nunen; 2nd Fife and Forfars with the Herefords had a stiff action near Zomeren and during the capture of Asten, as 107th Panzer Brigade were still full of fight. The 3rd RTR line of advance was from the outskirts of Helmond (8 miles north-east of Eindhoven), north-east, heading for the River Maas. With 3rd Monmouths, in pouring rain, 'A' and 'B' Sqns put an attack in towards Liesel. Strong opposition was met south of Ommeel on the Deurne road. By last light the advance had reached the outskirts of Vlierden where four A/Tk guns were disposed of. On the Liesel road a Panther and two 88-mms were knocked out and at 1900 hrs Liesel itself was reached; Second Lieutenant J. Miller was killed in action near Helmond, as was Trooper G. Horton at Bakel. By 1100 hrs on the 24th 3rd RTR moving north from Liesel cut the Venlo–Helmond railway and entered Zeilberg. And at 1445 hrs both 3rd RTR and 23rd Hussars entered Deurne which was later cleared by 8th RB and 3rd Monmouths.

On the easterly route through De Rips, 3rd RTR took over from 23rd Hussars and at the crossroads in St Anthonis disaster struck. Brigadier Roscoe Harvey with his Brigade Major met two of his COs, Lieutenant-Colonel H.G. Orr, 3rd Monmouths and Lieutenant-Colonel David Silvertop, to establish the appropriate line of advance. In heavy rain two German half-tracks were 'flushed' out of hiding at 1630 hrs by 15/19th Hussars and made a bolt for safety. In the mêlée at the crossroads, Roscoe

Harvey was slightly wounded, the Brigade Major seriously wounded and the two commanding officers both killed. The half-tracks were of course destroyed. Silvertop had led the regiment since 'Pete' Pyman was promoted, well into 'Supercharge II' in the North African campaign. He was probably the only cavalryman (14/20th Hussars) to command a regular RTR battalion during the Second World War. The 2 i/c Major N.H. Bourne DSO took over command. A memorial service was held the next day at 1730 hrs, taken by Father Ryan in the Roman Catholic church in St Anthonis. Lance Corporal M. Lock was also killed in the same tragic incident.

'VIII' Corps had made rapid progress north during Operation 'Market Garden' with 663 casualties and had advanced 15 miles north-east of Eindhoven. By the 25th Montgomery had ordered the remnants of the British 1st Airborne Division to withdraw across the Neder-Rijn from Arnhem.

On 28 September the battalion sent a recce patrol to the Oploo–Overloon area which got shot up and a 13th RHA OP tank was brewed up. At 1800 hrs a memorial service was held in Westerbreek church for the two fallen commanders – Silvertop and Orr – and all comrades fallen since Antwerp. The next day 'A' and 'B' Sqns sent out a stronger recce patrol, backed with artillery fire and indirect tank fire. A Mk IV was brewed up but 'A' Sqn lost a Sherman and Lieutenant J. Moorehead and Trooper G. Patterson were killed in action at Oploo. Meanwhile, Lieutenant Bill Yates, 'A' Sqn, went back to Bovington for a wireless course! From Metz on 30 September came Major-General Silvester's 7th US Armored Division with the specific tasks of capturing Overloon and Venray. On arrival he said to the GOC 'Pip' Roberts: 'Oh we'll turn on the heat and be down to Overloon in no time.' From 1 to 9 October 11th Armoured maintained a small mixed force watching the Deurne Canal to the east and fending off fighting patrols.

Helmond was now a popular 'resort' for mobile baths and ENSA shows. Major F.I.C. Wetherell went to Brussels to interview possible reinforcements and on the 7th, Lieutenant-Colonel A.W. Brown arrived to take command. He was previously GSO1 Operations of Hobart's widespread and ubiquitous 79th Armoured Division.

11th Armoured now heard that Sergeant George Eardley of 4th KSLI had gained the Victoria Cross in the Oploo–Overloon fighting. A conference was held on the 7th to take over the

American 7th Armored Divisional area. They had tried to achieve their objectives which were indeed very difficult. Operation 'Ascot' involved 3rd British Division in fierce fighting in the Oploo–Overloon–Venray area. 'B' Sqn were in support near Oploo, and 'C' Sqn to the north of 'Fingerwood', as 'Ascot' started on the 12th. The next day around Overloon Second Lieutenant E. Stower, Troopers A. Mauger and J. Ashby were killed in action. On 16 October in heavy rain the battalion moved back towards De Rips. Ijsselstein was the key objective and for five days the battalion was in action. Although 3rd British had occupied Overloon and Venray, the small enemy parties fought vigorously. On the 17th 'A' Sqn and 'B' Sqn linked with 'B' and 'C' Companies, 3rd Monmouths for several attacks towards the Deurne–Venray woods. These were strongly held and A/Tk guns caused casualties. Corporal C. Hanam and Lance Corporal R. Sutherland were killed at Volen. It rained incessantly and the going was miserable. Twelve enemy vehicles including three tanks were seen on the 18th and heavily 'stonked'. In return 'C' Sqn were also heavily bombarded as 100 POWs passed through in the Veulen–Schei area. For the next two days the enemy mortars and *Minenwerfers*, artillery fire and some AP fire landed in the battalion area. The rather curious autumn and winter of discontent had already started. *Every* day until the end of October the 3rd RTR War Diary reported laconically: '75 ORs to cinema show; heavy enemy shelling. "A" Sqn seemed to bear the brunt. On 21st keeps observation all day, 23rd 10 bombs in "A" Sqn area, 25th "A" Sqn sit rep, enemy shelling all day.' Indeed, on 27 October the enemy counter-attacks in the Meijel and Leisel areas caused considerable alarm at Corps and Army HQ. The battalion crews dismounted from their Shermans and manned slit trenches as infantry. There was a 100 per cent stand-to from 1800 to 2300 hrs.

Major Bourne, 2 i/c and DAAQMG, went into Helmond to recce the area for a rest centre, while Major Johnny Dunlop and Captain A.M. Dixon led an advance leave party for a five day rest into the same town. The truly indomitable 'Stubby', Captain Gibson Stubbs MC MM, was wounded at 1600 hrs on the 22nd and evacuated to hospital. On 26 October the first rest party returned from Helmond and the War Diary reports: 'stonks and counter-stonks, enemy infiltration on the flanks'.

During the autumn/winter campaign in the Peel country, the Padre Captain Taylor MC was killed in action, and the RMO,

Captain MacMillan MC, indestructible and valiant from Greece and the Western Desert, was wounded and did not return to the battalion; Captain D.B. (Barry) Whitehouse took his place. Lieutenant Hugh Abercrombie, the Regimental Signals Officer, was also wounded in October and evacuated.

26

Operation 'Nutcracker', and the brand new Comet

For most of November 1944 the division had only minor operations, although the 159th Infantry Brigade and gunner regiments were kept busy. Guarding villages such as Veulen, Griendtsveen and Horst under shellfire in wet, cold, stormy days and nights was the norm throughout the month, and the 3rd RTR War Diary often just mentions 'usual shelling and mortaring'. On the 4th forty unsuitable personnel were posted away to the CRC; Captain R.G. Dear went on a D+M course, lucky fellow, *in the UK*, and Lieutenant H.P. Brookshaw and three NCOs, lucky chaps, were sent on a special gunnery and Driving and Maintenance Course – *in the UK*. The main military operation was Operation 'Nutcracker' by 'VIII' and 'XII' Corps, starting on 19 November, to close out the last German pockets of resistance west of the Maas. Conditions were so bad on the ground that D-Day was put back to the 22nd. Deurne, Griendstsveen, Amerika, Meterik and Schadijk were sad little hamlets to start with and were rubble after 'Nutcracker'. Sherman tanks slipped sideways into ditches and the recovery tanks would also get bogged down. The 4th KSLI, 3rd Monmouths and 1st Herefords bore the brunt of these grim unpleasant operations. On the 19th, RHQ, 'A' and 'B' Sqns moved to take 'high' ground at 7919 and a few days later tried an approach march to Amerika, 'A' Sqn acting with 3rd Monmouths. Conditions were so bad that on the 28th the battalion provided a forty-five man fatigue party to help the REs clear demolitions and minefields on the Deurne–Amerika road.

Awards were announced on 26 November of a bar to his MC for Major Bill Close and MCs to Lieutenants Brookshaw, Johnny Langdon and Bill Yates. Sergeant 'Buck' Kite was awarded a second bar to his Military Medal, L/Sergeant Woodward a bar to his MM, and Sergeant Cooper, the MM. The 2 i/c Major Bourne organized a tank commanders' course. Large-scale leave parties went to Brussels and Antwerp, and day trips to ENSA, cinema and theatre in Helmond and Eindhoven were arranged. On the 29th the Corps Commander Lieutenant-General Sir Richard O'Connor gave a farewell address in the Deurne cinema. The next day 3rd Monmouth and 15/19th Hussars fought a savage battle to take one of the last Maas strongpoints, Broekhuizen 'Kasteel'. The fanatical SS Parachute Cadets inflicted nearly 200 casualties in the action. On the same day 'B' and 'C' Sqns moved into Helmond, with 2nd Fife and Forfars, while 23rd Hussars moved back to Deurne.

In late October came the news of a secret new tank destined only for 11th Armoured Division. It was British-made, called the Comet, in general style similar to the Cromwell but with thicker armour and mounting a new high-velocity gun – the 77-mm in place of the 75-mm. It was capable of firing HE as well as AP; the gun was likely to combine the virtues of the 75-mm and the 17-pdr. The tank would have the speed, low height and reliability of the Cromwell. Re-equipment for 29th Armoured Brigade was scheduled for 1 December. Major Bill Close, when he returned from his stint in hospital, noted: 'We were all involved in getting to know our new tank, the Comet. We found it to be an excellent tank. It was better armed than the Sherman, had a much lower profile, was very fast and manoeuvrable and the 77-mm gun was an extremely efficient weapon. We had hoped that the Comet would be armed with the 17-pounder as the Sherman Firefly but it had not been possible to fit it in the turret. We consoled ourselves with the thought that perhaps at this stage, we might not meet many Tiger or Panther tanks.' Close was quite right. The main defensive weapon encountered in the Rhineland and river battles was the cheap, one-shot, Panzerfaust.

For receiving and training with the Comets an area between Ypres and Ostend in northern Belgium had been allotted to 29th Armoured Brigade who were scheduled to stay there six weeks. They were the only formation in the British Army to have these new 'toys' and 3rd RTR was the only Royal Tank Regiment to be awarded this accolade. On 5 December plans were made for the disposal of the Shermans and a day later on St Nicholas's Day a party was given by the battalion in Venlo for 130 Dutch children and 'B' Sqn held a dance. The tanks were handed over in Helmond on the 14th, and the whole brigade with its 171st RASC Company and workshops moved back to Belgium, while 3rd RTR moved to Poperinge. The new Comets were collected from Menin and firing ranges and shoots had been arranged at Gravelines (where Major Bill Reeves had won his DSO in 1940). The 'overs' fell into Dunkirk still held by the Germans. A team of instructors were supervising the gunnery lessons with the factory-new Comets.

The news of a German offensive fell on 20 December when Christmas plans with friendly Belgian families were well under way. Trooper Allan Cameron Wilson, 'C' Sqn recalled: 'Promised a rest and new tanks. Dump our tanks at Bourg Leopold, finally came to rest at Poperinge. Instructor on Sqn conversion to Comets. Civilian billets. Landlord catches cats, feeds us on the meat, makes gloves from the fur, unknown to us.' Captain Barry Whitehouse RMO wrote in the RAMC journal: 'It was wonderful luck, we thought, to get out of the line for Christmas and everyone was in great spirits at the thought of the weeks ahead to be spent among the hospitable Belgians. Von Rundstedt's offensive and the Ardennes Bulge seemed a long way off and of little concern to us at that moment. It came as an unpleasant shock on the morning of 29 December to be told to be ready to move at 1400 hours as an operational reserve for the Ardennes Sector.

27

Christmas 1944 – 3rd Tanks in the Ardennes: 'our god-dam show'

General Dempsey's Second Army HQ phoned Lieutenant-General Horrocks early on 20 December. 'The Germans have smashed through the American front and the situation is extremely confused.' General Montgomery sent a dozen of his young 'gallopers' down into the Ardennes to find the form and report back. 21st Army Group HQ in Brussels ordered 29th Armoured Brigade to get back in action with their abandoned old Shermans. The 6th SS Panzer Army was thrusting for Liege with 5th Panzer Army on its left flank leading via Namur and Dinant for the seizure of Antwerp. It was a typical bold, brilliant Adolf Hitler plan, but doomed – although for nearly a week there was considerable panic in certain quarters. The brigade was allocated a 40-km north–south stretch of the River Meuse to defend; 3rd RTR were tasked with the defence of Dinant. 'G' Company, 8th RB – the old faithfuls – were soon to be reunited.

Captain Barry Whitehouse, the RMO recalled: 'After a long march, mostly in fog and darkness we reached the outskirts of Brussels at midnight and spent the night in an empty school. At the CO's conference we got our second unpleasant shock. It was thought that nine Panzer Divisions had broken through and were heading for the Meuse.' The next day: 'The atmosphere was rather tense in the towns we passed through, but the people seemed cheered to see British tanks arriving on the scene. Our confidence was not raised by the sight of L of C (Lines of Communication) troops digging slit trenches by the roadside, only 15 miles from Brussels.'

Trooper Les Slater, 'H' Sqn recollected: 'We were doing a church service at the Menin Gate Memorial in Ypres. Lots of us lost fathers in the First War and it was very touching to see all those names and gravestones. Then we were woken up in the early hours, rushed through Brussels to pick up some Shermans (at 256th Army Delivery Squadron) and off to the Ardennes. I didn't like it, knowing the bridges over the river Meuse. Once an American tank sergeant called down to me from his tank, "Go home, this is *our* god-dam show." Then he said "How you guys off for gas?" We gave him two Jerry cans.' The first casualty was Captain Neil Kent, 2 i/c 'A' Sqn, who at 2200 hrs on the 22nd was accidentally injured by the Americans and evacuated. Lieutenant Robin Lemon was sent off with his troop of Honeys to recce the battalion positions and contact the Americans. 'I found much chaos – American vehicles dashing backwards and forward and utter confusion reigned.' Eventually he found a defensive position manned by an American ordnance battalion. 'They seemed in good heart and I admired their spirit.' Sergeant Bill Jordan, 'B' Echelon, was a 3rd RTR veteran: 'It was bitterly cold knee-deep in snow and the ground frozen solid. The Mech QMS approached me carrying in his arms a starter motor. "It is from a motorised caravan captured from a German general. It has to be towed to start and the CO (Lieutenant-Colonel Alan Brown) wants it put right for his personal use. He said he doesn't care where you go, but get one" '. Jordan toured round various brigade workshops and ordnance stores and found a replacement starter motor. He told his truck driver to put it under the seat and say nothing. As bold as brass Jordan told the MQMS that only in Paris, Brussels or of course Berlin could it be found. 'Making sure we had plenty of money, bully beef, chocolate, toilet soap and eggs, we set off to enjoy Christmas Eve in Brussels.'

Immediately after 3rd RTR's campaign in the Ardennes, the CO, who went on leave to the UK on 2 January 1945, asked Captain J.A. Kempton, 2 i/c 'C' Sqn, to write this account:

When Von Rundstedt launched his offensive against the Americans with his 5th and 6th Panzer Armies in the Ardennes in mid December 1944, the 3rd Royal Tank Regiment, together with the other Armoured Regiments in the 29th Armoured Brigade, were on the way from Holland back to Belgium, in order to re-equip with the new British Comet Tank. En route the Regiments disposed of their Sherman Tanks with which they had fought from the Normandy Bridgehead. They were dumped, almost gladly, one might say, at the Armoured Replacement Unit in Brussels.

The drive to Brussels that afternoon was damp and miserable, a heavy fog hung over the whole countryside and our feelings were pretty gloomy, leaving comfortable firesides and easy chairs where we had looked forward to spending a pleasant Christmas, for the rigours of campaigning over a wintry countryside and we knew not what other unpleasantnesses besides.

In the meantime the colonel (A.W. Brown DSO, MC) had gone ahead to 21st Army Group HQ where he met the commander of 29th Armoured Brigade, Brigadier R. Harvey DSO. Information there was very vague. There was reputed to be one German Army heading for Liege and Namur and another further south in the Bastogne Area and other troops unknown and unaccounted for in between.

The Brigade task was to hold a sector between Namur and Givet both inclusive. That is to say, a line following the river Meuse between these two towns. The river here runs, to all intents and purposes, North and South, which means about forty miles of river line.

The harbour parties had arrived at a Convent some four miles away and soon had things organised. Cookhouses set up and accommodation allotted. The Colonel having seen that all was going steadily, returned to 21st Army Group. The Brigadier gave out the latest known situation on the map. Roughly it was the same as before except that for some reason the appreciation was that the main enemy force would strike North West towards Namur and Liege. It was known that there were three bridges in the Brigade area, one each at Namur, Dinant and Givet. How many others there might be or what Americans were in the area was unknown. The 8th Battalion of the Rifle Brigade, who we had left behind in Holland, were on their way down, one company to each bridge.

The Brigadier's orders were to move off the next morning, the 23rd Hussars leading and to go to Givet. Then ourselves bound for Dinant and the 2nd Fife and Forfar Yeomanry to go to Namur. Givet was then an open flank and no one knew what was on the Brigade's right. We were to take up initial positions to hold each bridge at all costs and to ensure the defence of the left bank of the Meuse. The Regiment's sector being Hastière-Lavaux to Anhée. The Colonel collected maps and gave out orders at the convent before midnight.

The next morning dawned bright and sunny and crews were

busy at work early. By 9 o'clock shape was forming, Squadrons were forming up ready to go, and sure enough we were ready to move off that Thursday morning at 10.30. A belated Squadron Commander arrived with eyes staring out of his head incredulous at the preparations going on. He was on 48 hours leave in Brussels and was called to the Armoured Replacement Unit from his hotel in Brussels, believing the Regiment still to be in Poperinge, and knowing nothing of the preparations afoot. In fact when the Squadron Commander arrived the Colonel said 'Hello Sam', and a few minutes later the whole Regiment moved off.

We arrived at Namur about 4 o'clock and found a strange assembly guarding the bridge, 17-pounder Shermans hull down in extraordinary positions. There was a story that an over zealous colonel had put one hull down in the river itself, with just the gun showing.

We carried on along the very lovely road by the riverside from Namur to Dinant. The road follows the winds and twists of the Meuse, all the way between steep cliffs. The scenery is very beautiful and dotted along the banks are hotels and restaurants with lawns and flower gardens running down to the river. We stopped near one hotel for a 20 minute maintenance halt. The hotelier was very pleased to see us and gave us some brandy. He said we were the first British troops in that area and we excited a lot of curiosity.

In the meantime the Colonel had gone ahead, once having sorted out things at the Armoured Replacement Unit. When he arrived at Dinant he contacted Colonel Murray commanding 'Murray Force', a mixed force of about six Sherman 75s and 17-pounders plus Royal Engineers who were sparsely scattered over the area. The tanks that we had seen in Namur were part of this force.

'G' Company of the 8th RBs, commanded by Major Noel Bell MC were in strong positions defending the bridge and its approaches, and appeared to have the situation well in hand. Major Bell had organised 20 American Military Police on the bridge and was quite happy although glad to hear of our coming.

Dinant was reached in the dark. 'A' Squadron staying in the town to give support to the 8th RBs, while the other two squadrons leaguered at Onhaye. The Echelon and LAD at Florennes.

Orders for the next day were for 'A' Squadron to stay supporting the RBs. 'B' Squadron to recce positions west of the river while the Colonel and Squadron Commanders did a recce East of the river as far as Marche. They reached the town to find it occupied by an American Battalion who were most kind once initial suspicions had been allayed, but they knew nothing.

As a result of this recce 'C' Squadron crossed the bridge and moved up the road to Ciney, followed by 'A' Squadron, while 'B' Squadron remained West of the river. While on the recce to Marche the Colonel had picked out a series of positions. These proved excellent and by 9 o'clock squadrons were in position. 'A' Squadron at Sorinnes, 'C' Squadron at Achene and 'B' Squadron at Dinant supporting the 'G' Company 8th RBs.

So that within 48 hours of being under training at Poperinge, we had picked up our tanks, put them in order, filled up and were in battle positions. The country was excellent tank country, open and rolling and the frozen ground made the going fair over all the area.

That night 'C' Squadron Commander and the Squadron Sergeant Major decided to try and contact the Americans at Marche again to get some more information from them. This they did after a very exciting ride in a jeep. The journey back being even more exciting, as according to the Squadron Sergeant Major, they passed four German Armoured Vehicles. They reported to the Colonel that an American Infantry Division was now in Marche and the General said that he would hold on there and the US 2nd Armored Divison was due to move in on our left flank to the North East.

That night the squadrons formed leaguers in the nearest village and most of the talk was about Cecile, a very pretty Belgian refugee from Liege. So far as could be judged, no less than six Tank Commanders had tried to show her the 'Golden Rivet' in the turret, but her attention seemed divided between the Squadron Commander and the Squadron Sergeant Major.

The next day, the 23rd, dawned foggier than ever and brought an even bigger drop of rumours. Regimental HQ had established itself in the fine Château at Sorrines. An Air Liaison Officer turned up, as did a Liaison Officer from the 2nd American Armored Division. The main snag was that American troops in half tracks were difficult to differentiate from Panzer Grenadiers in similar vehicles especially in the fog.

That evening a Liaison Officer, Lieutenant J.F. Langdon MC who was acting 2 i/c of 'A' Squadron was sent from the Regiment up to Ciney to contact the HQ of the 2nd US Armored Division, which was supposed to move in there. The story goes that Lieutenant Langdon asked the Colonel if the road was clear and the Colonel said, 'We'll know when you get there.' He set off in a scout car, passed through 'C' Squadron at Achene and arrived at Ciney, which he found deserted except for an American Sergeant of whom he enquired the whereabouts of Divisional HQ. The Sergeant replied "Don't ask me, I'm only the 'Commander of the Blade' ", later identified as an Armoured Bulldozer. Eventually the 2nd US Armored Division arrived and set up an HQ. A small detachment of them actually lost their way and two half tracks drove in to 'C' Squadron at Achene. It was a little later that an American jeep passed right through to the 8th RB's road block at Dinant, refused to halt and was blown up by the mines drawn across the road. It was found to contain three German SS. Two were killed and one taken prisoner. The same evening it was confirmed that German Infantry had got into Conneau with some half tracks at last light.

And though the squadrons went into leaguer certain precautions were taken, one of which was a 17 pounder hull down looking east along the Sorinnes–Ciney road with an officer in a scout car ahead acting as a Forward Observation Officer. This officer moved into an upstairs room in a cottage and with a long lead to the wireless set took up his vigil. He had only been there a short time when he found that German Infantry were in the house on the ground floor. Fortunately he got back to Regimental HQ using not a little cunning and temporarily abandoned the scout car. Since enemy infantry were now only some 400 yards from Regimental HQ, the Regiment was stood to by the Colonel.

Luckily the move out at first light into battle positions was accomplished without incident. The Americans confirmed that the Germans were in Celle.

First blood was to 'C' Squadron who brewed up a Mark IV about 9 o'clock. Full marks for the 17 pounder gunner as the Commander was relieving nature. Then the report came in that the road between 'C' Squadron at Achene and 'A' Squadron at Sorrines had been cut by infantry. This made 'C' Squadron's position very insecure and they were withdrawn to the North

West. The next contact with the enemy was at Boisselles when 'A' Squadron knocked out a half track and another vehicle.

Visibility was poor early on, and it soon became evident that the advanced elements of the 2nd Panzer Division were trying to push through to Dinant in the mist. However the mist cleared a little and two Panthers moving up to Sorinnes from the South East were knocked out by another troop of 'A' Squadron.

About this time the Brigadier visited the Regiment and later General Bols, commanding the 6th Airborne Division, and we learned that by Boxing Day a Brigade would have arrived from England and would be on the ground in our position.

We also learned that at last we had some Gunner support. Admittedly it was only two mediums, but medium stonks are very useful especially against tanks. About this time one troop of 'A' Squadron was pulled back and 'A' Squadron took up a closer position at Sorinnes. Two carriers of the 8th RBs in Foy Notre Dame (between Sorinnes and Boisselles) were extracted from an awkward position. It was certain that the Germans were in Boisselles and Foy Notre Dame in some strength and probably in or had passed through Achene.

The Colonel then decided that as the Germans might very likely have a go at the bridge that night, we should have to take up defensive positions in a semi circle to defend the bridge and as the rumour of parachutists was very prevalent (some had been dropped further south) 'A' Squadron were withdrawn behind the river in an anti-parachute role.

The position was 'B' Squadron on high ground South East of Gemmerchene with a detached troop well to the south in contact with an American Troop of 2 anti-tank guns, and 'C' Squadron to the north side of the Dinant–Ciney Road with Regimental HQ at Gemmerchene. That evening the Regiment fell back on Dinant in tighter positions, 'B' Squadron forward looking south, south east and east. 'C' Squadron, echeloned back a little, looking east and north east.

The order at this stage was to defend the bridge at all costs. It may be of interest to record that the Colonel had, either written or verbally, four different orders as to what he was to do to the bridge.

At 9.30 that evening fresh orders came through from Brigade, Squadron Leaders were called for and later that evening, Christmas Eve, we learned that the Regiment was to advance on the morrow. It was believed that the Germans were running short of petrol. Our objectives were to be Sorinnes, Foy Notre Dame and Boisselles. The advance was to be made two squadrons up. 'B' Squadron on the north route from Dinant to Sorinnes, 'C' Squadron on the south route from Dinant to Boisselles., 'A' Squadron in reserve, who were to follow 'B' Squadron.

That night was quiet but full of anticipation and Christmas morning dawned bright and clear. Each had a platoon of the Rifle Brigade attached to them and 'C' Squadron a section of Recce Troop.

The advance began at first light and 'B' Squadron occupied Sorinnes without much difficulty. 'C' Squadron got into Boisselles after a dash down a forward slope under fire from a German tank, all ran the gauntlet successfully except one tank of Recce Troop which was hit low down, the crew escaping safely. Lieutenant Robin Lemon personally evacuated wounded members of the Honey, took over another tank and remained on observation. The bag in Boisselles included an armoured car, a half track, a truck and a jeep. The position was unpleasant as the village was overlooked by a wooded hill to the north east, in which were four tanks, one identified as a Panther.

A 17 pounder was manoeuvred into position and eventually got a few shots in, whereupon the Panther pulled back. The next incident was a Squadron of US Lightning Fighter Bombers, half of whom bombed the German tanks, the other half ground strafing 'C' Squadron. This attack was repeated an hour later, fortunately the bombs again falling on the Germans; the machine gunning on 'C' Squadron. Very luckily the only casualty was one Infanteer from the 8th RBs, but it was not serious.

By this time 'B' Squadron had contacted the Americans again and had got into Foy Notre Dame. This village was ablaze and yielded up a very fair bag of German PoWs, vehicles and half tracks. 'B' Squadron and the infantry of the US 2nd Armored Recce Squadron doing a first class Allied combined Operation.

Unfortunately a premature report came in that Foy Notre Dame was clear and Major Dunlop MC, 'C' Squadron leader, called to a conference at HQ, now established at Sorinnes, decided to go the short way via Foy Notre Dame. He was most unlucky to be hit in the mouth by a German sniper, while travelling in a scout car through the village.

By nightfall the position was the Americans had occupied the

Farm Mayenne (Panther Farm), Foy Notre Dame was a smouldering ruin in which half of 'B' Squadron and the Americans leaguered for the night after going round the village and getting Germans out of the cellars like ferrets after rats.

Regimental HQ re-established at Sorinnes, with 'A' Squadron, 'C' Squadron and a Squadron of an American Recce Regiment holding firm in Boisselles. The night being Christmas night, both Americans and British had the same idea. So an immediate search was made for wines and spirits in the recaptured villages.

'C' Squadron were perhaps the most fortunate as the Squadron HQ along with the American Squadron HQ was soon established in the Chateau at Boisselles which was in perfect condition except for the fact that about four 5.5 shells had fallen in it on Christmas Eve. The cellar was undamaged. The RBs platoon produced Army Ration. The Americans a bottle of gin. 'C' Squadron some hastily gathered bottles of brandy from Brussels, and Christmas Night and a good day's work was celebrated with due solemnity and great gusto. It must be stated that the Americans were terrific. They produced wine, K Rations and stories equally quickly and at 1.30 a.m. when going round the guards with an American Captain carrying gin, brandy and rum one felt it had been one of the most exciting Christmas Day's of one's life. The tank and armoured car crews certainly needed the liquor ration as there was a heavy frost on the ground and we did not know if the Germans were five yards or five thousand yards away. All we knew was that they had taken a nasty knock. But we were celebrating Christmas and the fact that we had given the Boche a 'Bloody Nose' as best we could.

Boxing Day again brought perfect weather with glorious sunshine and a sharp frost. 'A' Squadron advanced early on and secured the high ground east of Sorinnes, 'B' Squadron moved forward from Foy Notre Dame and cleared the woods to the east.

Observation was obtained by Recce Troop and 'C' Squadron of Celle and the area to the south east. As a result of those observation of the road from Celle, south east, on which a great deal of German movement could be seen, air support was called for by Regimental HQ. Within 20 minutes a Squadron of Typhoons did devastating work on the Celle road, four Panther Tanks, various Mark IVs and half tracks were brewed up together with sundry soft vehicles. An extremely fine piece of work by the RAF as red smoke, the usual Allied method of indicating target for aircraft (at that time) was fired by the Germans on an American pocket staunchly holding out to the east of Celle. Fortunately the Typhoons took no notice of the red smoke, and set about the German reinforcement column with devastating results.

The next morning 'B' Squadron advanced from the leaguer area and brewed up two Panther tanks believed abandoned as a result of the air attack. Later 'A' Squadron moved into Celle and reported vehicles destroyed and abandoned in the woods east of Foy Notre Dame as two Mark IVs, four half tracks, three 88 mm anti tank guns, a 105 mm gun and various transport.

Later that day the American General, commanding the US 2nd Armored Division, visited the Colonel at Regimental HQ and though it would be invidious to say, congratulations were made on both sides. It is certain that every single trooper in the 3rd Royal Tank Regiment, who saw the American Medium Tank attack from Achene towards Celle (across our left flank) did and will have nothing but praise and admiration for the magnificently executed attack on Boxing Day morning by our Allies.

Sad to say the next morning we had orders to move south, the brigade was to concentrate in the Finnevauxe area. So our connection with some very good American friends was severed.

By this time 'XXX' Corps had come in to assist on the north of the Bulge. General Patton was coming up from the south and was soon to relieve Bastogne where the American 101st Airborne Division had held out so gallantly. General re-grouping was going on with a view to pushing the Germans back behind the Siegfried Line.

28

OPERATIONS 'VARSITY' AND 'PLUNDER' – 'REAPING THE WHIRLWIND'

The three armoured regiments post-Ardennes left their white-painted beat-up Shermans once again in Brussels and celebrated a more traditional Christmas around Ypres on 20 and 21 January 1945. 3rd RTR were back in Poperinge after a journey back from Dinant on icy roads, often driving at 2 mph. The tanks were out of control on all the hills owing to heavy frost on top of snow. The CO returned on 14 January and training with the Comets resumed on the 30th. Their place with 11th Armoured was taken by 4th Armoured Brigade commanded by the redoubtable Brigadier Mike Carver. They acquitted themselves with distinction in the Reichswald operations, the breaking of the Hochwald defences and Schlieffen support line to the main Siegfried Line. Major Bill Close had hoped on his return to the battalion to take over his old 'A' Sqn, but the new CO, Lieutenant-Colonel 'Teddy' Mitford, decided otherwise. Lieutenant-Colonel Alan Brown had left on 21 February and the new CO replaced him four days later. Mitford was a professional RTR officer, served first with 6th RTR, then CO 1st RTR in the desert, then back to command 6th RTR and later 1st RTR and finally commanded 3rd RTR for the crossing of the Rhine. Major John Watts after being wounded during Operation 'Goodwood' returned in November 1944 to command 'A' Sqn.

Bill Close was happy to command 'B' Sqn. His 2 i/c was Captain Freddie Dingwall and the troop commanders, Lieutenants Wadsworth, Pearson, Ricketts and Stewart Montgomery 'all of whom had been with the battalion since D-Day'. Major Norman Bourne DSO was the 2 i/c and Major John Dunlop commanded 'C' Sqn. On 2 March 'C' Sqn had a fancy dress ball; a few days later 3rd RTR held the Poperinge football club to a 4–4 draw. The ammunition scale of sixty-one rounds of storage in the Comets was exceeded by 23rd Hussars, who with ingenuity were able to carry twelve more rounds. So 3rd RTR and 2nd Fife and Forfars had to conform!

A series of lectures were given to officers and sergeants by Lieutenant-Colonel Bob Daniell DSO, 13th RHA (the author's CO), and by Brigadier Roscoe Harvey and by Lieutenant-Colonel A. Hunter DSO, MBE, MC, CO of 8th Rifle Brigade. These were in effect refresher courses of close tank/SP artillery/motorized infantry tactics. Major F.I.C. Wetherell was posted to 4th RTR as 2 i/c, and on 9 March an investiture rehearsal took place at Ypres. Field Marshal Montgomery presented medals to 29th Armoured Brigade. Major J.A. Watts, Captain Brookshaw, Lieutenant Johnny Langdon and Lieutenant Bill Yates were awarded MCs; Sergeants Cooper, Killen and Lister, the Military Medal.

The 11th Armoured Division after Operation 'Veritable' (the approach to the northern Rhine) were sent back from Germany on 9 March to the region of Diest and Louvain. They were joined there in the middle of March by the 29th Armoured Brigade, plus 8th RB. The battalion was stationed at Aeschof on the 17th and were addressed by the GOC in the Louvain theatre the next day, and inspected by him on the 20th. 'It was a real morale booster, the equipping with new Comet tanks throughout the armoured brigade. Monty held a conference of senior officers before the assault across the Rhine. Morale was very high and I thought we had the best of all chances. We were not taking part in the actual crossing at Wesel but would follow up and if necessary break out of the bridgehead', wrote the GOC 'Pip' Roberts in his memoirs.

Once over the Rhine the division, part of 'VIII' Corps with 6th Airborne Division was under the command of Lieutenant-General 'Bubbles' Barker. They were directed from Wesel to Holtwick and thence on to Osnabruck occupying the left forward position. 6th Airborne Division were going to drop and take a sector on the far side of the Rhine, then recover, consolidate and with Churchill tanks from 6th Guards Tank Brigade, race 11th Armoured Division up to the River Elbe to the Danish frontier. General 'Pip' Roberts reverted once again to the two mixed brigades formula that had worked so well during Operation 'Bluecoat'.

13th RHA and Ayrshire Yeomanry 25-pdrs took part in the ten-hour barrage to soften up the enemy defences on the far bank of the mighty River Rhine. Operation 'Plunder' was the appropriate codename for this terrible onslaught into the heart of the Fatherland. Montgomery had chosen 15th and 51st Scottish Divisions to make the initial crossing (Operation 'Varsity') to link up with the Airborne drops on the east bank. The German defenders included 6th, 7th and 8th Parachute Divisions with 15th Panzer Grenadier and 116th Panzer Division in reserve. On the 28th 3rd RTR crossed the Rhine at Wesel by a long Bailey bridge to Brunen, the next day to Velem while the whole division concentrated in the Wesel bridgehead.

'On our route we had first to secure Burgsteinfurt. This was done by night while the Royal Engineers with a company of 8th RB bridged a stream which held up 3rd Royal Tanks', wrote the GOC. 3rd RTR with infantry of 1st Herefords on the backs of tanks moved up to Burgsteinfurt, north-east of Horstmar, found to be heavily defended. 'A' Sqn in the lead lost two Comets, so under a barrage 4th KSLI and the Herefords mounted a major attack during the night. During the street fighting Panzerfaust teams brewed up two 'B' Sqn and three 'C' Sqn tanks. In the first battle eight brand new Comets had been knocked out. On the right flank 3rd RTR captured Holtwick then pushed on to Horstmar (on 30 March). The procedure was, armour leading, infantry following over very poor quality roads with every bridge blown. Lieutenant-Colonel 'Teddy' Mitford's 'O' group now planned for the capture of Emsdetten and the crossing of the River Ems.

At first light Major Jock Balharrie's 'C' Sqn led and reached the river at 0730 hrs; since the bridge was blown, a recce was made down to Mesum where the REs defended by 8th RB established a bridging party. A company of 4th KSLI was soon across and the bridge was completed by late afternoon. Major Bill Close's 'B' Sqn led by Lieutenant Frank Wadsworth's 2 Troop moved on quickly and soon reached the vital Dortmund–Ems Canal. Both bridges were destroyed and enemy activity in the huge wooded Teutoburger Wald on the far side was noted. It was a magnificent defensive position. At an 'O' group that night Brigadiers Roscoe Harvey (29th) and Jack Churcher (159th) decided that 'C' Sqn 3rd RTR would be ferried across the canal after dark by a ferry which the enemy – unusually – had left behind intact.

Together with a company of 4th KSLI they crossed over safely, and established a small bridgehead at Birgte. In a recce of the vast woodlands ahead 'C' Sqn lost two tanks to A/Tk fire. The 3rd RTR War Diary reported: '1st April two tanks bazooka'd. 4 ORs wounded an enemy SP KO'd another, 1 OR KIA 4 wounded.' Trooper A. Hickman was killed in action at Horstmar, and Troopers R. Russell and D. Leroy on the Dortmund–Ems Canal. A bridge was completed by 1430 hrs and 2nd Fife and Forfars with

1st Herefords under a barrage tried to expand the bridgehead but made little progress. 3rd RTR were in the Bevergern area on 2 April still tackling the expansion of the bridgehead towards Tecklenburg. Trooper K. Sims was killed and a desert veteran Major J.A. Watts MC was wounded and died the next day. A great loss to the battalion 'a charming gentleman and a good Adjutant,' recalled Bill Morris, 'C' Sqn.

15/19th Hussars had a field day on 2 April. With their Comets they blasted their way into Brochterbeck and through thick woods to Holthausen. The key village of Tecklenburg was heavily defended; by the time 23rd Hussars and 8th RB had cleared the place of defenders, the rubble and debris of wrecked vehicles blocked the route. 3rd RTR and 4th KSLI took a lower road through Brochterbeck and reached Tecklenburg from the south; 159th Brigade were given the responsibility of clearing the Teutoburger Wald defended by troops from an NCOs' training school at Hanover. 'The 3rd Monmouths took heavy casualties. Corporal E.T. Chapman won the division's second Victoria Cross in fierce fighting. The Hanoverian cadets went on fighting for another five days. The brave Monmouths fought their last battle with the division and were now replaced by 1st Cheshires', noted the GOC.

Possibly because 6th Airborne were still ahead in the race (for race it was) with 11th Armoured Division for Osnabruck, the GOC decided 'obviously we must do another night march as we had done at Amiens. As on the other occasion 3rd Royal Tanks were in the lead. But the way was not easy. The Germans resisted by night as they had by day and several defended road blocks had to be cleared before the Dortmund–Ems canal (north-west of Osnabruck) could be reached. Morning however brought the reward of this thrust. The southern of the two bridges at Eversheide was seized intact and the demolition charges removed.'

It was indeed a famous night. The moon shone fitfully and most of the 24 miles was covered in a downpour. 'B' Sqn led and Major Bill Close 'briefed my tank commanders to watch out for Panzerfaust parties. The way was not easy and the German resistance was determined. We encountered several defended roadblocks which had to be cleared under fire by the leading tanks. One of the tanks was fitted with a steel bulldozer blade. The radio call for the bulldozer "George George" was in constant use that night.'

Lieutenant Frank Wadsworth, leading, moved towards the river at Eversheide, and spotted two huge 50-lb bombs attached to the side of the bridge. Under fire he climbed out of his tank and cut the connecting wires to the explosives. The vital bridge was captured intact and Wadsworth later received the MC for his bravery. The 3rd Tanks had added another significant action to their impressive list. Lieutenant Robin Lemon was relieved of the Recce Sqn and took over 'C' Sqn Comet troop before Osnabruck. 'I was leading troop advancing on a single road centre line near Halen. The order was to push on as speedily as possible. Inevitably my tank, then leading was knocked out and my gunner Trooper Vosper was killed. I was wounded in the legs and lay in a ditch until picked up and given first aid by Lance Corporal Nation.' A sharp action followed next day at Levern, another at Rahden and on 5 April the battalion reached the River Weser where all the bridges were destroyed. The 3rd RTR War Diary shows that at Levern they took 200 POWs and at Lavelsich 'B' Sqn had to fend off bazooka teams who caused a lot of trouble. 4th KSLI were engaged until after dark in house-to-house fighting before the bazooka teams could be liquidated. To everyone's surprise including General 'Pip' Roberts the Luftwaffe put in an appearance at the Weser with Stukas, Junkers 88s and Focke Wulf 190s; 12th SS Panzer Division and 100th Pioneer Brigade produced strong resistance which RAF Tempests helped subdue. 3rd RTR were now out of the line for several days.

The River Weser was a major obstacle and well defended. The sappers lost a lot of men at Stolzenau building a floating bridge 346 feet long which the Luftwaffe destroyed by skip-bombing. 1st Commando Brigade came up to help establish a bridgehead but the indomitable 6th Airborne had already secured a bridge 15 miles south-west at Petershagen which they kindly allowed 11th Armoured Division to use. The Cheshires crossed on the 7th, but Loccum, Leese and Heimsden villages all gave trouble. 3rd RTR/4th KSLI group met heavy opposition in Rehburg on the morning of the 8th and it took five hours to clear the village. But 7 miles north of Husum the RTR/KSLI battle group met fanatical resistance from the Hitler Youth. Panzerfausts knocked out three RTR tanks. Sergeant A. Duff, Lance Corporal Nation and Trooper C. Ellershaw were killed in action. Snipers killed ten KSLI who had over forty casualties taking the village. The Comets' and Wasps' flame-throwers then killed 80 Hitler Youth and eventually 120 were captured. Many V-2 sites, explosive factories, ammunition dumps and some POW camps were concealed in large woods and were 'liberated'. 3rd RTR and 8th RB opened up first Lintzel, then Nienburg on 9 April which was eventually cleared by 4th KSLI. 23rd Hussars and 8th RB needed two set-piece attacks, supported by 13th RHA 'stonks' before Steimbke was taken on the 9th. At this stage 'A' Sqn's OC was Captain Graham Scott, 'B', Major Bill Close, 'C', Major Jock Balharrie (2 i/c Jack Kempton), and HQ Sqn, Major Johnny Johnson. 3rd RTR route was Stolzenau (bridgehead delayed), south-west to the Airborne bridge to cross the River Weser at Petershagen, east to Loccum, Rehburg, and around the Steinhuder Meer lake to the town of Neustadt on the River Leine. This was crossed on 11 April. From Wenden they followed the river line north via Helstorf, Vesbeck to Schwarmstedt in the triangle formed by the River Leine and Aller.

'On 11th April from Schwarmstedt my "B" Sqn was in the lead', wrote Major Close. 'Second Lieutenant John Pearson aged 19 with little battle experience, with Sergeant Cranston a very experienced troop sergeant, with Second Lieutenant Jeff Lomas a new subaltern acting as his troop corporal.' RTR practice was for young officers to gain battle experience initially as a tank commander. Lieutenant Johnny Langdon, 'A' Sqn, wrote an account of the River Aller battle: 'Our approach to the River Aller was via the village of Essel.' Pearson kept a sharp lookout for Panzerfaust men and moved on rapidly towards the river. 'It was difficult tank country, a straight road leading across the river, the ground on either side of the road very marshy, making it impossible to deploy off the road. About 100 yards from the river he could see the bridge was blown and that the river was about 40 yards wide at that point. Suddenly Crash! Bang! Pearson's and Cranston's tanks erupted into flames. One or two crew baled out but obviously wounded. Lieutenant Lomas in the third tank got off the road, took cover in bushes, engaged the A/Tk gun. His tank was now hit twice, but courageously with a direct hit on the enemy gun knocked it out.' Major Close moved up to the burning tanks and got out to help the wounded crews. John Pearson and two of his crew Shipley and Wyatt, his operator were lying in the long grass beside the road, all badly burned about the hands and faces. Trooper Rowe was not badly hurt. The driver Trooper J. Manning was killed instantly as were Sergeant W. Cranston and Lance Corporal M. Turnbull in the other tank. The remainder of the crew had only minor wounds. The RMO Doc Barry Whitehouse, with his two medical half-tracks, soon arrived and the wounded were evacuated. As the far bank was held in strength 3rd RTR remained until 1st Commando Brigade and 4th KSLI made a night assault crossing of the river. By the morning of the 12th a bridgehead half a mile in depth and a mile wide had been established. So 'A' Sqn was rafted across by 1100 hrs, while the REs built a bridge at high speed. Lieutenant Johnny Langdon led 1st Troop through thick woods up to the little River Drebber. The KSLI Wasp flame-thrower burned many of the enemy out of their slit trenches. It was a hot sticky day and Langdon gave orders for a brew while Corporal Brindle and Sergeant Elstob parked their Comets on either side of the road. Langdon recalled: 'Suddenly there was a great deal of noise around us caused by infantry carriers moving followed by the terrifying sound of an AP shot which whistled past me. I saw through my binoculars an enemy Tiger tank moving slowly through the trees at the corner of the road about 300 yards away.' Lance Corporal Bourne the WO/Loader replaced the HE shell already loaded with an AP. Trooper Rice the gunner was directed onto the tank. 'I saw its 88-mm gun slowly traversing onto us. We fired, I gave Trooper Charlton my driver the order to reverse. We were out gunned and I wanted to save my tank and crew.' Corporal Brindle's Comet had its offside track smashed by AP. A scout car and another infantry vehicle were blazing. Two more AP shots thudded into Brindle's Comet. RHQ said that reports of Tigers were generally unfounded! Lieutenant Denis Sullivan commanding 2nd Troop was sent up to give flank protection. The KSLI sent up a patrol, but the Tiger tank after a good morning's work withdrew – probably to have lunch. 3rd RTR leaguered that night near the River Aller with KSLI dug-in on the perimeter which was shelled during the night. Trooper Bourne went on leave, replaced by Trooper Ward in Langdon's troop. At first light on 13 April 'A' Sqn with 4th KSLI resumed their cautious advance through the very thick woods. Lieutenant Donald Collie, 3rd Troop led, followed by Lieutenant Denis Sullivan, 2nd Troop; Lieutenant Michael Bullock, 4th Troop, and Langdon's 1st Troop. The Tiger reappeared, fired a few AP rounds and brewed up a KSLI TCV: 13th RHA put down a heavy concentration which deterred the enemy, 'enabling us to niggle slowly up the road. Meanwhile "C" Sqn moved round our right flank. Sergeant Harding managed to get within 100 yards of the road concealed by trees, when the Tiger suddenly appeared broadside on to him.

Immediately he put two AP shots into its side which brewed it up. *This was the first Tiger the Regiment had knocked out.* There was a second Tiger who then withdrew down the road', Langdon recalled.

Sullivan's troop took over from Collie in the lead and Sergeant F. Probert was killed by a sniper's bullet. Worse was to follow: Lieutenant Bullock and his driver Trooper E. Bligh were killed by AP shot. Captain Graham Scott, the Squadron OC asked Langdon to confirm. 'I looked into the turret and saw his body lying across the gun. An AP shot had grazed the cupola and taken his head off.' During the day all the tanks of 'A' Sqn were bogged down by the little River Drebber in full view of the enemy. After a lonely, wet and miserable night, on the morning of the 15th, Captain Charles Adkins and the REME LAD recovered them.

Lieutenant Johnny Langdon recalled: 'Everyone was in good form, I filled my canvas bucket with water, splashed my face, then the hard job of getting off three days' growth of beard. Best of all a hot meal and a brew provided by the crew. That night we leaguered at Engehalsen rejoining the rest of the Brigade. Comfortably settled in our bivvies, bottles of wine and a very welcome double rum ration were issued.' The CO, Lieutenant-Colonel Teddy Mitford, wrote: 'Our leading Sqn engaged Tiger tanks on Friday, 13 April. We had a fairly bad day with casualties and we were being pressed to get a move on.' One Tiger fired AP at Mitford standing beside his scout car and took off the pocket of his tank suit.

The battalion made sure, now that squadrons were rotated in turn, that troops were also rotated, and that individual tanks were rotated within troops. The point troop, and almost certainly the lead tank, was in constant danger to a bazooka team, a sniper at a roadblock or in a house, and to the occasional A/Tk gun, SP or Tiger. Young schoolboys in uniform could and did handle and fire the one-shot Panzerfaust. As Major Bill Close remarked: 'No one wanted to take any risks any more. The crew in the lead tanks knew they would be the first to get it if we bumped into a last ditch battlegroup. It was necessary to ring the changes. People were reluctant to drive round corners. I gave orders that no chances were to be taken with bazooka merchants.' Hamlets and small villages were often 'stonked' by the two gunner regiments at the slightest sign of trouble. 'They have sown the wind, and they shall reap the whirlwind' – Hosea VIII.7.

29

HEADING FOR THE BALTIC – 'I KNEW THE THIRD WOULD COME'

The knowledge about the appalling concentration camp of Bergen-Belsen only came slowly to light. Preliminary negotiations began on 12 April 1945 at Bucholz, when the commander of the German garrison troops appeared at 159th Brigade HQ. The German party were blindfolded and sent back to HQ VIII Corps. In exchange for an exclusion zone for medical reasons around the infamous camp (with 60,000 mostly political prisoners suffering from typhus and starvation) the German garrison would give 11th Armoured Division free passage, including access over the bridge on the River Aller at Winsen. Negotiations went back and forth until a local agreement was concluded fixing a limited typhus zone around the camp itself. The enemy then blew the Winsen bridge! Alerted to the danger of typhus every member of the division was doused with white DDT powder. 'We were sprayed with DDT', recalls Trooper Les Slater, 'under the arms and down the trousers because of a "typhoid" camp ahead. We were told "don't interfere with the Hungarian guards who wore yellow armbands and were armed". After going through the camp we smelled for days.'

1st Commando Brigade made a small bridgehead and took Hademstorf, a mile north of the river but efforts by 3rd RTR and 4th KSLI to continue due north to Ostenholz were frustrated by tanks and A/Tk guns firing straight down the road. 4th KSLI were then counter-attacked from the right flank. So the Essel bridgehead was left and the sappers started to build a bridge at Winsen, 10 miles due east. It took the Cheshires and Herefords a day and half before Winsen was clear. The road due north through woods went to Walle (5 miles) then Belsen (5 miles) and Bergen (2 miles). The infamous Josef Kramer, his twenty-year-old woman assistant, Irma Grese and their staff of forty-four were lined up to watch the Comets of 23rd Hussars and 3rd RTR trundle very slowly along the road through the camp; slowly because of the 24-hour truce to allow the German/Hungarian staff to get away and for medical supplies and help to arrive. There were two camps, one with 35,000 men, the other with 25,000 women. When 11th Armoured Division arrived there were 13,000 *unburied corpses*. Many of 3rd RTR who saw this horrifying scene and smelt the dreadful stench of death would never forget it.

The battalion and 4th KSLI pushed on at dusk on 14 April to Wietzendorf, to be met by heavy shelling. The next day they advanced to Hermansburg, 5 miles east through thickly wooded country defended by roadblocks and bazookas. Rarely was it possible for cross-country movement. 3rd RTR accidentally set the dry heathland on fire, attracting two Messerschmitts which bombed the column, destroyed a truck and a jeep and damaged a Comet, causing casualties. The bridge at Muden 4 miles north was blown, but the battlegroup advanced on the 16th by a deviation through Forst Lintzel to Ebstorf nearly 20 miles further on. On the way 3rd RTR captured a mixed bag of seven Luftwaffe bombers, an airfield, a large store depot, a poison gas factory at Wriedel, a POW camp at Hagen with 230 guards and 10,000 POWs, who were set free. At one such camp RSM 'Tiny' White and officers and men taken prisoner at Calais, in Greece and in the desert battles were found and released. Major Close met a particular Sergeant pal, 'Socker' Heath who clambered on to the Comet saying 'always knew the Third would come for me.'

A strong enemy force at Uelzen, a large town 25 miles south of Luneburg, was trying to escape northwards. On 17 April, 29th Armoured Brigade blocked them at Tatendorf, while 3rd RTR and 4th KSLI captured Medingen (where Trooper F. Iles was killed) and Bevensen. Since the River Aller battle the division had taken 6,000 POWs and destroyed 13 guns. The line of advance was now directed due north towards the large town of Luneberg, Luneburg Heath (the German equivalent of Salisbury Plain) and then the wide-flowing River Elbe. The battlegroup using the main road cleared Bienenbuttel and Melbeck where 400 Allied POWs were freed. The bridge 2 miles ahead was destroyed, so by turning eastwards across the railway to Wendisch Evern, 'A' Sqn and the armoured cars of the Inns of Court Regiment carried out several converging attacks. During the evening they cleared the eastern half of Luneburg against slight opposition and leaguered for the night of the 18th around Scharnebeck. The division was allotted a sector of the River Elbe, from Winsen to Tespe, a 9-mile stretch well west of Lauenburg.

In an effort to seize the railway bridge opposite and south of Lauenburg on the morning of the 19th, 4th KSLI edged forward through Sassendorf in an endeavour to surprise the defenders; 3rd RTR, 'C' Sqn, stood ready to drive down the road from Hittbergen (the author was FOO with 4th KSLI that day and received six grenade fragments for his efforts).

'The idea of capturing a bridge over the Elbe seemed an exciting objective. Luneberg was taken without much difficulty (by Inns of Court, 15/19th Hussars and 1st Cheshires). It was reported that the railway bridge at Lauenburg was still intact', wrote General Roberts. 'A combination of 3rd RTR and 4th KSLI were up against the enemy who held the near side of the river with a force of 200 men with plenty of machine-guns and Tiger tanks. They were supported by artillery fire from the other side of the river, but targets the other side of the river were engaged by our own artillery (especially 13th RHA!) and several German guns were knocked out. Gradually 4th KSLI closed in while 3rd RTR were within 200 yards of the bridge, but at this moment the Germans blew the bridge. This was on 19 April.' Many pockets of enemy resistance had been bypassed in the strong surge towards the Elbe.

The GOC was convinced that if 11th Armoured Division had managed to force the Lauenburg railway bridge on 19 April, then the route to Berlin was wide open. 'Pip' Roberts was sure that the division would have been 25 miles east within 24 hours. Would Eisenhower have refused to let Montgomery's armour reach Berlin?

3rd RTR crossed the Artlenberg sapper-built bridge over the Elbe late on 30 April through a 15th Scottish bridgehead. 23rd Hussars led the breakout from Schwarzenbeck under a protective screen of RAF fighters; 3rd RTR were teamed with 1st Herefords and on the left flank found many mines and roadblocks as they pushed for Havekost and Mohnsen, but Trittau needed a set-piece attack. On 2 May the village of Rethwischdorf with 20 guns and 500 POWs was taken. At 1115 hrs came the order to press on for Lubeck which 2nd Fife and Forfars and 1st Cheshires were first to enter. Now 3rd RTR and 1st Herefords pushed northwards and accepted the surrender of Bad Segeberg which they occupied. 23rd Hussars and 8th RB progressed to Travemunde and Neustadt, and the Baltic had been reached. Among the 70,000 POWs taken by the division since crossing the Elbe were some 25 generals and admirals. When 3rd RTR probed into Rickling, they met the German garrison commanders of Neumunster and Rendsburg both anxious to surrender. Captain Johnny Langdon attended an 'O' group on the 5th; the battalion were warned to prepare for an attack across the well-defended Kiel Canal but the news of the unconditional ceasefire came through – just in time.

A strong force of SS troops was holed up in Forst Segeberg on the Luneburg plain and would only surrender to a British unit (and certainly not to the Russians). So Major Bill Close with 'B' Sqn was 'invited' by the CO to assist, with a company of KSLI, in the rounding up of the SS. Nursing severe hangovers, in due course they met a complete SS A/Tk battalion recently come from the Russian front, drawn up in full array. The German CO would only surrender to a British officer of field rank. Bill assured him that he was and the seventeen Comets were sufficient back-up. The SS were escorted back to Bad Segeberg where 3rd RTR spent two weeks.

30

ENVOI

The rejoicing on 8 May – the official Victory in Europe Day was the third consecutive day of celebration. From the moment late on 4 May when the wireless broke the news of the surrender to Field Marshal Montgomery of those German armies facing the 21st Army Group, the joy and relief was profound; but there was sadness too for those who had fallen beside the long centre lines. For most of 11th Armoured Division it had been a furious, exciting and dangerous near-year of battle. But for 3rd Tanks it was just the last campaign of many. No other formation in the British Army – let alone among the twenty-eight Royal Tank Regiments involved – had fought in so many theatres of war. Captain Johnny Dunlop, the battalion military poet, wrote perhaps a trifle optimistically:

> Oh I wear a green tab on my shoulder
> And a little white tank on my arm
> 'Twas the Third Tanks that taught me to soldier
> And with them I will come to no harm!

It had taken 3rd Tanks a long, long time to 'Tame the Panzers'. They were overwhelmed by panzer divisions in Calais, by Stukas (and poor tank tracks) in Greece; in Operation 'Crusader' they had been crushed; but in Operations 'Gamebirds', 'Lightfoot', 'Supercharge', the entry into Tripoli, and the famous left hook at Mareth, the battalion was beating the panzers all the time. True, in Operation 'Epsom' honours were even, and 'Goodwood' was a disaster, but 'Bluecoat', the breakout to help close the corridor, the 'Great Swan' (and the taking of Amiens and Antwerp), were great consistent victories with the panzers in general retreat. The week-long battle in the Ardennes was successful. Uniquely armed with new Comets they swept all before them after the Rhine, the Dortmund–Ems Canal, the Rivers Weser, Aller and Elbe, and the final triumphant dash for the Baltic. There is little doubt the 3rd Tanks, after many vicissitudes, eventually tamed the panzers. As the sergeant in the desert said to the Staff Officer, 'The two Thirds are at it again, the 3rd Tanks taking on the Third Reich.'

This book is dedicated to the many heroes of the 3rd Tanks – wearers of the Brunswick Green – some of whom have already reached the 'green fields'. Many of them have helped to make this book come alive. Theirs was an exciting story and if there are errors of names, dates or places, then they are mine alone.

APPENDIX I

ABRIDGED TALK BY LIEUTENANT-COLONEL H. PYMAN DSO, FEBRUARY 1943

Problem to be solved basically *Fire and Movement*, i.e. first neutralize anti-tank artillery of hostile rear guard and movement to cut off the line of withdrawal of rearguard and destroy it.

At the battle of Sidi Rezegh I saw the Squadron of Crusaders which I had commanded until a week previously, destroyed by German A/Tk guns, in ten minutes. They were gallantly charging an A/Tk screen. It was the only way in those days. It was very costly and very ineffective. On the aerodrome at Sidi Rezegh 120 Stuart tanks were launched into the battle after both sides were otherwise fully committed. This intervention of a reserve should have been decisive. Instead it only staved off a defeat and forced a draw. The reserve had no supporting fire plan and never reached its objective. Throughout the rest of that fine campaign the remnants of the Stuart Brigade teased and harassed the German withdrawing columns right across Cyrenaica in a way that was tactically a fine test of tank command and technically a triumph of tank design. But however bold the movements there was never fire to support the thrust on to its objective. Tank for tank we were outclassed and we had no answer to the anti-tank gun.

In the battles of May–August 1942, armoured regiments were equipped with a few Grants and supported by a battery of 25 pounders. An Armoured Regiment might muster eighteen HE guns. This was a great improvement. But the armoured grouping was rigid. The batteries of 25 pounders could not be linked to produce a regimental shoot with twenty four guns. Some COs thought that tanks haphazardly and inadequately supported could charge A/Tk guns. Our tank casualties were very heavy.

A typical enemy rearguard was (a) frontal screen of 50 mm, (b) main lines of 88 mm, (c) supporting artillery, (d) armoured mobile reserve of tanks. _Importance of Recce Squadron_. Needed an eye for country, axis of advance suitable for _all_ vehicles of group. Intimate knowledge of enemy's equipment, habits; understand how RHA and medium squadrons operate; be capable of directing fire from 25-pounders and 75-mm guns. They need to be experts with field glasses, compass, maps and confident of describing vividly what they see. Finally their lives will depend upon their ability to see without being seen and to fight with A/Tk and MGs once they have been spotted. _Medium squadrons_ are chief mobile firepower the CO has. Medium tanks both in attack and defence are the principal means by which their CO can switch firepower to bear. The squadrons are vulnerable to un-neutralised A/Tk guns and to enemy tanks more favourably positioned than themselves and when resting in leaguer at night to hostile infantry.

A tank Brigadier has under command 94 X 75-mm guns, 24 X 25-pounders and can call on further field and medium artillery and nearly always has A/Tk guns under command. In a straight fight the A/Tk guns will beat the armour every time. Therefore we tank men must not be straight – we must be crooked! Pound the A/Tk gunner, the basic weapon of all German rearguards, with artillery fire until he yells for help from the meagre tanks and guns supporting him. When these reserves disclose themselves, neutralise them. Then, and only then, drive the armoured assault home from a _flank_, supported by crash after crash of every HE weapon available. These are the conditions in which armour should challenge an A/Tk rearguard.

APPENDIX II

MAPS

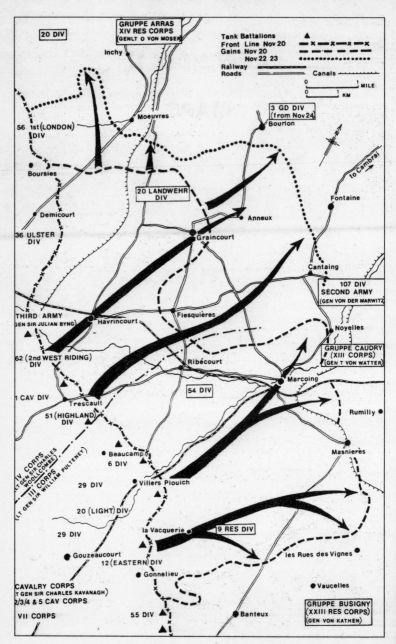

The Battle of Cambrai, November 1917.

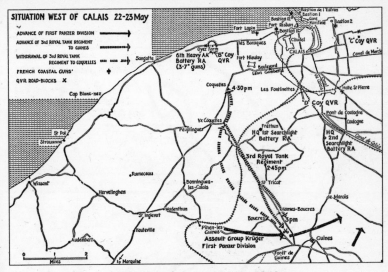

Battle for Calais, 22–23 May 1940.

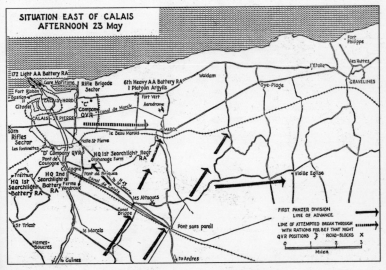

Battle for Calais, p.m. 23 May 1940.

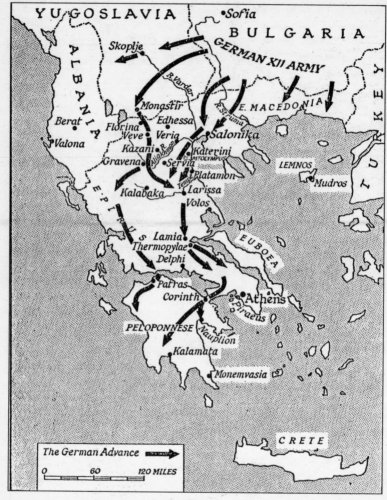

German invasion of Greece, March 1941.

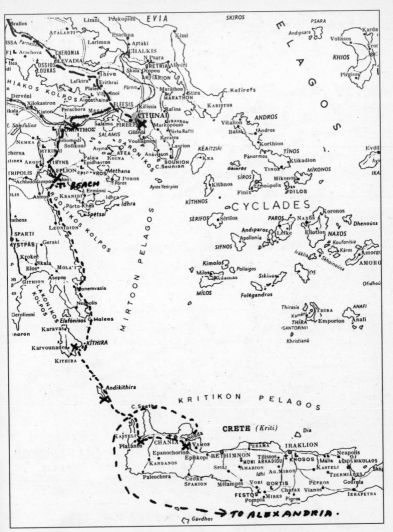

Final withdrawal from Greece and Crete.

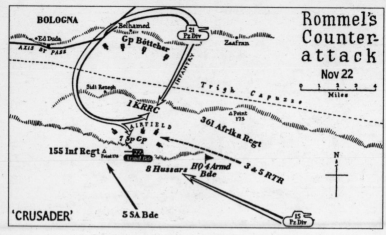

Operation 'Crusader', 21 November 1941.

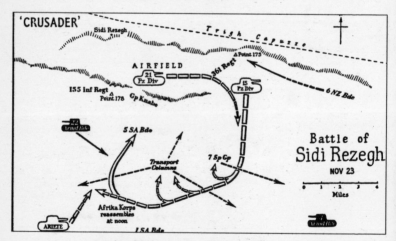

Battle of Sidi Rezegh, 23 November 1941.

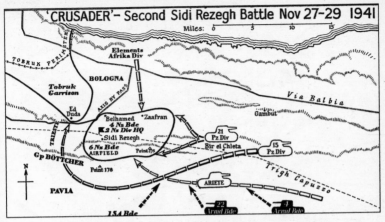

Second Battle of Sidi Rezegh, 27–29 November 1941.

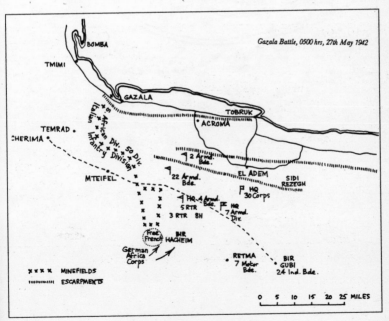

Battle of Gazala, 27 May 1942.

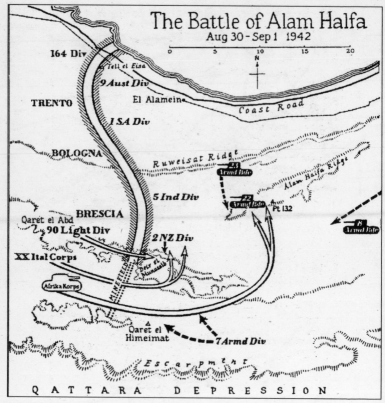

Battle of Alam Halfa, 30 August 1942.

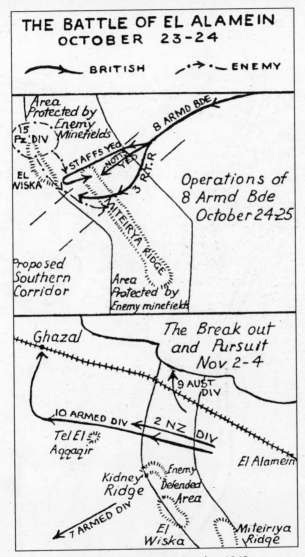

Battle of El Alamein, 23 October 1942.

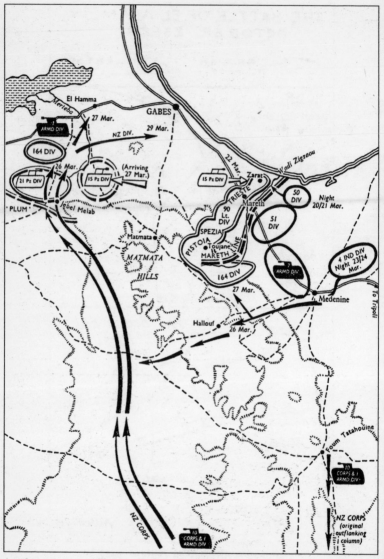

Battle of Mareth, 19–29 March 1943.

Tebaga gap battle, 26 March 1943.

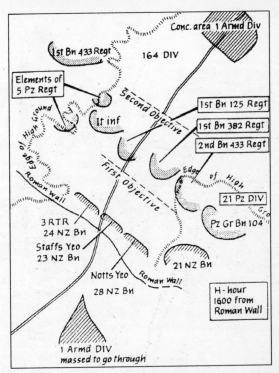

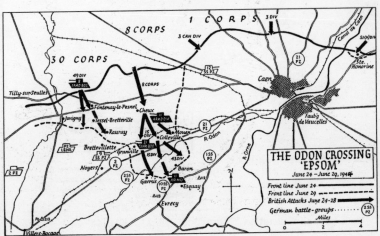

Operation 'Epsom', 24–29 June 1944.

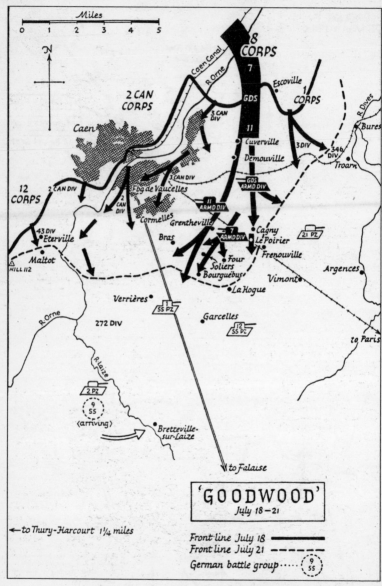

Operation 'Goodwood', 18–21 July 1944.

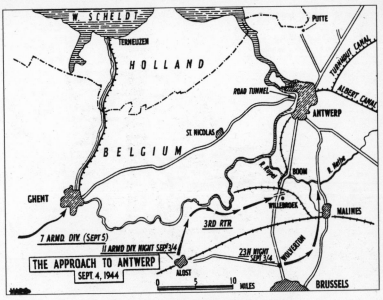

Approach to Antwerp, 4 September 1944.

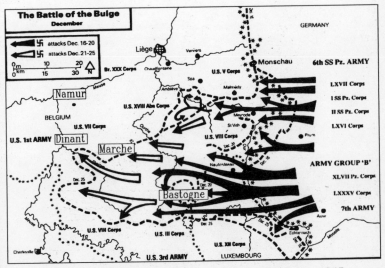

Battle of the Bulge, Ardennes, December 1944–January 1945.

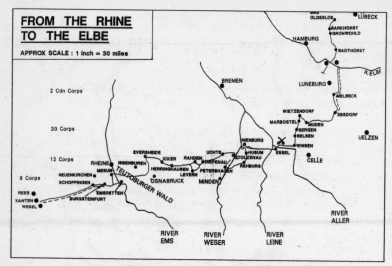

3rd RTR and the five river battles.

BIBLIOGRAPHY

Close, Major W., *A View from the Turret*, Dell & Bredon, 1998
Crisp, Major Robert, *Brazen Chariots*, London, Frederick Muller, 1959
— —, *The Gods were Neutral*, London, White Lion, 1975
Delaforce, Patrick, *Black Bull – History of 11th Armoured Division*, Stroud, Sutton, 2002
— —, *Monty's Marauders (4th and 8th Armoured Brigades)*, Stroud, Sutton, 2003
Joly, Lieutenant-Colonel C., *Take these Men*, London, Buchan & Enright, 1985
Morris, George, *The Battle of El Alamein and Beyond*, Lewes, Book Guild, 1993
Neave, MP, Airey, *The Flames of Calais*, London, Grafton, 1972
Pyman, Lieutenant-General Sir H., *Call to Arms*, London, Leo Cooper, 1971
Roberts, Major-General 'Pip', *From the Desert to the Baltic*
Ross, Peter, *All Valiant Dust*, Dublin, Lilliput, 1992

Journals, Letters, Articles:
Denis Bartlett; Bill Bourne; Jim Caswell; Fred Dale; Major John Dunlop; Bert Hobson; H.T. Jarvis; A.E. Jobson; Bill Jordan; Lieutenant-Colonel R.C. Keller; Major J.A. Kempton; 'Buck' Kite; Major Johnny Langdon; Robin Lemon; Stewart Montgomery; R.C. Payne; 'Geordie' Reay; Lieutenant-Colonel W.R. Reeves; Dick Shattock; Les Slater; Jock Watt; Barry Whitehouse; Cliff Wicks; A.C. Wilson; R.N. Wilson; Major George Witheridge; J.F.C. Wollaston.

INDEX